Revolting Indolence

Latinx: The Future Is Now
A series edited by Lorgia García-Peña and Nicole Guidotti-Hernández

BOOKS IN THE SERIES

Frank García, *Clicas: Gender, Sexuality, and Struggle in Latina/o/x Gang Literature and Film*
Regina Marie Mills, *Invisibility and Influence: A Literary History of AfroLatinidades*
Jason Ruiz, *Narcomedia: Latinidad, Popular Culture, and America's War on Drugs*
Rebeca L. Hey-Colón, *Channeling Knowledges: Water and Afro-Diasporic Spirits in Latinx and Caribbean Worlds*
Tatiana Reinoza, *Reclaiming the Americas: Latinx Art and the Politics of Territory*
Kristy L. Ulibarri, *Visible Borders, Invisible Economies: Living Death in Latinx Narratives*
Marisel C. Moreno, *Crossing Waters: Undocumented Migration in Hispanophone Caribbean and Latinx Literature and Art*
Yajaira M. Padilla, *From Threatening Guerrillas to Forever Illegals: US Central Americans and the Cultural Politics of Non-Belonging*
Francisco J. Galarte, *Brown Trans Figurations: Rethinking Race, Gender, and Sexuality in Chicanx/Latinx Studies*

Revolting Indolence

The Politics of Slacking, Lounging, and Daydreaming in Queer and Trans Latinx Culture

Marcos Gonsalez

University of Texas Press *Austin*

Copyright © 2024 by Marcos Gonsalez
All rights reserved
Printed in the United States of America
First edition, 2024

An earlier version of chapter 1 was published in "Glimpsing Angie Xtravaganza: The Trans Latinx Imaginary of *Paris Is Burning*," *Camera Obscura* 39, no. 3 (2024), and an earlier version of chapter 4 was published in "Fantasies of Valentina: *RuPaul's Drag Race* and the Performance of Trans/Queer of Color Spectacular Obfuscation," *Transgender Studies Quarterly* 9, no. 4 (2022): 587–608.

Requests for permission to reproduce material from this work should be sent to permissions@utpress.utexas.edu.

♾ The paper used in this book meets the minimum requirements of ANSI/NISO Z39.48-1992 (R1997) (Permanence of Paper).

Cataloging in Publication Data is available from the Library of Congress

Names: Gonsalez, Marcos, author.
Title: Revolting indolence : the politics of slacking, lounging, and daydreaming in queer and trans Latinx culture / Marcos Gonsalez.
Description: First edition. | Austin : University of Texas Press, 2024. | Includes bibliographical references and index.
Identifiers: LCCN 2024004419 (print) | LCCN 2024004420 (ebook)
  ISBN 978-1-4773-3050-0 (hardcover)
  ISBN 978-1-4773-3051-7 (paperback)
  ISBN 978-1-4773-3052-4 (pdf)
  ISBN 978-1-4773-3053-1 (epub)
Subjects: LCSH: Hispanic American sexual minorities—Political activity—United States. | Laziness—Political aspects—United States. | Laziness in literature—Political aspects—United States. | Laziness in motion pictures—Political aspects—United States. | Sexual minority culture—Political aspects—United States. | Neoliberalism—United States.
Classification: LCC HQ73.4.H57 G667 2024 (print) | LCC HQ73.4.H57 (ebook) | DDC 306.76089/68073—dc23/eng/20240426
LC record available at https://lccn.loc.gov/2024004419
LC ebook record available at https://lccn.loc.gov/2024004420

doi:10.7560/330500

Contents

List of Illustrations vi

INTRODUCTION
Liberating Indolence 1

1. **GLIMPSING ANGIE XTRAVAGANZA**
The Trans Latinx Imaginary of *Paris Is Burning* 39

2. **LOUNGE LIZARD AESTHETICS**
Los Angeles Nightlife Visualities 63

3. **THE POETICS OF LATIN NIGHT**
The Literatures of the Pulse Nightclub Shooting 89

4. **SLACKING OFF ON THE MAIN STAGE**
RuPaul's Drag Race and the Performance of Spectacular Obfuscation 109

5. **THE TEXTURES OF OUR DAYDREAMING**
Justin Torres's *We the Animals* and the Art of Sarah Zapata 131

CODA
Nobody Wants to Work Anymore 157

Acknowledgments 161
Notes 163
Index 181

Illustrations

FIGURE 1.1 Angie chitchatting in Spanish, Union Square, NYC. 52

FIGURE 1.2 Angie and the scratch on the reel. 52

FIGURE 1.3 "¡Ay lo que ha hecho, loca!" 53

FIGURE 1.4 Angie laying her head on a friend. 60

FIGURE 2.1 Reynaldo Rivera, *Untitled, Downtown*, 1993. 71

FIGURE 2.2 Reynaldo Rivera, *Performer, Silverlake Lounge*, 1995. 73

FIGURE 2.3 Reynaldo Rivera, *Performer, Silverlake Lounge*, 1995. 73

FIGURE 2.4 Reynaldo Rivera, *Silverlake Lounge*, 1995. 77

FIGURE 2.5 The New Jalisco Bar front. 84

FIGURE 4.1 Valentina's bejeweled claws obscuring her face. 117

FIGURE 4.2 Valentina lounging on the couch before her lip-synch. 119

FIGURE 5.1 Jonah daydreaming in the trench. 138

FIGURE 5.2 Sarah Zapata, *A Little Domestic Waste I* and *A Little Domestic Waste VII*, 2017. 145

FIGURE 5.3 Sarah Zapata, *In vastness of borrowed time (The taxing of a fruitful procession)*, 2020–2021. 147

FIGURE 5.4 Sarah Zapata, *In vastness of borrowed time (The taxing of a fruitful procession)*, 2020–2021. 148

FIGURE 5.5 Sarah Zapata, *I want you to know how hard I am*, 2019. 155

FIGURE 6.1 David Antonio Cruz, *Puerto Rican Pieta*, 2006. 159

Revolting Indolence

INTRODUCTION

Liberating Indolence

THE RUSE OF WORK; OR, THE WORLD-MAKING PLEASURES OF INDOLENCE

In 2023, Florida's state legislature passed Senate Bill 1718, barring the issuing of work documentation for undocumented laborers in Florida and prohibiting the use of any other forms of documentation issued by other states.[1] The bill also mandated that hospitals inquire over immigration status upon admission. In response, undocumented farmworkers fled the Florida workforce out of fear. This blatantly xenophobic, white nationalist juridical criminalization of undocumented peoples fulfilled its intended goal; yet not too long into the bill's tenure, Florida Republican legislators bemoaned how the bill was only meant to scare, and serve a political purpose.[2] Posts on social media circulated, calling out the bill, particularly highlighting how Florida agriculture would suffer significantly from the absence of migrant labor. Photos and videos proliferated of grocery stores devoid of fruit and vegetables on the shelves, as well as images of migrant farmworkers laboring expediently and productively, in efforts to rhetorically emphasize how this labor is truly "skilled" labor though popular belief posits it as "unskilled." Appearing on the video-sharing social media site TikTok, one video, where various types of laborers are shown harvesting grapes, presents itself as a before-and-after of the passing of Senate Bill 1718. Intending to be humorous, the fourteen-second video opens with a nonwhite, masculine-looking laborer rapidly, efficiently, and expediently harvesting green grapes into a basin in a Florida field.[3] The video cuts midway to white women, presumably US citizens, laboring slowly, inefficiently, and inexpediently, collecting the grapes at a lackluster pace. The juxtaposed laborers, and the disparities between their work practices, are further accentuated through a sonic coding: a distinct Mexican trumpet fanfare that for the nonwhite laborer is upbeat and jovial while for the white laborer is downbeat and cartoonishly sluggish. The video aims to poke fun at the white laborers' underwhelming working, victims of their Republican legislators' own xenophobic legislation. The video's logic is strikingly clear: nonwhite, undocumented Latinx workers are valuable to the state of Florida and the larger US nation-state, because they work hard, a lot, and under grueling environmental conditions—performing work that white citizen-subjects fail to do properly or refuse to do at all. Work, and hyperproductive work at that, determines the worthiness of a life, and such work-inflected axioms have become a staple rhetorical strategy for defending nonwhite, migrant people, and a means of legitimizing pro-immigrant discourses within the United States. However, a cruel logic undergirds this now commonsense argument: undocumented, nonwhite farmworkers deserve dignity and respect only if they work hard and fast enough, if they can prove themselves as "skilled" and thereby hyperproductive, able-bodied labor US capitalism can exploit, violate, and make expendable accordingly on behalf of the needs of capital. In both the pro- and anti-immigrant imaginary, there is no room for the underwhelming, sluggish nonwhite migrant laborer. There is no rhetorically or theoretically viable means to make a case for the nonwhite migrant farmworker who might be a little too slow, who paces themselves, takes their sweet time, isn't as "skilled" as their peers lauded on TikTok. The nonwhite migrant farmworker's right to life is a right to work. Ontologically, the indolent migrant farmworker can't exist under capitalism. They are a categorical anomaly.

Since its inception, work has been integral to the formation, expansion, and legitimization of the United States. Various workforces and modes of work were required to inaugurate the new nation: the work of white European colonists to displace, dispossess, and commit genocide against Native peoples across Turtle Island and Abya Yala; the work of white slave-traders and slave-owners to inaugurate chattel slavery across the Old and New Worlds; the work of enslaved African peoples to build the US nation and then, once emancipated, transitioning into exploitative systems of sharecropping and indentured servitude; the work of migrant workforces from China, Mexico, Puerto Rico, and elsewhere allowed to work for cheap in the United States under ever-fluctuating, conditional arrangements. In the twentieth century, discourses of work, the valorizing of waged labor, and productivism congealed into US public consciousness, forming a value system both internalized by subjects and externalized into public policy and general consensus. This paved the way for concentrated moral panics and legislative attacks upon the welfare system, the poor, and nonnormative subjects (nonwhite, queer, disabled). In this way, notions of proper respectability, bootstrapping, and a work ethic latched onto conceptions of individual self-making and communal uplift. Working hard, working a lot, and work as both an individual moral good and a collectively ethical enterprise became intimately tied to US statecraft and capitalist entrenchment that served to discipline, control, and quell unruly nonwhite populations.

These regimes of work also see the emergence of popular tropes and types constituted by notions of laziness, or the refusal to work properly or participate effectively in waged labor. Figures like the welfare queen, the idle Native, or the sex-obsessed indolent queer became dangerous figures haunting the US nation's work ethos and productivist mandate, the stability of the cisgender-heterosexual nuclear family, and the well-oiled capitalist system undergirding it all. These various types morphed into indolent pathologies in need of fixing or, if need be, elimination. The necessary foil to the imagined productive, hardworking, and respectable nonwhite worker became the lazy Other. In this way, nation-building, normative gender and sexuality that propagate the productive family, and capitalism go hand in hand. Defending the value of work has become a commonsense and lucrative industry shared by all classes and races, a rhetorical stance deployed to assert value, worth, and deservingness in comparison to unproductive, indolent Otherness. Moreover, the ongoing COVID-19 pandemic has made indolence—workers quitting, workers not wanting to risk their lives for work, workers wanting to not spend the majority of their lives laboring—a straw man for governmental ineptitude and capitalist retrenchment. Both the hyperproductive worker and the lazy person of color have been instrumental for US nation-building and the advancement of neoliberal capitalism. Neoliberalism designates a turn in the late twentieth century toward privatization, deregulation, and globalization, opening up new sectors for profit and accumulation. Formerly disavowed subjectivities and groups, like people of color and LGBTQ+ people, were now seen as viable, and lucrative, demographic markets to tap, a way in which to systematically coerce subjects into believing individual autonomy and freedom are exclusively achievable through accumulation of capital and cooperating with capitalism's dictates. What this enabled was the dismantling of public resources and social welfare services through austerity measures, market deregulation, cuts to wages and benefits, corporate tax breaks, and the privatization of all aspects of social life. Neoliberalism has become a totalizing ideology for ordering and systemizing both human and nonhuman ecologies, with neoliberal capitalist tenets concretizing into commonsense logic. One's ability to labor properly, and the subsequent ability to fashion an identity in relation to one's labor, has directly entwined itself into notions of proper, acceptable humanity within neoliberal capitalism, a model of humanness dependent upon ideas of bootstrapping, self-sacrifice, respectability, and the desecration of life and community for the sake of work, the family, capitalism itself.

These concerns over work, waged labor, and *indolence* are at the heart of *Revolting Indolence*. This book examines how styles of queer and trans Latinx indolence challenge capitalist logics and oppressive structures organizing the US nation-state. Its primary thesis theorizes upon various aesthetic strategies and world-making practices deriving from queer and trans Latinx cultural producers that undermine commonsense notions related to neoliberal capitalist work and productivity, normative representational rubrics affixed to minoritized peoples, and the procedures involved in valuing life and relationality under capitalism. Through a series of case studies analyzing literature, photography, television, film, and installation art, the queer and trans Latinx cultural producers profiled in *Revolting Indolence* vitalize indolence as a radical refutation of the norms of aspirational citizenship tied to cisheteronormative patriarchy, bourgeois respectability, assimilationist drives, and minoritarian uplift. Scenes of the spectacularly unremarkable and extravagantly mundane that encompass indolence, such as dozing, slacking off, lounging about, daydreaming, and other such indolent styles and comportments, revolt through the relishing in spatiotemporal slowing down and sensorial laxity as well as the aesthetically and performatively undercharged. The indolent styles I track operate in a two-pronged manner: (1) flagrant refusals of work and capitalist productivism by nonwhite queer and trans subjects, critiquing existing capitalist work paradigms; and (2) the inventing of alternative aesthetic strategies, sensoriums, and world-making practices that imagine elsewhere from neoliberal, cisheteronormative, white supremacist capitalism. The case studies examined aestheticize indolence as a pleasurable, enthralling practice activated through indolent styles that make possible antiwork critique and postwork imaginaries. Highlighting various indolent styles allows for "an action of coordinating form and content," as Michael Dango provocatively theorizes about style's ability to resolve the form-content debate in order to more effectively respond to crisis.[4] *Revolting Indolence* importantly expands the parameters of Latinx studies and literature, queer and trans of color theory, visual studies, film and television studies, and negative affect theory through reclaiming indolence as a category, and reevaluating how indolence generates liberatory practices that challenge oppressive, exploitative regimes of thought and valuation tied to capitalist work ethics, productivism, and respectability politics. By situating indolence as the central analytic framework of reading texts and objects, *Revolting Indolence* demonstrates how this underexamined mode reorients what is thinkable for, and how we can theorize anew, minoritized cultural production like that created by Latinx and queer and trans peoples. Indolence as a critical reading method directs the study of queer and trans Latinx aesthetics and culture away from needing to fit into neoliberal capitalist scripts that seek to make respectable and productive citizen-subjects. Instead, indolence as an analytic foregrounds liberatory agendas that work to redress majoritarian logics and imagine other forms of sensing, knowing, and worlding.

"I would prefer not to" is the maxim guiding the eponymous clerk in Herman Melville's short story "Bartleby, the Scrivener." The scrivener refuses to work; in fact, he prefers not to, as he continuously repeats to the Wall Street lawyer who employs him, instead opting for "looking out, at his pale window behind the screen, upon the dead brick wall,"[5] or what the narrator-boss coins as "one of those dead-wall reveries of his."[6] The boss is vexed by the worker's refusals and his lackadaisically dispirited behavior, and unable to deduce precisely why Bartleby believes he can *choose* to not adhere to the contract of waged labor, of working correctly and properly under capitalism. The scrivener even goes so far as to squat in the office. Eventually, Bartleby's refusals and squatting become far too noticeable to the other employees and clients. The scrivener's behavior stirs the narrator-boss's fears over what such lazy insubordination could foster: "The idea came upon me of his possibly turning out a long-lived man, and keep occupying my chambers, and denying my authority; and perplexing my visitors; and scandalizing my professional reputation; and casting a general gloom over the premises; keeping soul and body together to the last upon his savings (for doubtless he spent but half a dime a day), and in the end perhaps outlive me, and claim possession of my office by right of his perpetual occupancy."[7] Bartleby, the "intolerable incubus" haunting the offices of Wall Street, jeopardizes the seamless perpetuation of capitalist production and regimented work. The scrivener's slackerly example threatens to rub off on all who come into contact with him, or worse, to outright seize the property of the bourgeois capitalist. Bartleby's indolent insurrection is too glaringly in-your-face for the boss to let go unchecked. Ultimately, he is imprisoned for vagrancy and dies while incarcerated, because, according to the narrator, he seemingly refuses even to labor to keep himself alive.

Bartleby provides a poignant example of the worker's disenchantment with work under capitalism, and how the refusal of work troubles the routinized machinery upholding capital's flow. He also proves an illustrative case of how work under capitalism demands compliance through disciplinary measures juridically enforced by the carceral state. In *The Problem with Work: Feminism, Marxism, Antiwork Politics, and Postwork Imaginaries*, Kathi Weeks persuasively deconstructs how work in the United States has become a disciplining mechanism, maintained by conceptions of work as, individually, morally good and, collectively, productive for society. Following Weber's theorization on the Protestant work ethic's seamless integration into secularized capitalist systems, Weeks debunks the governing ideological premise that work functions as social uplift and societal betterment. "Challenging the present organization of work requires not only that we confront its reification and depoliticization," Weeks contends,

> but also its normativity and moralization. Work is not just defended on grounds of economic necessity and social duty; it

is widely understood as an individual moral practice and collective ethical obligation. Traditional work values—those that preach the moral value and dignity of waged work and privilege such work as an essential source of individual growth, self-fulfillment, social recognition, and status—continue to be effective in encouraging and rationalizing the long hours US workers are supposed to dedicate to waged work and the identities they are expected to invest in them.[8]

Work is socially and fiscally productive for capitalism, with citizen-subjects trained to internalize a sense of value and identity around waged labor, one that encroaches into every facet of life. In this way, valorized and virtuous conceptions of waged labor and work overwhelmingly constitute the grounds for human relation to others and the world. According to Weeks, discourses concerning work, not class, are the theoretical site upon which to challenge regimes of capitalist exploitation and production. This allows for various antiwork politics and postwork imaginaries to emerge that confront routinized conceptions of productivist work, waged labor, and the valuation of life tout court governing all forms of relation and axes of social difference under capitalism. Laboring and productivity are not in and of themselves practices or behaviors that are inherently exploitative or detrimental to the flourishing of human life. After all, we must labor in some capacity to maintain life and a functioning society; however, capitalism distorts and hijacks wholesale notions of labor, activity, purposefulness, and productivity to shore up neoliberal capitalist accumulation and state power. Weeks posits resistance premised upon "the refusal of work," "a refusal of central elements of the wage relation and those discourses that encourage our consent to the modes of work that it imposes. It comprises a refusal of work's domination over the times and spaces of life and of its moralization, a resistance to the elevation of work as necessary duty and supreme calling."[9] Mandating a basic universal income and shortening the workday is one such tactic that enacts alternatives.

This refusal of work echoes earlier theorizations by Italian Marxists in the 1960s and 1970s who operated under the banner of the *operaismo* movement. Roughly translating to "workerism," *operaismo*, spearheaded by thinkers like Mario Tronti, Romano Alquati, and Antonio Negri, put the struggle over the worker's labor, and the ability for the worker to refuse their labor-power, at the center of Marxist critique in an unprecedented way. According to the operaists, the refutation of work and of the status of being a worker in capitalism is the source of anti-capitalist possibility. Only when the worker recognizes themselves as being indubitably part of capitalism, when the worker acknowledges that even attempts at negotiating working conditions with the capitalist bourgeoisie are still working within the system, can the worker use that critical awareness to overturn capitalism: "Italian *operaismo* didn't glorify workers and proletarians: it wagered on the possibility that there was a force in them that they could mobilize against themselves, not to extend but to destroy their own condition. It was therefore a workerism against work, refusing a naturalized subjectivity imposed by the capital relation."[10] The worker becomes an antagonist to capitalism by negating the very condition of being a worker, by seeking the destruction of such an identity that capitalism will always find a way to exploit. As Steve Wright put it in his sober history of the movement's successes and flaws, "[*operaismo*] would force attention towards an exploration of the inherently contradictory experiences of workers, whether waged or otherwise, and from this to the terms upon which their struggle to turn such contradictions against the capital relation become feasible."[11] Mario Tronti theorized it in terms particularly salient for this study, when, for instance, discussing the power of the strike: "Living labor's refusal of activity is the recovery of its autonomy, which is to say, precisely the autonomy that the production process has to break."[12] Though Tronti does not outline at length upon passivity as anti-capitalist strategy, his abbreviated inquiry, nevertheless, urges a reconsideration of how inactivity and passivity, as theoretical frameworks and anti-capitalist tactics, are not apolitical, or not without radical force to effect change: "Once passivity is extended to a mass social scale, it can be a very high form of working-class struggle. We should never confuse the lack of open forms of struggle with a lack of struggle itself."[13] Recall Bartleby's Wall Street employer, who narrates his frustration at his slacking scrivener in this way: "The passiveness of Bartleby sometimes irritated me. I felt strangely goaded on to encounter him in new opposition, to elicit some angry spark from him answerable to my own."[14] Elsewhere, the narrator describes the clerk as having a "cadaverously gentlemanly *nonchalance*"[15] and a "wonderful mildness."[16] When the clerk refuses to vacate the premises after refusing to do any work, he is given an ultimatum:

"Either you must do something or something must be done to you."[17] His (in)action is to stay put, finding himself hauled off by the police for the crime of vagrancy. The worker not doing anything, total inaction, seems to bother Melville's lawyer above all else. From within the apparatus of capitalism, according to the operaists, the worker labors, deploying various tools and schemes, according to the situation and context, to undermine it from within. "Conditioned by the social relations of production," as Jacopo Galimberti postulates of *operaismo*'s approach to understanding the working class, "but that remained in an ongoing state of becoming, an ephemeral objective reached during struggles rather than a solid starting point."[18]

The "labor of love" myth is what Sarah Jaffe formulates as neoliberal capitalism's governing ideology, which coerces workers into believing a love of work will produce a sense of belonging, value, and fulfillment.[19] Workers internalize a commitment to work and capitalist mandates for accumulation and productivity premised upon a belief in reciprocal exchange, where loyalty to capitalism is supposed to generate individual satisfaction, interpersonal meaningfulness, and monetary reward. "Work has the appearance of informality," Amelia Horgan writes, "bound up with social relations and personal social capital, promising to be indistinct from sociability—offering friendship, or even family—in both good and bad jobs."[20] However, "turning our love away from other people and onto the workplace serves to undermine solidarity," Jaffe notes,[21] where the compulsion to love work not only authorizes capitalist exploitation for the sake of profit but rationalizes as commonsense that all kinds of exploitation (overwork, little pay, health-endangering labor, etc.) are in fact acceptable, and laudable, under the rubric of the labor-of-love myth. This bolsters Jennifer Ponce de León's diagnosis that "liberal ideology elaborates a hegemonic aesthetics of violence that works to naturalize and render imperceptible the violence inherent in capitalist social relations, including the violence capitalist states exercise to secure processes of accumulation and guarantee the reproduction of class relations."[22] Jaffe provocatively calls for a severing of love from capitalist work, in order to reprioritize solidarity, collective action, and nontransactional relations, where, day by day, workers "discover the pleasures that are to be found in rebellion."[23]

Critiques of valorized wage labor and moralized notions of productivist work under capitalism have been around for some time. Marx's son-in-law, Paul Lafargue, in 1883 penned a pamphlet titled *The Right to Be Lazy*, a diatribe against capitalist productivist values, which the proletariat, he believes, follow unquestioningly. "A strange madness has taken hold of the working class," begins Lafargue's polemic,[24] echoing his father-in-law and Friedrich Engels's famous opening line from *The Communist Manifesto*: "A spectre is haunting Europe—the spectre of communism." Ahead of his time, Lafargue refuses concessions to capitalist timescales and imperatives, stating the matter plainly:

> If the working classes would root out the vice that domineers them and debases their nature, they would rise up in all their terrible strength and call not for the Rights of Man, which are only the rights of capitalist exploitation, or the Right to Work, which is only the right to be poor but for the passage of an ironclad law prohibiting any man from working more than three hours a day, and the Earth, the old Earth, trembling with joy, would feel a new universe of life leaping within her. . . . But how can we ask such manly resolution of a proletariat corrupted by capitalist morality?[25]

Lafargue here epistemologically shifts the terms of the debate by urging the working class to refuse the tenets of liberal humanism ("Rights of Man") and valorized labor ("Right to Work"), which ascribe the value and meaningfulness of human life as inherently tied to work. Bertrand Russell, in his 1932 essay "In Praise of Idleness," likewise proclaims: "A great deal of harm is being done in the modern world by belief in the virtuousness of work, and that the road to happiness and prosperity lies in organized diminution of work."[26] Russell importantly links waged labor and moral virtuosity, a matrix crucial to capitalist common sense that subjugates the working classes, but his armchair philosophical approach abstains from a full-throated indictment or direct critique of capitalist machinations. A four-hour workday, as Russell posits, leads to more happiness for the proletariat, and that's morally good because it continues the operations of society as it already exists. This line of argument for better working conditions that doesn't necessarily require challenging capitalism, and, in fact, can make capitalism run more effectively, finds theoretical purchase in a growing corpus of popular self-help-styled literature on burnout, the attention economy, and the power of rest. Coping with capitalism is the animating thesis of works like Devon Price's *Laziness Doesn't Exist*, which debunks what they term "the Laziness Lie," those "source[s] of the guilty feeling that we are not 'doing enough'; it's also the force that compels us to work ourselves to sickness."[27] Price provides various strategies to unlearn the myth of our laziness under capitalism, and to find better ways of working in capitalism, neatly summing up the solution to burnout under capitalism as "boundless compassion."[28] Many of the lazy solutions Price advocates for promise to not disrupt capitalism but only help make it run smoother, because, as Price points out throughout, rested, contented workers create better profit and production for managers and businesses. *New York Times* best-selling book *How to Do Nothing: Resisting the Attention Economy* finds author Jenny Odell mounting a critique of how our attention and lives have gravitated to online spaces for a sense of self-worth and valuation, feeding into capitalist systems that prioritize individuality over community, human over nonhuman, productivity over inactivity, careerism over connection. "I want to argue for a new 'placefulness,'" Odell contends, "that yields sensitivity and responsibility to the historical (what happened here) and the ecological (who and what lives, or lived, here)."[29] Odell provides a multitude of examples from literature, technology, social movements, art, and her own lived experience to support her compelling thesis, but questions how minoritized social differences, and how they intersect with capitalism's choke hold over our attention, are too frequently sidelined or not given extended consideration. She herself emphasizes that resisting the attention economy depends upon various degrees of privilege that, inevitably, rely upon capitalism and capital to grant such resistance.[30] While I am sympathetic to the various strategies this body of work sets forth for living better under capitalism, what we find are solutions premised upon fashioning individualized escape routes (for those whose waged labor is flexible enough to do so, for those who have enough capital to do so) and narrow horizons for imagining a life beyond capitalist structures. Recall Marx's warning over capitalism's disregard of human well-being even when society dares to question its protocols: "[Capital's] answer to the outcry about the physical and mental degradation, the premature death, the torture of overwork, is this: Should that pain trouble us, since it increases our pleasure (profit)?"[31] Thinking under and beyond the terms set up by capital is imperative for world-remaking liberatory practice.

Revolting Indolence does not take a valorized, virtuous, or moralized conception of work, one's ability to demonstrate proper, legible, and deserving forms of waged labor or capitalist productivity, as the organizing framework for avowing the worthiness and valuing of human life. The rhetorical and epistemological temptation to turn to discourses of work as morally good, and productivism as ethical and thereby constituting the valuableness of marginalized human life, require refutation. Instead, I advocate for thinking indolence as a means of enacting liberatory practices that seek to critique, challenge, and imagine elsewhere from neoliberal, cisheteronormative, white supremacist capitalist dictates and structures. *Indolence* as the operative term used in this study closely aligns with other terminology that espouses antiwork and postwork sensibilities like idleness and lethargy. L. H. Stalling's *Funk the Erotic: Transaesthetics and Black Sexual Cultures* forwards a notion of funk disruptive to anti-Black, white supremacist capitalism. "Sexual expressivity and performance in black culture signals funk as a multisensory and multidimensional philosophy capable of dismantling systems of labor that organize race and sexuality for commercial profit," Stalling notes, introducing funk, and all its attendant sexual openness and embracing of filthiness, as a conceptual apparatus that provides alternatives to the paradigms of capitalism.[32] Stalling importantly locates how work, and the imperative to legibly operate through waged labor under capitalism no matter what the form of labor is, including sex work and pornography, becomes synonymous with proper morality and a functioning civilization. All labor is valuable to white supremacist capitalism, Stalling proffers, and therefore, embracing the abjection of funk allows for an antiwork and postwork politics to emerge, one that detaches itself from the governing logics of Enlightenment humanism. For philosopher Brian O'Connor, idleness resonates as a "state of not working" that "involves a departure from a range of values that make us the kinds of people we are supposed to be in order to live well," experienced as having "no guiding purpose" and as "noncompulsion and drift."[33] Tung-Hui Hu theorizes a notion of "lethargy," a kind of absence of emotion and inactivity, brought about by the digitization of everyday life and relations that people must navigate under capitalism. Lethargy, in Hu's formulation, becomes a coping response to the quotidian digital sphere that has become completely entwined with capitalist production and exploitation: "Lethargy is concerned with enduring a condition rather than refusing it. What on first glance seems like a lack of engagement, action, or responsiveness (*argos*, not-working, not-acting) is in fact a way of abiding, remaining intact, or tolerating the intolerable; it is generally a set of tactics to survive within a condition (e.g., delaying tactics that forestall the inevitable), rather than a way of overturning the condition."[34] Whereas Stalling's theorization of funk attends explicitly to sexual expression as a stankiness that counteracts capitalism, O'Connor's notion of idleness describes a kind of pleasurable drift distinct from capitalist purposefulness, and Hu's concept of lethargy illustrates an enduring of capitalism, my sense of indolent laziness diverges from these theorizations by focusing on how indolent laziness's popular connotations as a pejorative designation and an abject category markedly averse to capitalist sensibility, mediated *as* nonwhite, feminine, and queer in comportment, is precisely what supercharges indolence for radical critique and world-making otherwise. In this way, indolence becomes "a counter-time and counter-sense of the world" that "spurns activity as the sole destiny of man and civilization," as Pierre Saint-Amand poignantly puts it.[35]

Laziness, as an appellation and category unique unto itself, is closely examined by Nick Salvato in his fascinating book *Obstruction*, which charts scholarly inquiry into genealogies of literary and artistic laziness within a generalized US-European cultural context. Salvato theorizes laziness as a form of obstruction, a generative impasse that stimulates intellective inquiry through a variety of liquid, slack styles of aesthetic comportment. Through a close analysis of a genealogy of writers like Samuel Johnson, Oscar Wilde, and Robert Louis Stevenson, Salvato proffers "an active form of lazing, distinguished from a more passive or even ossified state of laziness," where a "liquid set of styles" and "liquidification of the contingent norms governing work and value" become possible through lazing modes of writing and thinking, a "proof that slacking, in the sense of un-tautening thought, is not coeval with thought's abandonment or, less dramatically, with the abandonment of its concretion."[36] Lazing enables another kind of intellective action and purposefulness, one that invigorates an otherwise frowned-upon category like lazy, a revaluation of how meaningful thinking can look and feel differently than the concretized norms of scholarly style and productiveness. In order to provide critical heft for his sense of lazing, Salvato stresses a distinction between being lazy and the practice of lazing, where the latter functions as "a phenomenal cultivation of attention and rumination that we might profitably distinguish from the sense of stasis or ossification (as well as pejorative judgement, so often classed and racialized) connoted by the nominal form of laziness."[37] Salvato attempts to redeem lazing (a practice or style) as a productive, purposeful intellective undertaking by definitionally disassociating it from the loaded *lazy* (ontologically determined), or its descriptive counterpart, *laziness*, which he notes as overtaxed by class and race significations. Salvato's conceptual parsing here is underwritten by the anxiety-inducing spectre of laziness, which demands for posterity's sake a disavowal and distancing from laziness's weighty stigmatized baggage that manifests as ontological status or descriptive truth, in order to endow a sense of intellectual seriousness and appropriate productivity. From this, the critical wager I proffer is as follows: What if we lean in to the classed and racialized dimensions of laziness? What occurs to conceptions of lazy indolence when theorized as liberatory styles, praxis, and aesthetics? What avenues of intellectual inquiry, social critique, and political transformation are possible if we do not seek to disavow or delink *lazy* from its historical saturation in stereotype, tropes, and abjection that have been overwhelmingly configured as nonwhite, poor, feminine? What happens if we give in to the fullness of the messy, unsavory, and discomfiting complexity of laziness's historical baggage and stigmatized underpinnings, which have long been construed as ethically, socially, and politically compromised?

This series of questions instigates a necessary revision of the laziness genealogy, one that extends into earlier epochs, and one that grapples with the nonwhite refusenik and the Global South loafer. This genealogical extension leads to a confrontation with Enlightenment philosophy and the aesthetic theory of Immanuel Kant. The eighteenth-century German philosopher conceived a sense of work as the ability to produce aesthetic judgement and to discern regimes of beauty through fantasizing (fetishizing?) about purposeful, productive vigorousness and about the feminized nonwhite Other's laziness. In order to ascertain the radical shifts indolence may usher in, we must rethink the procedures of valuation, and orient ourselves anew to the relations constituting life, community, and world. This proposition requires a troubling of an inheritance given to us by Enlightenment philosophy, one whose ramifications are long overdue in addressing.

KANT'S VIGOR, BORED CARIBS, AND INDOLENT UNENLIGHTENMENT

During the long eighteenth century, Western Enlightenment, an age where reason, science, and knowledge were being systematized and incorporated into conceptions of everyday modernity, needed industry. The age of Enlightenment required industry of the attitudinal kind, the need for individuals to be industrious for the sake of human ennoblement, knowledge production, and civilizational advancement, as well as the mechanical kind, the need for profitable industries to emerge organized around waged labor, plantation slave economies, global commerce, and other industrious technological innovations. Enlightening oneself was hard work, with work functioning as an ennobling and edifying procedure, and no one espoused such views more so than Immanuel Kant, eminent philosopher of Enlightenment and aesthetic theory. Laziness and cowardice are the preeminent obstacles in the way of free-thinking, rational, autonomous subjectivity, Kant argues in his 1784 response, "An Answer to the Question: 'What Is Enlightenment?,'" a polemic serving as his diagnosis of the state of reason and philosophical enlightenment. The ability for "Man" to think for "himself" (for it was always intended to be a *he*, to be a man) depends upon exercising a free will that counters a "self-incurred immaturity," or a "lack of resolution and courage to use [one's understanding] without the guidance of another."[38] This lazy, cowardly dependence on others to guide one in rational thinking, what Kant terms "immaturity," prohibits self-possessed, free-thinking individualism from flourishing: "Laziness and cowardice are the reasons why such a large proportion of men, even when nature has long emancipated them from alien guidance (*naturaliter maiorennes* [Those who have come of age by virtue of nature]), nevertheless gladly remain immature for life."[39] Overthrowing this compromised state of immaturity, according to Kant, requires hard work, masculine determination, and a penchant for bold autonomy apart from the masses. Kant is hard-pressed, however, to distinguish how public enlightenment happens at a large scale when his argument, paradoxically, hinges on a virtuosic, "chosen one"–type paradigm, "a few who think for themselves,"[40] in contradistinction to those "who must behave purely passively" and "must simply obey."[41] Kant's theses on enlightenment are understood by Michel Foucault as "neither a world era to which one belongs, nor an event whose signs are perceived, nor the dawning of an accomplishment,"[42] but more, "a process in which men participate collectively and as an act of courage to be accomplished personally."[43] Foucault here highlights how Kant envisions enlightenment as disciplined self-improvement, requiring a masculinist, individualized work ethic and attitudinal disposition that fosters the appropriate conditions for bringing wider civilizational enlightenment. The "greatest" achievement of Enlightenment thinking, and its most prized possession, which capitalism would adopt and refine to disturbing proportions, here takes shape: the discrete, objective, masculinist, work-oriented, and heroicized individualist emerges, a quintessential figure of moral good and ethical soundness, upheld as *the* valorized, virtuosic, and idealized subject for *all* humans to measure up to and aspire after. The bar has never been higher.

Kant's vaunting of masculinist work as a necessary means for enlightenment of oneself and the public unfolds in a more intricate, and convoluted, manner in his third critique, *The Critique of Judgement*, where he attempts to articulate a proper aesthetic judgement according to degrees of vigor. In it, Kant postulates upon the differences between the beautiful and the sublime, aesthetic judgement, proper forms of taste, and ideas on what constitutes genius. The famous treatise is much more fragmented, unsystematic, and roving than his *Critique of Pure Reason* or *Critique of Practical Reason*: "a disorganized and repetitious work, which gains little from Kant's struggle to impose on its somewhat diffuse subject matter the structure of the transcendental philosophy."[44] Nevertheless, the third critique has proved formative across generations of thought for theorizing aesthetic judgement and the sublime and has become the philosophical bedrock to aesthetic theory. Kant establishes a dialectic of vigor in order to differentiate how the aesthetic judgement of the beautiful and the sublime operate. For Kant, sublimity occurs not in the object but rather in the subject, who produces an "attitude of thought."[45] This aesthetic response induces in the part of the judging subject a kind of vigorousness. "The mind feels itself *set in motion* in the representation of the sublime in nature," postulates Kant, "whereas in the aesthetic judgement upon what is beautiful therein it is in *restful* contemplation."[46] Kant goes so far as to emphasize the polarities of vigor each judgement requires, expounding upon the differential vigor in this way: "Every affect of the STRENUOUS TYPE (such, that is, as excites the consciousness of our power of overcoming every resistance (*animi strenui*)) is *aesthetically sublime*, e.g. anger, even desperation (the *rage of forlorn hope* but not *faint-hearted despair*). On the other hand, affect of the LANGUID TYPE (which converts the very effort of resistance into an object of displeasure (*animum languidum*)) has nothing *noble* about it, though it may take its rank as possessing beauty of the sensuous order."[47] Affect in nature and the fine arts becomes a means of discerning what constitutes the sublime and the beautiful through degrees of vigor. These degrees rely upon superimposing onto the sublime and the beautiful various binaries, active and passive, strong and weak, and exertive and lethargic, though these descriptive binaries prove unwieldy for Kant, as he uses the various terms interchangeably and unevenly. The neat, binaristic divisions are hard for Kant to maintain: "Even sorrow (but not dispirited sadness) may take its place among the *vigorous* affects, provided it has its root in moral ideas. If, however, it is grounded upon sympathy, and, as such, is lovable, it belongs only to the *languid* affections."[48] Though Kant's classificatory schema deploys many conflicting descriptors that end up producing dizzying imprecision rather than clarity, he does not propose a moralistic distinction between the beautiful and the sublime. They are two polarities of vigor, which function differently though both may traffic in an indolence that Kant establishes as unsuitable for proper aesthetic judgement. For instance, Kant maintains language that equates proper aesthetic judgement with a moralism premised upon disavowing laziness: "Romances, maudlin dramas, shallow homilies, which trifle with so-called (though falsely so) noble sentiments, but in fact make the heart *enervated*, insensitive to the *stern* precepts of duty, and incapable of respect for the worth of humanity in our own person and the rights of human beings (which is something quite other than their happiness), and in general incapable of all *firm* principles." Or, as Kant espouses over the "vigorous resolution" needed to overcome base inclinations, his denouncing of the "passive frame of mind" is supposedly needed in order to be acceptable to God.[49] Ultimately, Kant constitutes proper aesthetic judgement upon a masculinized, hardworking, hyperattentive, and laboring vigorousness that casts as morally suspicious anything determined as feminine, lax, unfocused, or improperly vigorous.

Kant's third critique hinges on the consensus of a public where the subjective tastes of all coalesce into an objective, commonsense logic, "sensus communis," a universal agreement over what properly counts as beautiful and how one *works* to attain such aesthetic discernment. This communal agreement of aesthetic judgement of the beautiful and the sublime coheres over a moral goodness contingent upon "a *public sense*, i.e. a faculty of judging which in its reflective act takes account (*a priori*) of the mode of representation of everyone else, in order, *as it were*, to weigh its judgement with the collective reason of mankind, and thereby avoid the illusion arising from subjective and personal conditions which could readily be taken for objective, an illusion that would exert a prejudicial influence upon its judgement."[50] When the consensus is met over what gets deemed beautiful, "the mind," summarizes Kant, "becomes conscious of a certain ennoblement and elevation above mere sensibility to pleasure from impressions of the senses, and also appraises the worth of others on the score of a like maxim of their judgement."[51] How we come to such a *sensus communis* of proper taste is left unclear in Kant's system. However, it is well enough evident that in Kant's system, not only one but all must work hard to cultivate such objective, universal aesthetic discernment, with work functioning as the unifying basis of individual and communal intellectual worthiness as enlightened subjects in a modernizing age. If left unchecked, an indolent imperative threatens to toxify (intoxicate?) not only the individual but the entire *sensus communis*.

Whatever conceptual integrity and systematic dichotomy Kant seeks to uphold in his critique, even though descriptively confounding and riddled with contradictions his philosophy may be, relies upon a suppressed third vigor: the indolent vigor. The sensuous, indolent subject figures within Kant's dialectical system as those who derive pleasure and enjoyment from sensory impressions and who are unable to refine their aesthetic judgement or taste through a subjective universality that all have in common. These types, "who have no *feeling* for beautiful nature (for this is the word we use for susceptibility to an interest in the contemplation of beautiful nature), and who devote themselves to the merely sensuous enjoyments found in eating and drinking,"[52] are the exception that constitutes the dialectical norm, useful precisely to be dismissed as inappropriate for aesthetic discernment and undeserving of serious consideration. This diminishment of the sense of taste finds further traction in the later aesthetic philosophy of Hegel, where "smell, taste, and feeling remain excluded from being sources of artistic enjoyment," counting only as a sensation of pleasantness.[53] Hegel here abets the link made in Kant between the senses of taste, smell, and touch as too sensuous, a sensuousness inducing one into the vices of sloth, and, therefore, improper for aesthetic judgement. The sensuous, lazy subject is one who is unable to appropriately extrapolate sensations into a schema of aesthetic judgement that perceives pure forms, especially natural forms, as Kant's preferential interest in the natural versus the arts of humans attests.

This third term of the indolent vigor haunting the dialectic finds further elaboration in *Anthropology from a Pragmatic Point of View*, a series of lectures given across the years and published near the end of Kant's life, a highly commented upon work in which Kant expands the scope of his philosophical system to address questions of the human condition and social difference.[54] The *Anthropology* is not only an application of his more abstract, universalizing theories on concrete, particular case studies but also an extension and further concretization of his earlier thinking. In a section entitled "On the Highest Physical Good," Kant articulates how "the greatest sensuous enjoyment, which is not accompanied by any admixture of loathing at all, is *resting after work*, when one is in a healthy state."[55] Loathing for oneself arises only when "rest[ing] without having first worked" occurs, his description for laziness, wherein recreation and relaxation are only tolerable to the degree that they prepare the person to work again, to restore the worker for another day of toil. "Among the three vices: *laziness*, *cowardice*, and *duplicity*, the first appears to be the most contemptible," Kant asserts, but attenuates the force of the statement: "Nature has also wisely placed the aversion to continuous work in many a subject, an instinct that is beneficial both to the subject and to others, because, for example, a man cannot stand any prolonged or frequently repeated expenditure of power without exhaustion, but needs certain pauses for recreation."[56] Although brief, a flicker of antiwork sensibility emerges in this sentence-long qualification to Kant's disparaging of laziness, a minor deviation from his own staunch orthodoxy on work as ennobling and edifying above all else.

These remarks on laziness in *Anthropology from a Pragmatic Point of View* may seem, at first blush, racially unmarked, another instantiation of Kant taking the white European man as the implied universal. However, one remembers that these postulations are subsumed within the work's larger apparatus structured around grappling with racial, cultural, and civilizational differences. Foucault, in his doctoral thesis study of the *Anthropology*, frames the book and Kant's approach as "rooted in a German system of expression and experience," with a bias revealing a "geographical and linguistic space from which it cannot be quite disassociated."[57] Tracking the world-shifting pleasures of daydreaming in the work of Black artists and writers, what she terms "wandering as philosophical performance," Sarah Jane Cervenak demonstrates how wandering proves vital for defying the impositions of Enlightenment rationality and comportment that philosophers like Kant wanted to resist. "Racialized and sexualized deviations (unprincipled movements)," notes Cervenak, were the conditions of possibility for Enlightenment reason, and manifested in Kant's precritical writings, *Observations on the Feeling of the Beautiful and Sublime* (1764), where "wandering described a movement antithetical yet indispensable for reason."[58] In this early writing, Kant needed to disavow the errant, perverse Black subject in order to set up an appropriate, idealized rational subjectivity befitting an Enlightenment sensibility. The pathologizing of nonwhite Others, and the various descriptive-semiotic associations white European philosophers ascribed to them, was crucial for legitimizing Enlightenment thought as an enactment of moral freedom and human progress, with Kant here orchestrating one of the first theories of race.[59] As Cervenak illustrates convincingly, Kant himself practiced a methodological waywardness across his oeuvre, "someone with a promiscuous relationship to space, place, and principle,"[60] and "colonialist wandering,"[61] activated through his readings on colonial travel reports—a raced sense of waywardness Kant needed to reject in order to authorize his thinking. Errant movement, exemplified best by nonwhite and feminized Others, was both disturbing *and* enticing for the eminent philosopher of the Enlightenment.

The indolent vigor I have been schematizing materializes most visibly in the *Anthropology* as a distinctly non-European, nonwhite figure: the Caribbean Native. "The Carib," as Kant designates a people he imagines to be indigenous to the region of the Caribbean, appears in a footnote in book 2 describing "the feeling of pleasure and displeasure" in a section explicating upon the nature of boredom. For Kant, boredom is a difficult state to exist in, because one does not know how to make meaningful and valuable one's passing of time. Boredom, Kant writes, induces a "void of sensation" that demands "the striving to fill up" one's life "with something or other,"[62] surmising, melodramatically, that unresolved boredom leads to suicide. Either way, the logic undergirding

Kant's boredom postulate is that when one is bored, work, and the attendant value one is supposed to derive from the purposefulness and meaningfulness of working, does not occur, and this proves frightening for the father of Enlightenment philosophy. In order to drive home the seriousness of boredom's threat, Kant turns to example as proof, a methodological tool he shies away from in his magnum opus, *Critique of Pure Reason*, and uses only sparingly in *Critique of Judgement*. "Because of his inborn lifelessness," Kant writes,

> the Carib is free from this arduousness. He can sit for hours with his fishing rod, without catching anything; thoughtlessness is a lack of incentive to activity, which brings pain with it, from which this one is spared.

In Kant's view, the Caribbean Native is immune to feeling boredom, because they have not acquired the ability for self-possessed, free-thinking individuality paramount to Enlightenment rationality and, therefore, cannot cultivate a suitable work ethic and productivist sensibility in which to even need to stave off boredom. The trope of the idle Native is not new or unique to Kant, reaching far back into the colonial record, but it is torqued by the philosopher to fit into his larger philosophical apparatus, which synonymizes a Protestant, vigorous work ethos with intellective capacity and human worthiness. Moreover, in his earlier precritical writing, *Observations on the Feeling of the Beautiful and Sublime*, Kant, ever the taxonomist, cleaves a distinction between "the savages" of North America (particularly those of Canada, a settler designation for a colony that would belong in the course of Kant's life to France, then England) and those of South America, "indifferent and phlegmatic,"[63] with the former serving as a useful example of the noble savage trope pervasive in the white European imagination. "The Canadian savage," according to Kant's racialist hierarchy, "is moreover truthful and honest. The friendship he establishes is just as adventurous and enthusiastic as anything reported from the oldest and most fabulous times. He is extremely proud, sensitive to the complete worth of freedom, and even in education tolerates no encounter that would make him feel a lowly subjugation."[64] Here the North American Native, in contrast to the Carib and the South American Native as well as the Black African (of whom Kant asserts, "not a single one has ever been found who has accomplished something great in art or science or shown any other praiseworthy quality"[65]), is valiant, honorable, and vigorously masculine and shares, to the degree possible that they can since they are still nonwhite in Kant's terms, in the white European man's pursuit of possessive individualism and free-thinking. Some Natives are lazy, some Natives aren't, and for Kant the distinction matters for reifying his conception of what qualifies as valorized humanness.

In the same footnote on boredom in the *Anthropology*, and immediately after his comment on the Carib fisherman, he wags his finger in another direction:

> Our reading public of refined taste is always sustained by the appetite and even the ravenous hunger for reading ephemeral writings (a way of doing nothing), not for the sake of self-cultivation, but rather for *enjoyment*. So the readers' heads always remain empty and there is no fear of over-saturation. For they give the appearance of work to their busy idleness and delude themselves that it is a worthy expenditure of time, but it is no better than what the *Journal of Luxury and Fashion* offers to the public.

Kant here explicitly indicts the white European, who is the arbiter of Enlightened personhood and a civilizational emblem. Within the space of this footnote, Kant condemns both New World Native and Old World European according to a metric of sensuous, indolent vigor. In this way, boredom, not knowing exactly what to do to make one's time and life purposeful and productive, and its resulting vice of laziness that both nonwhite Native and white European can commit, in effect, becomes the glue synthesizing Kant's various disparate and convoluted threads of thought around what constitutes the proper enlightened subject. Indolent vigor amounts to the ultimate affront to Enlightenment rationality that enlightened Europe and the unenlightened darker continents share in common, an unseemly, transcendent obstacle in the way of civilizational progress and capitalist modernity. In this light, the rebelliousness of laziness had to be quelled at all costs. The best method of suppressing such indolent revolt was by "enlightening" as many as possible across all corners of the globe, by any means necessary, into believing in a system where work, above all else, above even a good life itself, had to be the supreme reason of why one lives at all, in toto.

What I am alighting on in this turn to Enlightenment thought is that thinkers like Kant relied upon a metric of vigorousness as a means of rationalizing proper and improper forms of aesthetic judgement and comportment. By doing so, this naturalized the idea that laziness is an ultimate affront, a primordial embarrassment to notions of societal progress, knowledge production, and modernity, wholly antithetical to what it might mean to be a human and relate to other humans, non-humans, and the world. A person nominally affixed with an indolent epithet—the idler, the lounge lizard, the vagabond, the couch potato, the welfare queen, the layabout, the loiterer, the indolent queer—does not identify as such, does not lean in to the unbecoming, unruly energies inherent within such pejoratives, because to do so is to prove the tastemakers of proper forms of civilization and humanity, like Kant, right, an avowal that, if committed, categorically confirms sweeping representational truths about various groups that make them exploitable, violable, and disposable. The perversity of sensuous indolence, and the various racialist discourses it was refined through, may have gained ground in Enlightenment philosophy, but it is under post-Enlightenment, the instantiation of neoliberal capitalism, where it truly soars free. Kant's abhorrence toward the sensuous, indolent vigor, which he had to denounce and exorcise at all costs to legitimize his system of aesthetic judgement, is precisely why I locate in indolence a radical, liberatory charge to unmake and remake conceptions of how the world can be. Retooling castigated indolence provides a way to reroute sensibilities that can counter the Western Enlightenment colonial-capitalist project.

SLACKERS, DAYDREAMERS, AND OTHER LAZY TYPOLOGIES: RECLAIMING INDOLENCE AS LIBERATORY PRACTICE

Indolence is revolting to capitalism. The threat of laziness entails the delegitimizing and dismantling of ideologies of normative gender and sexuality premised upon the white, moneyed, masculine-centered, and monogamous nuclear family, which has so laboriously worked to rationalize the deception that capitalism is the only viable, only imaginable arrangement for understanding oneself as a person and living together well in a society. The pejorative, abject connotations indolence invokes are precisely what makes this affective-performative category primed for critiquing and imagining elsewhere from exploitative capitalist work logics, bourgeois respectability, and normatively rendered citizenship aspirationally tied to cisheteronormative white supremacist patriarchy. In fact, the overwhelming menace that indolence is chalked up to be, those various practices and imaginaries of unseemly unruliness it traffics in, demonstrates exactly why it is instrumental for developing the conceptual tools and aesthetic strategies needed to disrupt and imagine elsewhere from capitalist systems. I follow in Tom Lutz's articulation that "slackers are precisely those who argue that the good life is better than the good job," who have "encouraged us to think of work, whether we are compensated financially or not, whether it fulfills our obligations or not, in terms that complement rather than compete with our sense of life worth living, replacing duty and necessity with pleasure and satisfaction."[66] Taking seriously the undertheorized indolent liberatory schemas I track across this book crucially demonstrates how to devise aesthetic strategies, sensoriums, and world-making practices that yearn for what José Esteban Muñoz formulates as "a *then and there*" of queer utopia that aims elsewhere from the "here and now's totalizing rendering of the present," where "we must dream and enact new and better pleasures, other ways of being in the world, and ultimately new worlds."[67]

Indolence concentrates various disparate yet interanimating nodes of minoritized difference, which is what makes it a long-standing target, and boogeyman, for US neoliberal capitalism. However, activity, productivity, usefulness, purpose, and work are not diametrically opposed to indolence, often understood to exist upon a matrix of passivity, inactivity, frivolousness, aimlessness, and nonwork, though they can be that too. Indolent enactments may have goals or outcomes in their purview.[68] The problem at hand is that white supremacist capitalism has completely hijacked the means of how we understand these various terms, attitudes, and modes of comportment, in effect binarizing them in order to codify the work value system that has become entrenched in popular discourse and public consciousness. As Thorstein Veblen aptly diagnosed it at the turn of the twentieth century, "the propensity for achievement and the repugnance to futility remain the underlying economic motive."[69] I aim to think capaciously about what constitutes indolence, opting for an expansive scope of how and under what conditions it may manifest. For instance, Brian O'Connor makes a sharp distinction between the possibilities of idleness and that of capitalist-granted leisure time away from work. "The boundaries of leisure, though, are to be found in the degree to which leisure can be incorporated within the general model of the modern social actor," he writes, where

> in today's world leisure may be considered a liberation of a sort, yet many labor regimes make leisure—paid vacation leave—obligatory. Leisure is good, apparently, not only for the worker but also for the employer. The general model of the effective social actor within a system of work is partly sustained in this way. Idleness, by contrast, threatens to undermine what the model requires, namely, disciplined, goal-oriented individuals. For that reason, idleness cannot be incorporated within the productivity model—unlike leisure—since it is a noninstrumental break from all that is required to make us useful.[70]

I agree with O'Connor in that, definitionally, leisure is time away from waged labor ordained by capitalism in order to restore the worker for future capitalist laboring, thereby making leisure an acceptable form of nonwork because it adheres to capitalist morality and productivity. However, I depart from the categorical bifurcation O'Connor sets up in slotting discipline, goal-orientedness, and instrumentality as features of regimes of labor in contrast to idleness, with such a descriptive matrix only reifying the overarching framework rationalizing the capitalist work value system. The allure of this neat dichotomy for theorizing antiwork modes and practices—productive or unproductive, useful or frivolous, active or inactive, purposeful or aimless—succumbs too easily to an apolitical, decontextualized, and universalizing philosophizing that discounts the radical purposefulness, productivity, usefulness, action, and labor involved in imagining indolence as a viable means of enacting political critique and social transformation. In his study of "loiterature," those loitering practices and loiterly styles depicted in literature, Ross Chambers illustrates how loitering pleasurably toggles between these apparently steadfast binaries of active/passive, purposeful/aimless, useful/frivolous, productive/unproductive, etc etera. Loiterature "casts serious doubt on the values good citizens hold dear—values like discipline, method, organization, rationality, productivity, and, above all, work—but it does so in the guise of innocent and, more particularly, insignificant or frivolous entertainment," Chambers explicates,[71] where loitering operates as a stealthy subterfuge of digressiveness that, nonetheless, poses a challenge to commonsense values appended to the work value system. He goes on to describe loiterature as "loitering with intent" and "attacking all possible objects of attention without attaching itself to any,"[72] where "its art lies not in not moving but in moving without going anywhere in particular, and indeed in moving without knowing—or maybe pretending not to know—where it's going."[73] Loitering waywardly flies under the radar, but that does not preclude it from being an active, purposeful, useful, productive, and engaged practice. "In a larger universe that seems committed to directness, speed, and immediacy (doing it fast, getting there right away)," Chambers elucidates, "delay and indirection—the phenomenon of mediacy—become at once sources of pleasure and devices of provocation."[74] La Marr Jurelle Bruce similarly focuses on loitering as political praxis for Black queer world-making and speaks to the radical energies in loitering for mapping out other worlds distinct from white supremacist capitalist ones, where loitering's sense of "aimlessness might conceal a truth of deliberation, strategy, and care" for a radical "slowness or stillness that violates [proper movement in anti-Black capitalist spaces] mandates."[75] Loitering does something by doing nothing. Loitering, like its taxonomic relative, indolence, busies itself with subtle subterfuge, if one leans in closely enough to sense it.

Additionally, I theoretically diverge from O'Connor's critique of leisure by contending that leisure, even if granted in part by capitalism's need to restore the vitality of a labor force, still leaves room for antiwork and postwork possibility. In those far-too-few hours of not working, of capitalist-granted leisure, we must excavate, too, the lines of refusal and lines of flight that emerge, especially for those whose only respite from waged labor and capitalist productivity are snatches of leisure time. We cannot predict what inventions for radical change may reside after a shift has ended, through the course of a weekend off, or following an extended vacation away from a job. To put a finer point on it, under the totalizing reach of twenty-first-century capitalism, there is really no pure relation to passing one's time distinct from capitalism, no way to bracket off a space-time that is not in some way structured by capitalism. Any deviance of indolence operates in some relation to capitalism, but that does not minimize or preclude its ability to challenge, or imagine elsewhere, from it.

Existing scholarship on Latinx negative affect, performances, and aesthetics importantly reclaims modes like shame, ugliness, and unbelonging for social critique and liberatory practices. In his influential book *Dead Subjects: Toward a Politics of Loss in Latino Studies*, Antonio Viego, utilizing Lacanian psychoanalytics, provides alternative pathways for rendering Latinx subjects apart from the white supremacist assimilative demand to be whole, unified, and transparent selves. In order for racism to function smoothly, Viego argues, it depends upon the transparency of the racialized subjectivity, "bank[ing] on the faith and conceit that these subjects can be exhaustively and fully elucidated through a certain masterful operation of language," where nonwhite, raced subjects are only able to redress injustice in the very terms and frameworks that, paradoxically, are used to dominate them.[76] One of the "most generative internal principles" for racist discourse to flourish is for aggrieved racialized subjects to present themselves to state power as an "undivided, obscenely full and complete ethnic-racialized subject, transparent to itself and to others." One must refute one's racialized violation of mind/body, one's abjection by the state, in order to appeal to a hegemonic model of appropriately recognized, violated subject. In a similar vein, José Esteban Muñoz's posthumously published *The Sense of Brown* is also instructive for outlining queer and trans Latinx subjectivity against the grain of conceptions of Latinx wholeness and respectability. Muñoz formulates Latinx affect as "off," a failing of sorts in relation to affective US whiteness, which constructs itself as minimal, underwhelming, and unmarked, "revolv[ing] around an understanding of the Latina/o as affective excess."[77] For Muñoz, the myriad social differences and complexities of latinidad might be more generatively accounted for through the articulation of a racialized brownness, a "feeling like a problem, in commonality," that enables a better sense of struggle in common against hegemonic forces.[78] Brownness, conceptualized as a diversity of affective and performative utterances deriving from Latinxness, is a potential unifier of Latinx people conceived through nonwhite abjection, Muñoz suggests. However, I do not ascribe Latinxness to a distinct racial category like *brown*, which I have elsewhere explicated upon at length.[79] I understand *brown* or *brownness* as a nominal designation to signal nonwhite racialized experience rather than an ontologically stable racial formation between Black and white. Think, for example, of the euphemism "Black and Brown peoples," oft said in common parlance to signal "Black and non-Black racialized Latinx peoples," a way of addressing the experiences of nonwhite racialization for people who share to varying degrees and combinations the characteristics of being brown-skinned, undocumented or temporary documentation statuses within the Global North, non–English speaking or multilingual, living in distinct ethnic enclaves or barrios, and so on. "Brown is not an identity. Brown, along with its nominal form, *brownness*, are also not objects of knowledge in the ways that identity markers such as 'Latina/o' or 'Chicana/o' are in the late twentieth and early twenty-first centuries," as Joshua Javier Guzmán explains.[80] If brownness understood as a positionality between white and Black, as it is often rendered, is synonymous with Latinx, then it inevitably must eject any iteration of Latinx Blackness in order to guarantee distinctiveness, intelligibility, and legitimacy. Ren Ellis Neyra puts it succinctly in their assessment of brownness: "Blackness is not a position in brownness's semiotic world but material for its becoming."[81] Blackness is not an add-on to Latinx, and, as Alan Pelaez Lopez argues, "the liberation of all Latinx people necessitates the liberation of Black Latinxs. If this does not happen, systems of racism, colorism, and anti-Blackness will prevail in the Latinx community."[82] Tracing a historical analysis of how Dominican peoples have disassociated from Blackness and Black identity due to white supremacist imperialism and ideologies, and how contemporary mobilizations of Latinx identity formation in the United States actively distinguish it as not Black, scholar Lorgia García-Peña notes how "the common practice of referring to Latino/a/xs as a race—rather than as an arbitrary conglomerate of ethnic and racially diverse peoples who trace their origins to Latin America—further erases Black Latinxs from literally every space, institution, and possibility of representation."[83] In *Decolonizing Diasporas: Radical Mappings of Afro-Atlantic Literature*, Yomaira C. Figueroa-Vásquez importantly postulates how "Atlantic modernities are contingent upon forms of racialization and domination that are most often expressed through modes of anti-Blackness," opting to use the prefix "Afro" for her studies of Black Latinx writers, which "allows for Africa to be central to the configurations of Atlantic circuits."[84] García-Peña's and Figueroa-Vásquez's interventions here are paramount for addressing the rhetorical distinctions made by non-Black Latinx people to distance themselves from Blackness, and in hopes to carve out a kind of raced category distinct from it in the United States such as *brown*. An unspecific, pseudouniversal racialization of the Latinx category or latinidad in general is no longer viable if we want to ensure anti-Blackness's much-needed end, demanding a "keener awareness of specificities and internal complexities . . . across the amplified range of groups."[85] "Thinking of black trans women experiences," as scholar Dora Silva Santana articulates in her study of Black Brazilian travesti peoples, "is about how we reassemble the ways we understand racialization of black bodies as gendered, with as many genders as we encounter, but at the same time that blackness also ungenders and is trans-ing bodies."[86] Santana's work on Blackness in a Brazilian context is Latinx studies work, highlighting forms of Black trans latinidades that seek to dismantle anti-Black and anti-trans worlds, which puts pressure on the conceptual viability of brownness. Not all iterations of Latinxness are racialized as nonwhite, nor are all Latinx people automatically nonwhite, whether in the United States or Latin America, but the various cases I examine throughout *Revolting Indolence* are unapologetically nonwhite, queer, and trans.

Following in Viego's and Muñoz's theoretical lineage, Leticia Alvarado's *Abject Performances: Aesthetic Strategies in Latino Cultural Production* and Marissa López's *Racial Immanence: Chicanx Bodies beyond Representation* are formative examples in evidencing how aesthetic, performed, and literary depictions of abjection by Latinx cultural producers advance critiques of minoritarian respectability and coherent forms of latinidad. Alvarado calls for "abjection not as a resource for empowerment fueled by a desire for normative inclusion but as a resource geared toward an ungraspable alternative social organization, a not-yet-here illuminated by the aesthetic,"[87] while López elaborates upon interpretative strategies for reading Chicanx aesthetics against the grain of racialized essentialisms, observing, through her concept of "racial immanence," "how racialized bodies flicker between indexical and material understandings of language," one that "remains socially and politically aware, that is, but refuses to clearly signify."[88] Whereas Alvarado and López are motivated by the imperative to free up Latinx identities from prescriptive majoritarian demands, I move aslant from this analytical angle by postulating how queer and trans Latinx indolent liberatory practices activate through embracing stereotype, troping, and excess that flies in the face of neoliberal capitalist sensibility. The lazy Latinx styles, shot through with the pejorative, find affinity in Frances Aparicio's call for a "construction of a new social imaginary" in Latinx studies in order to diversify the frameworks of how we interpret the scope and parameters of latinidad, "transcend[ing] the old paradigms and nationality-based conflicts."[89] I likewise situate my notion of indolent Latinx in what Carlos Ulises Decena formulates for *dominicanidad*, "as a contested repertoire of meanings, practices, and institutional arrangements," in his study of same-sex desiring Dominican men.[90] Embracing the pejorative status of indolence for another framework for understanding Latinx identity and Latinx studies in general speaks to Joshua Chambers-Letson's cogent remarks on "minoritarian performance" as "temporary and never fully authorized, but its ephemerality and lack of authority give it the capacity to remain fugitive from the majoritarian and totalitarian tendencies of the revolutions of historical communism, while appropriating and amplifying their most revolutionary impulses and drives toward democratic and collective being."[91]

Discussions of minoritized aesthetics and cultures are frequently grafted onto a dialectic premised upon debating whether the group in question is complicit in the proliferation of majoritarian representational schemas (the welfare queen, the sex-obsessed indolent queer, the spitfire, etc.) or properly resists them by presenting valorized, virtuous alternative subject positions that actively contest the majoritarian image (the hardworking immigrant; the married, monogamous, same-sex couple; the pious; the nonviolent political protestor, etc.). A category like indolence, understood as either reifying majoritarian scripts about minoritized peoples or a mode to aspire away from by embracing more laudable contestatory categories, becomes the disavowed, unbecoming Other haunting the representational politics undergirding the dialectic. This complicity/refusal dialectic, in effect, needs a category like indolence to distance from and repudiate tout court in order to resolve the quandary of how best to represent marginalized peoples and what strategies should be utilized to do so. Ultimately, this dialectic condemns indolence by deceptively presenting it as an impossible subject formation or set of practices one can lay claim to, or, more aptly, one *should not want to* lay claim to because they are morally, ethically, and representationally vacuous. However, what this framework occludes from view are the radical energies inherent in stereotyped and stigmatized modes like indolence, which, when their pejorative associations and qualities are supercharged and strategically deployed, can short-circuit majoritarian logics and reorient sensibilities. Embracing indolent positionalities confounds any neat paradigms of proper or improper minoritized representation, especially ones organized upon how legibly conformist or resistant a subject is according to majoritarian dictates. Rather, indolence functions as an unsettling, and unruly, category to representational discourses, because it constitutes itself through forming intimacies with stereotypes, tropes, and excess, embracing a charged, unsavory semiotics that disturbs the very bedrock of representational frameworks in toto that we are beholden to think within. Latinx aesthetics and performances premised upon indolence defy representational logics by embracing that which has been deemed abhorrent and disreputable, that which none of us should aspire to be: the slacker, the lounge lizard, the loafer, the couch potato, the daydreamer, the loiterer, and the refusenik. This understanding of indolence underscores how "improper behavior," as Dixa Ramírez theorizes of Black Dominican women's performance strategies of empowerment in US and Dominican media, "becomes a performative stance against or, at least, in tension with the status quo, whether Dominican nationalism or the patriarchal and white supremacist leanings of dominant U.S. Latinx culture."[92] In other words, indolence finds its theoretical thrust precisely in the discomfort it has historically and contemporaneously aroused, akin to Kadji Amin's call for de-idealization in queer studies to "inhabit unease" as a "generative heuristic for politicized scholarship" that doesn't "quickly rid [unease] to restore the mastery of the critic, the unassailability of her politics, and the legitimacy of her trained field expectations."[93] For Amin, the object of inquiry is often hamstrung between idealization and critique, a promise of radicality upheld or the failure to not be radical enough, leaving little room for a broader array of scholarly responses that can attend to unease or disappointment. Discomfort is a primary attitude driving my conceptualizing of indolence, requiring an assessment of how its pejoratively charged status evokes discomfort and in what ways it does so in subjects and disciplines, while also evaluating the discomfort in recognizing how indolence may be limited or its application untenable in particular contexts. The potential limits of indolence become an important site from which to think the category, a needed reminder that all critical practices and liberatory strategies worthy of the name require scrutiny, testing out, revision, and sometimes retiring in order to continue being useful or efficacious.

The reclamation and revalorization of indolence undertaken in *Revolting Indolence* lays the groundwork for an interpretive practice that draws out, and luxuriates over, various enactments of what I am calling indolent liberatory practices. This critical reading practice recalibrates majoritarian affective, performative, aesthetic, and sensorial affinities through intensely descriptive and theoretically inventive analyses of queer and trans Latinx indolence. Following Juana María Rodríguez's provocative theorization over the radical charge of gesture in mapping out latinidades, the "reading of gesture" allows for "register[ing] what cannot or should not be expressed in words. And sometimes it signals what one wishes to keep out of sound's reach."[94] Reading for indolent Latinx modes calls for similar methodological approaches, deploying an analytical toolbox that allows for the discernment of what has flown under the radar or has been written off as apolitical or embarrassingly backward. The practice of reading for indolent liberatory practices will be developed chapter by chapter, focalized through styles of indolence that demand different types of attunement to indolence's liberatory potential. The indolent liberatory schemas evidenced throughout serve as unique blueprints for another sense of the world, an array of eclectic misfires and strategies for unmaking and making anew what is and what can be.

Chapter 1, "Glimpsing Angie Xtravaganza: The Trans Latinx Imaginary of *Paris Is Burning*," takes as its focus the trans Boricua mother of the House of Xtravaganza, Angie Xtravaganza, who was notably featured in the cult-classic documentary film *Paris Is Burning*. Through an extensive examination of the film's outtake recordings and supplemental footage like fundraising trailers, and the ways in which indolence manifests in outtake and supplemental footage of Angie, this chapter proposes my critical close-reading practice. The indolence documented in the outtake and supplemental footage, and the method such footage demands in order to be apprehended, calls for more capacious theoretical foundations for imagining historically queer and trans of color subjects besides those made legible by neoliberal capitalist regimes, which valorize narratives of tokenism, uplift, bootstrapping, and premature death. Indolently quotidian and lazy scenes in the supplemental footage, like the Xtravaganzas road-tripping and hanging out on Forty-Second Street, I contend, durationally slow down and stall cisheteronormative temporalities, obviating from the showy and profitable queer and trans of color performance-work crucial to the filmic gaze and capitalist drives, and scrambling representational coherence and narrative linearity.

The reading practice outlined in the first chapter finds further elaboration through queer and trans Latinx nightlife. Whereas chapter 1 focuses on documentary film and turn-of-the-century New York City, chapter 2, "Lounge Lizard Aesthetics: Los Angeles Nightlife Visualities," homes in on queer and trans Chicanx Los Angeles as rendered in the photographs collected in Reynaldo Rivera's *Provisional Notes for a Disappeared City* and the contemporary mural work of artists rafa esparza and Gabriela Ruiz. This chapter primarily centers on Rivera's photographs documenting queer and trans Latinx Angelenos lounging in bars and hanging out at house parties, sipping cocktails and beers— ordinary nights out on the town. Unlike the moving image of film, the photograph of the lounger or partygoer, recording a moment of quotidian lounging, presents indolence as a hypervisible and unavoidably ostentatious encounter that hails the viewer to engage with it on its own terms. In this way, a photographed moment of queer and trans Latinx lounging becomes a relational intensification of indolence, an intensifying procedure produced in and because of the static singularity of the still image, challenging the normative rubrics of aesthetic valuation and sensorial experience. The intensified attention on the mundanity of these loungers across time and space is precisely what propositions sensorial rearranging that encourages unexpected aesthetic responses, affective attachments, and modes of attention. The chapter concludes by examining a collaborative project by artists rafa esparza and Gabriela Ruiz, who were commissioned to create a mural for a downtown Los Angeles queer Latinx bar, the New Jalisco Bar. Informed by the Mexican artist José Guadalupe Posada's drawing of the Dance of the Forty-One, a 1901 Mexico City raid of a queer ball held in a private home, the mural, prominently displayed on the exterior of the New Jalisco, boldly affirms the historical and contemporary importance of queer Latinx nightlife spaces. Latinx indolence materializes as a visual landmark all can see.

Building off the second chapter's focus on queer and trans nightlife in Los Angeles, chapter 3, "The Poetics of Latin Night: The Literatures of the Pulse Nightclub Shooting," pivots attention to the growing array of literatures on the 2016 Pulse nightclub shooting that occurred in Orlando, Florida. I closely examine various writers like Maya

Chinchilla, Roy Guzmán, Edgar Gomez, and Justin Torres for the ways they aestheticize Latinx nightlife in relation to the anti-queer and anti-trans violence that transpired at Pulse. The poetics of Pulse, as I identify it, memorializes queer and trans Latinx life through poetic intensities that focalize bodies seeking pleasure and community, bodies under disco balls and on dance floors, bodies transcending time and space. These writers figure Latin night at the queer club as an indolent spatiality distinct from the cisheterosexist white supremacist one outside the walls of the club. The literary scenes of queer and trans Latinx partying, hanging out, and euphoria enacted by these writers proffer aesthetic and sensorial strategies for critiquing anti-queer and anti-trans violence and oppression.

Indolence takes the main stage in chapter 4. From Latinx ball culture and nightlife to contest reality television, "Slacking Off on the Main Stage: *RuPaul's Drag Race* and the Performance of Spectacular Obfuscation" advances the theoretical purview of indolent liberatory schemas by observing how *RuPaul's Drag Race* fan favorite Valentina performs the nonbinary femme Latinx slacker as global entertainment. Her slacking on the couch instead of properly rehearsing for a lip-synch, the frequent ditzy referencing of "living in her fantasy" as a means of negating judges and contestant critiques, and her overall affective-performative blasé leisureliness put into disarray the bourgeois respectability, professionalism, and minority uplift undergirding the show. *RuPaul's Drag Race* is known for its unique production techniques favoring snappy and flashy editing that accentuates, and manufactures, drama, conflict, and theatricality, which is conducive to attracting and retaining audience interest. Similar to the close reading for indolence developed across the first three chapters, discerning the racialized queer and trans Latinx slackerliness Valentina embodies requires an even more concentrated and anatomizing slowing-down and dragging-out of analytic attention, sensorially dawdling in the televisual mechanics like pausing, rewinding, rewatching, and slow-motioning. Such fine-tuned investigating crucially surfaces Valentina's glamorously fantastical slackerliness, which reframes queer and trans Latinx value not according to majoritarian paradigms but according to different logics of valuation. Living in anti-queer, anti-trans, and racist worlds, as Valentina expressed in various interviews about her drag, sometimes calls for one to occupy the space of fantasy, where fantasy becomes the reconfigured reality of another world entirely.

What happens when queer and trans Latinx indolence encounters the surreal and nonhuman? When it transforms itself into the more-than-human sensorium? The final chapter, "The Textures of Our Daydreaming: Justin Torres's *We the Animals* and the Art of Sarah Zapata," extends the conceptual horizons of the indolent reading practice by evidencing how analytic attention to surrealist techniques and nonhuman intimacies, as depicted in the novel and film adaptation of Justin Torres's *We the Animals* and in the installations of queer Peruvian American artist Sarah Zapata, stages provocative strategies for queer and trans Latinx world-making. Chapter 5 begins with a critical focus on *We the Animals* premised on a particular scene in both the book and the film where indolence manifests in an unusual juncture: the queer of color child lying in a muddy, worm-riddled trench dug out by the patriarch of the family. The trench serves as a spatiotemporal dislocation from the cisheterosexist white supremacist world structuring the child's everyday life, where such a dislocation functions as both a pleasurable escape from the world writ large and a sensorial immersion into another, activated through a nonhuman and magical idiom. The aesthetic differences and renderings of the trench scene between novel and film enlarge the scope and scales of critically reading for indolence to new proportions. The novel, on the one hand, depicts the scene of the child lounging in the trench as a syntactically digressive, loose, and daydreaming internalized experience, a simultaneous sinking into oneself and the earth that is a sinking into queer and trans of color tempos. The film, on the other hand, represents the sinking into the trench as a sensually charged audiovisual experience of nonhuman intimacies between mud, worms, and child, culminating in a magical uprooting of the child from the trench into the sky as he soars across the landscape, an abstracted shadow moving at his own pace. For the latter half of the chapter, I turn to Sarah Zapata's shaggy abstracted sculptures and installations. Informed by Andean textiles and practices of tufting and weaving, Zapata's works are unusual mixtures of boldly garish colors, lush fabrics, and other found materials like synthetic hair. These variously textured constructions seem to slack to the side, frumpy and lethargic, couch-like and loungy in appearance, and, by being so, they materialize indolence on the gallery floor. These works of sculptural indolence invite the viewer into indolently pleasurable worlds of soft asymmetricalities, plush unevenness, and the indulgence in unlike textures. Zapata's zanily homey and multitextured works manifest, in the here and now, queer and trans Latinx indolence as an experience to be felt, to be touched, to lounge with in space-time. Tactility is the presence of another kind of world. These filmic, novelistic, and sculptural examples torqued to nonhuman and magical grammars evince how racialized queer and trans Latinx indolence generatively transforms our sense of scalar attention and possibility: from the minuscule intimacies with the earthworm, to the shadowy human-like abstraction that is soaring across the planet, to the shaggy textural intimacies of the gallery floor. These more-than-human amalgamations tap into what indolent modes can unlock for Latinx liberatory aesthetic practices and sensorial imaginings.

Finally, in the coda I turn to the paintings of queer Puerto Rican artist David Antonio Cruz to reflect on the current state of indolence and the continued promises it may offer.

TOUCHING WORK, DREAMING INDOLENCE

As a child, I marveled at my father's hands. I'd grasp their dark-brown thickness, and outline the many cuts and scrapes, the lumpy calluses, a scar of unknown origin, the firmness of the palms. He returned each evening, late, the sun having fallen, and held me with those hands weather-worn and labor-scarred. Their roughness gave comfort, but also cruelly reminded me of my father's taxing, grueling work. My father's hands materially cited the fact that he labored, from sunrise to sundown, in the fields. Since the age of six, his hands have toiled, trimmed, plucked, pruned, and dug across Mexico and the United States on behalf of a wage. He has worked since the late 1980s growing all kinds of trees and shrubs for the lawns of middle- and upper-class homes, small businesses and corporate complexes, and public schools and Ivy League college campuses. He works for wages that will never allow him to retire. He has no healthcare coverage, no union protection, no security of permanent employment or housing. He works while undocumented, hoping his white, moneyed, and propertied benefactors will not pull a fast one on him. He works under a precarity that is all too exhaustingly real for the proletariat and nonwhite masses who labor across the Global North and South. His hands are hands in common with so many.

My father's hands narrate a story of work. The life of the undocumented migrant, the nonwhite Mexican farmworker. This project arose in part from a concern over my father: his aging body and the inability to continue working as he once did. A set of questions weighs heavily upon the mind: How will he and I cocreate a present and future for him that promises rest, relaxation, and, ideally, a life free (as much as remotely possible) from the stress of colonial-capitalist systems? When can the man who has worked for a wage his entire life be free to be indolent, liberated to not worry about work anymore? How do we dream up a world where work and the wage do not constitute the worth and value to live a good, dignified, healthy, and fulfilling life? As I write this, I do not have a viable means in which to secure a life of indolent rest for my father. But what I do know is that my father's hands, his loving touch, have taught me how to rethink how I think about work and its role in measuring the value of human life. His hands upon mine have guided me in reading against the ruse of the capitalist work ethic's false promises. My father's hands have instructed me to figure out, to yearn achingly for, ways of reading a worthy life *beyond* work, into a beyond arranged by a radically different and unfamiliar conception of the world. Work will never love us back, nor capitalism for that matter. We are more than how hard we work, how much we work, how much of our body-minds and time we sacrifice at the altar of work. Only the intimacy of a touch longing for something else will love us in the fullest sense of the term. Love is the dream of indolence we extend to the other.

1 | Glimpsing Angie Xtravaganza

THE TRANS LATINX IMAGINARY OF *PARIS IS BURNING*

There is nothing impressive about the footage. No spectacles of high-energy vogueing, no dramatic arguments, no theatrical shade-throwing. No noteworthy testimonies of trauma. It's not even that long, lasting only mere seconds, the camera surveilling the bus for something of filmic interest, something for the final cut. These mundane seconds of the Xtravaganzas on a road trip never get their big premiere, as the record shows. It's just a glimpse of a couple of chicas in the late eighties on a road trip, chitchatting in Spanish. One of the women in this outtake footage is Angie Xtravaganza, the mother of the House of Xtravaganza during the late eighties and early nineties.

This outtake footage is included in the Criterion Collection edition of *Paris Is Burning*, a 1990 film documenting queer and trans African American, Afro-Latinx, and non-Black Latinx ball and house culture in 1980s New York.[1] Released in 2020, and nearly two hours long, the outtake footage features extended views into the interviews undertaken by Jennie Livingston with notable cast members like Dorian Corey, Pepper LaBeija, and Venus Xtravaganza. We also see some people not featured in the film. For instance, Marcel Christian, who is not identified in the documentary, details in the outtakes how he creates what he calls "idle sheets": witty pamphlets about etiquette and decorum handed out during the balls. In another outtake, "Let's Play Lawyer," we see several unidentified children, some Xtravaganzas, hanging out on the West Side Piers. The clip shows one of them explaining the intricate rules of the game and the subsequent confusion. The outtake highlights a game played in the throes of boredom, to pass time. Additional footage highlights the House of Xtravaganza road-tripping to Washington, DC, ball-goers carousing through Times Square, and other such idle, quotidian scenes. What we get across this additional footage are filmic snatches of extraordinarily banal trans and queer of color lifeworlds: brief close-ups of nonverbal interactions like walking down the street side by side, instances of dialogue in Spanish, a writer discussing craft. This is not the stuff of award-winning film spectacularity.

That said, the extra outtake recordings and supplemental footage of the *Paris Is Burning* filmic universe reveal alternative trans of color quotidian histories, aesthetics, and worlds. The footage showcases leisure, hanging out, boredom, and a generally languid unproductivity, which starkly contrasts with the high-energy, fast-paced performing in the theatrically entertaining, cinematically spectacular scenes highlighted in the film proper. Through a conceptual schema I identify as "critical otiosity"—a process through which to vitalize with trans Latinx liberatory possibilities the seemingly superfluous, unproductive, irrelevant, and other pilloried or overlooked affective comportments found in places like filmic outtakes—this chapter mounts a rereading of *Paris Is Burning* against the grain of neoliberal, cissexist capitalist regimes, which valorize above all else narratives and displays of spectacle, bootstrapping, tragedy, assimilation, uplift, and premature death. In particular, I look to how the brief, seconds-long, and fleeting glimpses of Angie Xtravaganza—idly chitchatting in Spanish, sluggishly dancing, napping, or doing nothing cinematically productive across this extra footage—evidence what I have termed an indolent liberatory practice. The critical otiosity documented in the outtake footage, and the method such footage demands in order to be apprehended, calls for more capacious theoretical foundations for imagining historically trans and queer of color subjects besides those tethered to neoliberal capitalist regimes. The unspectacular, leisurely, and mundanely quotidian scenes across the outtake and supplemental footage, like Angie road-tripping with the Xtravaganzas, I contend, durationally slow down and stall cisheteronormative temporalities, obviating from the showy and profitable trans and queer of color performance-labor crucial to capitalist imperatives, and scrambling representational coherence and narrative linearity. In order to draw out the indolent Latinx and trans liberatory possibilities of the additional footage, I propose critical otiosity as a conceptual tool that contributes to reading for indolent liberatory practices. Otiosity is an enactment of indolent liberation, which I will sketch out shortly.

Paris Is Burning has garnered substantive critical, artistic, and scholarly attention throughout the years. Critical response to the film has varied, ranging from scathing indictments to lukewarm gratitude, with different questions and concerns arising depending on who is doing the viewing. Lucas Hilderbrand puts it soundly: "That the film has sparked such vibrant discussion is testament to its power to challenge audiences to recognize the complexity of identity and social relations."[2] Despite these varying perspectives on the film, popular debates have generally gravitated toward three primary concerns: (1) whether Livingston, a white lesbian filmmaker, had any right to make the film; (2) whether the film accurately and positively represents the marginalized trans and queer people of color it documents; and (3) whether the film and its subjects adequately subvert the elitist, white supremacist ideologies underpinning US culture writ large, or merely reinscribe them. For example, bell hooks's oft-cited essay "Is Paris Burning?," written upon the film's initial release, questions Livingston's directorial gaze and postulates that the film merely reifies the allure of Eurocentric bourgeois whiteness to a white audience. The film, according to hooks, "turned the black drag ball into a spectacle for those presumed to be on the outside of this experience looking in," with the film's aesthetic trafficking in spectacle overshadowing any other ways of understanding the lived realities of Black queer life in the United States.[3] A *New York Times* article in 1993 documents the ravages AIDS wrought upon the ball communities and cites lawsuits against Livingston for their share of the profit by ball members featured in the documentary—all of which highlights how the material realities of HIV/AIDS and poverty were glossed over in the film.[4] In his 1999 monograph *Disidentifications*, José Esteban Muñoz identifies the film as "a highly sensationalized rendering" that is "overexposed" and which "glamorize[s] the experience."[5] In later writing, Muñoz emends his more critical assessment of the film, noting how "queers watched *Paris Is Burning* because it promised a world, glimmering and glamorous, tinged with criminality and discord, haunted with the specter of tragedy. So many learned the word 'shade,' as in 'throwing shade,' from that film, and while that phrase is not new, its descriptive force has not waned when discussing contemporary queer of color life."[6] "Does the denaturalization of the norm succeed in subverting the norm, or is this a denaturalization in the service of a perpetual re-idealization, one that can only oppress, even as, or precisely when, it is embodied most effectively?" queries Judith Butler in *Bodies That Matter*, where they conclude that the film, emblematized for Butler in the life and death of Venus Xtravaganza, stages an irresolvable tension between subverting and idealizing, neither fully one nor ever fully the other.[7]

A decade or more later, trans of color critique would mount important pushback against arguments like Butler's that figure Venus's as well as other modes of gendered variance and trans embodiment in the film as simply idealizing or facilely imitating cisnormative comportment and life.[8] "The metaphorization of the transsexual body," writes Jay Prosser, levying a trenchant critique of Butler's dematerialized, abstracted theorizing of Venus, "transcends the literality of transsexuality in precisely a way in which Venus cannot—Venus who is killed for her literal embodiment of sexual difference."[9] Following hooks, Prosser also goes on to note how the documentary sidesteps any meaningful filmic engagement with Venus's death, where "the moment is rapidly overridden by the spectacle of the ball, and, now that she can no longer function in the service of this spectacle, Venus is abandoned." The documentary's preoccupation with trans and queer of color spectacularity, the productive laboring of trans and queer of color vitality, leaves little room for an exploration into the violences of anti-trans antagonism and mourning of trans life. Moreover, Prosser suggests, Butler's observations fail to account for the actualities of transsexual and transgender women living in violently cissexist societies. Jian Neo Chen poignantly redirects Butler's reading: "Can we understand Venus's murder not so much as socially enacted punishment for her failure (and desire) to make her body—her 'remaining organs'—compliant with symbolic norms but rather as punishment for daring to exist at all as the woman she already was and would have continued to be if she had lived (with or without bottom surgery)—a woman differentially constituted by a transiting of racial gender that barred her from being 'real' . . . ?"[10] Reconceptualizing how we understand the filmic and historical lives of trans of color and Latinx people, distinct from the cisnormative, capitalist-driven productivity of spectacle, is eminently crucial for enacting trans of color counterhistories and counterdiscourses.

These long-standing debates over the spectacularizing of trans people of color and the ethics of representation in *Paris Is Burning* have largely set the terms through which the documentary and the people comprising it are discussed, to the exclusion of other interpretative frameworks. Films like *The Stroll* (2023), *Pier Kids* (2019), and *Wildness* (2012) showcase alternative representational schemas for depicting trans and queer people of color and communities. The additional footage included in the 2020 Criterion Blu-ray edition with its indolently otiose and quotidian seconds offers other avenues of inquiry that move aslant from the established critical debates. Undertaking an analysis of Angie allows us to ask: What other trans Latinx imaginaries and lifeworlds are possible if we pivot our attention to the outtake recordings and other supplemental footage? What does the supplement of outtakes and supplemental footage do, exactly, to how we understand the film, its reception, and any alternative trajectories for thought that it makes possible? How does a close attention upon glimpsing Angie through technological mediation, of being-with her through mundanely quotidian and ephemeral filmic moments, unlock possibilities for trans of color liberatory aesthetics and imagining? Critical otiosity may help in exploring these questions.

Otiose etymologically derives from the Latin word *otium*, which means to be in leisure, to have free time. The *OED* defines otiose accordingly: "having no practical result; unfruitful, sterile; futile, pointless" and "at leisure; at rest; idle; inactive; indolent, lazy."[11] *Otiosity*'s meanings perfectly capture the force of what the outtake footage does to imagine elsewhere from overdetermined and overrepresented demands for spectacularized productivity. Generally, outtake footage contains those moments designated unnecessary, irrelevant, or superfluous to the primary narrative or thematic concern of the film. Extra footage makes it into archives and, if lucky, special DVD or digital editions; if unlucky, into the trash. In this light, outtake footage finds itself peripheralized, characterized, through its sheer displacement into archives and "deleted scenes," as not as important, relevant, or consequential for audiences.

The outtake footage of the Criterion Collection edition bluntly attests to this by highlighting low-energy, slow-paced, and languorously underwhelming indolent quotidian moments in which the characters play games out of boredom on the West Side Piers or chitchat in Spanish on the street, in contrast to the film's abundant attention on the balls, dances, and colloquialisms, which have since been expeditiously disseminated, appropriated, and monopolized. The outtake and supplemental footage's critical otiosity produces nothing that warrants inclusion into the final cut. However, this is precisely what instantiates its theoretical merit, an extravagant otiosity giving conceptual heft to these seconds and scenes, the imagining of alternative trans of color histories and lifeworlds that strive for elsewhere from ciscentric neoliberal capitalist white supremacist legibilities and imperatives.

Critical otiosity, then, is a process through which to supercharge the unspectacular, unproductive, unremarkable, lazy, and other such overlooked modes for trans of color radical critique and Latinx liberatory possibilities. In this way, the otiose becomes extravagantly trans, nonwhite, and Latinx, a fabulously low-energy, slow-paced, and indolent deployment that reconfigures reality. The various examples of critical otiosity in the extra footage are astonishingly brief and fleeting. Attunement to critical otiosity demands an intensive critical attention and sensorial enmeshment into the unfolding of seconds: the pausing of an instant, the zooming in and out of an astoundingly ephemeral gesture or expression, the rewinding and fast-forwarding of a frame to experience the audiovisual encounter again. Such attunement lavishes in the techniques of modern video viewing in efforts to tease out as much as possible from a glimpse, extending a second into indefiniteness, a recorded instant into a multiplicity of transgenerational encounters. This cinematic horizon made possible by technological mediation is akin to D. A. Miller's concept of "in detail" with the study of art house films viewed on DVD, where the pursuit of filmic detail stages "fracture points in the image's presumed obviousness, and as such, they put the glib flow of meaning on pause,"[12] or that of Boyd McDonald's cruising of classic Hollywood film stills, for how "they can be studied in silence and solitude at length, and can offer a more detailed experience of actors and acting than do fast moving pictures. Sometimes stills reveal information that is hardly available in a motion picture, sometimes even information that is in conflict with the point of the movie."[13] Reading for critical otiosity pursues the detail in hopes of erring from dominant discourses. Reading against the grain "helps to free movement in cinema from a teleological understanding of an endpoint or purpose"[14] for what Jeffrey Geiger, paraphrasing Agamben, remarks upon as the force of the gestural and the ephemeral in queer cinematic experience, which "heighten[s] attention to the gestural so often suppressed in everyday modern life, and cinema, to articulate the intermediacies of movement, which for Agamben signals a release from teleological impulses towards commodification and epistephilia."[15]

The trans of color otiose details and impressions enacted by glimpsing Angie across the *Paris Is Burning* filmic universe defy the narrative teleology and coherence inextricably bound to neoliberal progressivist fantasies and to capitalist impetuses to commodify such narratives. These extravagantly otiose details and indolent impressions do not combine to tell a story, or *the* story, of trans Latinx life, not adding up to delineate some tidy narrative of sentimentalized or entertaining progressive upward mobility. As Jules Gills-Peterson aptly cautions, in the widespread attempt at jettisoning categories like transsexual and transvestite, which Angie and Venus Xtravaganza used to identify themselves in the film, the transsexual and transvestite become "atavistic" fixtures of an unfortunate past that requires overcoming, "recuperated, one day, by the inexorable rise in liberal trans inclusion that is supposed to typify the twenty-first century despite the overwhelming evidence that nothing of the sort is occurring but for the whitest, most propertied."[16] More fittingly, my approach in reading these extravagantly otiose trans and transsexual Latinx seconds, details, and impressions aligns with trans Latinx and Latin American thought like that of Cole Rizki's elucidation over travesti identity in Latin America as that which "subverts both normative expectations of femininity and trans politics structured around assimilation and respectability,"[17] and Dora Silva Santana, whose work on Black Brazilian travesti communities and knowledge production is focalized through "nonlinear, undirected, dislocated, and localized movement."[18] For Giancarlo Cornejo, travesti desiring of "idealized forms of femininity and stereotypical notions of (cisgender) feminine beauty" places pressure on Western-focused queer studies' sanitizing mechanisms writ large, where travesti identity expresses "a refusal to signify only one thing and in only one way."[19] Trans Latinx critical otiosity dwells in the unfixed, aberrant epistemic zone where "transness and brownness as frames reveal processes of materialization, a mattering that is *moving*," as Francisco J. Galarte succinctly expresses in his groundbreaking book *Brown Trans Figurations*.[20] In this vein, my approach generates decadent descriptions and errant imaginings that do not align with liberal progressivist teleology, do not result in coherent and conclusive narratives, and are not commensurable or equivocal to ready-made categories and typologies. I dally insurgently in seconds; gestures; screenshots; snippets of inaudible conversation; countenances muddled by deteriorated, scratched footage; and other such details deemed inconsequential, forgettable, unremarkable. I wander in these trans Latinx space-times forging a nexus of emancipatory pasts, presents, and futures.

ANGIE'S SHIMMY

The House of Xtravaganza goes to Washington, DC. The intertitle introducing the outtake footage reads, "The Extravas Host a Ball in DC," and this portion of the outtakes is arranged linearly. We watch as the Xtravaganzas (and some non-Xtravaganzas) hang out outside Union Square waiting to board the bus, their time on the bus, participating in the ball in DC, and then their return home on the bus. The sequenced outtake is composed in the standard montaged quality of the film proper, defined by fly-on-the-wall observational recordings and quick cuts, a chronological arrangement of microscenes. The camera roves from person to person, recording for a few seconds, then cutting to the next point of interest.

From the front of the bus, the camera records. Marshall Jefferson's house music classic "Move Your Body" plays from someone's boom box. In the last seat in the back of the bus, Angie, in pink rollers and a white cashmere sweater and propped up on one knee, dances. "Give me that house, music, set me free," rings out as she does a sluggish shimmy, a modest twist and turn, "lost in house, music, is where I wanna be." Her dancing is nothing out of this world. Just vibing to the music with the others around her. In these several seconds, there is nothing remarkable for the camera to seize upon. There is no need for it to focus in on her, to move up closer and get a clearer perspective for the viewer, to make consumable some action or saying. In the far distance from the camera, Angie remains, in a world of her own.

Her distance from the camera provides a fascinating contrast to the numerous close-ups found in other parts of the outtake footage. Close-up shots signal to the viewer a cinematic moment of interest, asserting that something is of note here to record and document, something to impart to the viewer. Yet what of Angie in this long-shot footage? What becomes possible in the impersonal, unfocused faraway perspective we get of Angie? What relation forms between her and us in the distance? The clarity of her face is muddled, probably due to the aging of the footage, and lacks the distinction of a close-up shot. Here we know she is not the center of the camera's attention. Our eyes and senses are not compelled by the camera in any way to home in on her, to make a distinction of her. She's not sassily performing or shouting an entertaining phrase, after all, not producing anything the camera can necessarily turn a cinematic profit from. She is merely part of the group shot, a person enjoying herself on a road trip, doing a languid shimmy. And such comportment, too, is crucial for imagining historical trans Latinx life.

Drawing together historiographic and theoretical approaches, L. Heidenreich's *Nepantla Squared: Transgender Mestiz@ Histories in Times of Global Shift* illuminates the challenges of writing the histories of trans Latinx and mestiz@ peoples. In order to understand trans mestiz@ lives, Heidenreich argues, we need to trace the various historical, economic, political, spatial, and gender conditions that constitute those lives in their situatedness. Following ideas developed by Gloria Anzaldúa, Heidenreich utilizes the term *Nepantla* for their historical recovery of trans mestiz@ lives and movements. Heidenreich sees Nepantla, a Nahuatl concept translating roughly to "in-betweenness," as a means of "view[ing] the world through motion-change," where "motion is generative, allowing for structural change, in fact driving and shaping it."[21] Motion-change is a way for trans mestiz@ peoples to resist the interlocking oppressions, a way to explore other ways of being foreclosed by racial, sexual, and transgender violence. Through a rigorous historiographical sketch of Jack Garland, a transmasculine Mexican European person from turn-of-the-twentieth-century California, Heidenreich provocatively illustrates how gender informs and structures movements in historical colonial-capitalist systems, particularly for racialized trans people. Garland, for example, fashioned a transmasculine life by dressing in men's clothing, serving as a Spanish translator in the Philippine-American War, and working as a newspaper reporter in Stockton,

California, despite the scrutiny and chastisement he was subjected to by the community for his comportment and self-presentation. Heidenreich's incisive contribution to the understanding of Garland's transness attends to the ways his gender-crossing intersects with his biracial identity, and how those intersections condition the possibilities of living a trans Latinx life across various historical junctures under capitalist systems of labor, settler occupation, and US empire in Asia.

Given this, I work with the documentary camera in order to draw out the radical charge of critical otiosity, and reading for indolent liberatory practices. This is not a reenactment of the disinterested, disembodied Enlightenment critic, trying to cleave a fine distinction between critic and film, subject and object. Rather, distance from what the camera does, and how it does it, allows me to know trans Latinx lives like Angie's—so widely observed and distributed across screens for decades—differently, a sensuously errant critical practice. The moving camera of documentary film is configured "not as the neutral picturing of reality, but as a way of coming to terms with reality by means of working with and through images and narrative."[22] I take seriously not only how the camera moves and what it does, but also what it doesn't do, and what it could have done differently. The conditional grammar is of especial interest for trans of color theorizing, and a means of moving aslant from either/or dichotomies that pigeonhole how we can discuss and imagine trans of color life, texts, and histories. This theoretical movement elsewhere is informed by Black trans and feminist thinkers like C. Riley Snorton, LaVelle Ridley, Marquis Bey, and Saidiya Hartman, who have devised formative frameworks and methodological strategies for working with trans of color subjectivities and imaginaries. Snorton situates the speculative mode as a means of vitalizing archives of anti-Black erasure and violence, allowing for stories and histories to emerge despite the impossibilities of ever fully knowing: "The task of writing invention is beset with difficulties, surrounded and beseeched by failure, which is to say that a litany of failure sometimes feels more readily accessible than a litany for survival."[23] This approach to writing historiography corresponds with Saidiya Hartman's notion of critical fabulation and her idea of close narration, which reads Black ciswomen and trans and queer people through the centuries against the grain of the archives produced and managed by white supremacist carceral state apparatuses. In her work, Hartman takes what she can from various archives—a case file, a newspaper article, a diary, a police report, a photograph—and constructs accounts of Black experience against the disciplinary goals that those who held people in slavery, the sociologist, the philanthropist, the police, and other forces from the late nineteenth century into the twentieth had in mind. "The beauty of the black ordinary," as Hartman writes on the intentions behind her project, drawing particular attention to the liberatory possibilities of historical Black quotidian experience, "the beauty that resides in and animates the determination to live free, the beauty that propels the experiments in living otherwise." She continues: "Beauty is not a luxury; rather it is a way of creating possibility in the space of the enclosure, a radical art of subsistence, an embrace of our terribleness, a transfiguration of the given. It is a will to adorn, a proclivity for the baroque, and the love of *too much*."[24] Her fabulative method is one that works with and against existing archives and accounts in order to imagine mundane and everyday instances of Black freedom. Her method is not about archival recovery, or filling in the historical record, nor trying to tell a full story of becoming fully human within liberal humanist constructs. "Narrative restraint, the refusal to fill in the gaps and provide closure, is a requirement of this method," Hartman explains, "as is the imperative to respect black noise—the shrieks, the moans, the nonsense, and the opacity, which are always in excess of legibility and of the law and which hint at and embody aspirations that are wildly utopian, derelict to capitalism, and antithetical to its attendant discourse of Man."[25] The epistemic allure for finality, completeness, and narrative is seductive, as Hartman suggests, but courting other critical trajectories for imagining oppressed historical subjects is key for enacting anti-capitalist, anti-racist, liberatory schemas. LaVelle Ridley, theorizing on the Black trans epistemologies and futurities emerging from the film *Tangerine*, incisively articulates the concept of "imagining otherly." In a close reading of a singing performance in the film, Ridley explicates the important ways in which imagining otherly affords "possibilities that lie in moving beyond the polarizing ways of engaging with power: to resist or comply," in order to posit a sense of Black trans life and futurity that "foreground[s] the possibility of escape to some imagined elsewhere . . . instead of reveling in the supposed arrival of equality and change that ideas such as the 'transgender tipping point' herald."[26] Ridley's conceptualizing of imagining otherly corresponds closely with Marquis Bey's postulation of "black trans feminism," a radically nonnormative and anti-identitarian political praxis putting into orbit gender radicality and abolition in efforts of "doing away with the state. And since the state is a relation rather than the mere establishment, the state-relationality takes myriad forms, racial taxonomization and gender binaristic impositions and hierarchical sex classification among them. More than just resistance, abolition as made here to engender black trans feminism is committed to moving 'beyond the state in the service of collective liberation' making a founding coalitional drive constitutive of it."[27] The proposition on offer here by Bey is that Black trans feminism promises an undoing of ontologically essentialist and hegemonic metrics that demarcate in advance what is thinkable and what can be, and, rather than operating within preordained schemas and categories that colonial-capitalist modernity has handed down, we might see what abolitionist imaginaries arise when "gender and sexual normativity are destabilized, creating a crisis that becomes an opportunity to enact new forms of assemblages, coalitions, collectivities, affinities, and life."[28] What these various theorizations on Black gender and transness elucidate are the possibilities of speculative inquiry and intellective waywardness for yoking together trans of color pasts and futures with liberatory aesthetics and schemas.

I return to Angie's casual, sluggish dancing. I relish the fact she dances to lyrics that repeat the refrain "It's gonna set you free." I want to imagine her in those seconds on that bus in the eighties feeling the words of those lyrics, feeling free. Her there among her kin and kind, no virtuosic dancing and fierceness, no documentary-worthy performance, just the most mundane shimmies, the most unimpressive of dances. I want to imagine those others around her doing their own modest, lethargic shimmies as also feeling the words in those lyrics, all together radiating freedom. I want to imagine how the slightest, most minimalist of gestures and movements, in the briefest of moments, can produce a sense of freedom. To fantasize that in that grainy footage Angie can make "many more unimagined configurations of gender, sexuality, and other forms of difference, as well as the forms that have been said to not exist for so long," as micha cárdenas aptly theorizes in her work on trans of color poetics.[29] Even if only for but a few seconds, a transient moment of road-tripping, I overindulge in the idea that freedom was known there and then: Angie feeling trans Latinx liberation in the casual shimmying of her body.

GLIMPSING ANGIE

Seated on the sidewalk in New York City's Union Square, Angie, in one of the microscenes composing the outtake footage, speaks in Spanish with, presumably, one of her daughters (see fig. 1.1). They wait to board the bus, which will take them to the nation's capital. Dangling in Angie's hand are what appear to be Polaroid photos of her dressed sumptuously for a ball. Angie uses that distinctly Nuyorican Spanish: the tongue loose and snapping out vowels, the hands gesturing riotously to make meaning, the lips wide and evocative. I can't make out what Angie is saying. Something or other about someone's sister. There's too much noise from the surrounding environs, too much traffic, and too many other people for the camera to catch exactly what the discussion is all about. Scratches on the film reel scar the footage, a reminder of what is all too ephemerally material, the pinkish, lightning-like patterns splashing across the image of Angie (see fig. 1.2). The camera lingers on their discussion for a few seconds. Then it moves on, leaving them behind in the eighties.

Throughout the outtakes documenting the Xtravaganzas' road trip to Washington, DC, we see Angie speaking Spanish often, in momentary shots of her in pink rollers, chatting and cracking up with the other girls. While on the bus, an emphatic Angie sputters from the lap of another, "¡Ay lo que ha hecho, loca!" (see fig. 1.3). Her speaking in Spanish here, and the deployment of the term *loca*, a word of playful endearment used between Puerto Rican queer and trans people, participates in what Lawrence La Fountain–Stokes theorizes as "transloca practices," "serving as a mechanism for historical memory and for intergenerational transmission of knowledge."[30] This passing scene is an instance of the historical trans Puerto Rican intimacy and belonging that the outtakes crucially provide. Many of the other Spanish-speaking women and femmes do not make an appearance in the documentary. Or, if they do, they are shown for a mere second, in the back of the ballroom, a human detail, a facial expression or bodily gesture responding to the ball, a blur that perception cannot fully acknowledge, not even intended to be taken in, because they are window dressing to the film's overall narrative and thematic construction of high-energy, fast-paced trans and queer of color spectacular ballroom performance. If one wants to find these unidentified others in the film proper, then one

Figure 1.1 Angie chitchatting in Spanish, Union Square, NYC. *Paris Is Burning*, Criterion Collection edition outtakes.

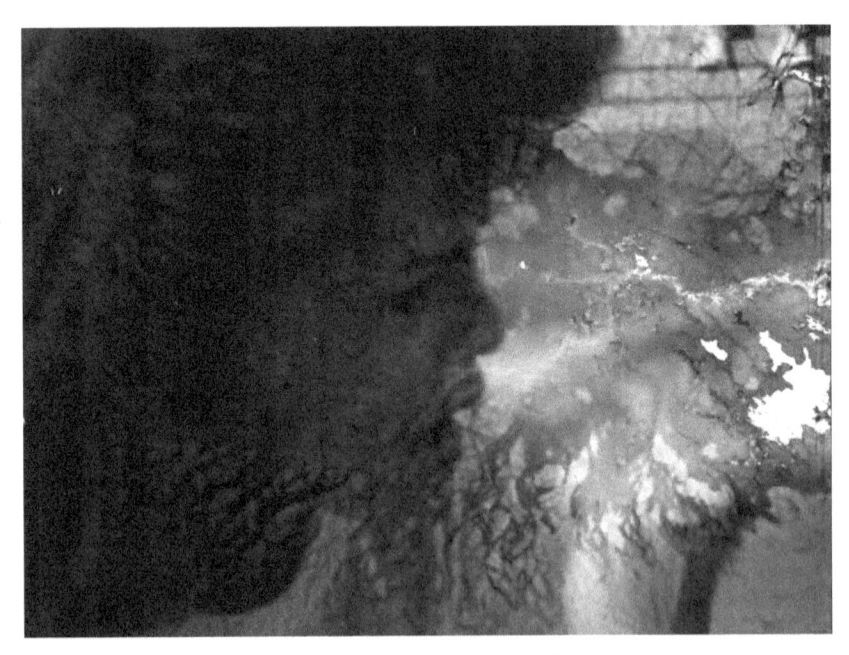

Figure 1.2 Angie and the scratch on the reel. *Paris Is Burning*, Criterion Collection edition outtakes.

Figure 1.3 "¡Ay lo que ha hecho, loca!" *Paris Is Burning*, Criterion Collection edition outtakes.

must search dutifully, must deploy technological mediation in order to render them. This is what I must do to glimpse Angie.

I rewind this brief recording of Angie idly chitchatting in Spanish, in hopes of deciphering what she's saying. I want to know the exact words, piece together the meaning of her sentences, try, in vain, to understand the context in which she discourses. I already know the futility of this interpretive endeavor, yet the impulse to know this chitchat lingers. What mundane event or situation was she recounting? Why do I yearn to know so intimately, so exactingly, the contours of this discussion that occurred well over thirty years ago? I don't believe this impulse to know this idle chitchat in Spanish is an attempt at reenacting an Enlightenment fantasy of mastery over or ethnographic voyeurism over the footage. Rather, I understand this impulse as an intense, transhistorical desire to know a form of trans Boricua comportment and living, of being together, that already existed there in the eighties on that curb in Union Square. This seemingly unseemly attention to the most micro units of interaction, this interpretive scaling-down so far into the weeds of decoding words and fixating on facial expressions, this extravagant otiosity, bears possibilities for apprehending trans Latinx quotidian flourishing. This yearning for transhistorical trans Latinx intimacies calls for what Leah DeVun and Zeb Tortorici explicate as "plural historicities," where the enacting of trans histories and historiographical writing "rejects the imposition of any single narrative of events that would demand coherence or continuity," which "refocuses us on the pleasures (of identifying or disidentifying; of avowing or disavowing; of imagining, filling in, or leaving blank)."[31] DeVun and Tortorici's theorizing of trans historicities is compelling for how it opens up space for the affective, embodied, messy, open-ended, and, above all, pleasurable process of creating historical trans experience and phenomenon. This approach to trans history-making remembers the researcher in the processes of making trans history matter, where the experience of histories of sexed gender variance and comportments across time requires a sensitivity to the variations in contexts, terminologies, and subjectivities.[32]

I linger longingly over Angie idly chitchatting in Spanish on the sidewalk, because it offers another vantage point from which to understand the capaciousness of historical trans Latinx life in a film like *Paris Is Burning*. The representation of and cultural visibility of transwomen of color has largely been determined by narratives of violence, suffering, and premature death. On the other hand, they have also been overdetermined by narratives of spectacle and theatricality that circumscribe them into exchange value for cisnormative white supremacist capitalist exploitation. Far too often, these narratives interlock, becoming mutually indistinguishable and reifying the other, forming master narratives that perpetually delimit how we apprehend and imagine trans of color experience and lifeworlds. Therefore, these seconds of idle chitchat in Spanish, these glimpsings of Angie across the archive, evidence another way of presencing historical trans of color personhood and communities. They provide more expansive, while still situated, liberatory imaginaries of lives like Angie's beyond the well-trod, and at times limiting, narratives and dichotomies that are so easily affixed to historical trans subjects.

At the time of this writing, the film's archive housed at UCLA, containing more additional footage and recordings, is embargoed. I must make do, then, with Angie there on the sidewalk idly chitchatting in Spanish. I make do because I know Angie there on the sidewalk is more than enough. We make do with much less, after all, making do with what little we have by way of archives. In those brief seconds of deteriorated footage, I let her reach out to me, and I to her, to foster a trans Latinx world from this bountiful brevity, where seconds amount to more than enough for emancipatory dreaming. These filmic moments are "always open and receptive to the gift of gender and a language of proliferation and transformation," as Giancarlo Cornejo elegantly puts it.[33]

There is a fundraising trailer included in the Criterion Collection edition of the film. The fundraising trailer rehearses many of the sequences and segments seen in the film, with additional material that never made it into either the film or the theatrical release trailer. "The House of Xtravaganza. The House of Ebony. The House of Dupree. Who the hell are they?" asks the narrator at the conclusion of the fundraising trailer. The trailer's answer? "They're nobody in society's eyes. You know they're somebody when they're in that little ballroom. Other than that, nobody knows who they are." Interestingly, this monologue is never heard again in the theatrical release trailer or the film.

As the voice-over addresses potential funders, we glimpse Angie. The fundraising trailer concludes with footage of ball-goers leaving a ball. The night is over, and early morning has arrived. The camera records from between the ballroom hallway and the Harlem street outside. The double doors burst open as the cameraperson documents the chaotic hubbub of ball-goers dispersing around them, trophies in hand and fur coats across bodies. In what amounts to the camera merely pivoting around, we see Angie in the hallway, one among the throng of trans and queer of color people. The hallway contains minimal lighting, so she is awash in a thick, textured darkness, the camera unable to provide much clarity to her image. In its no-more-than-a-second-long moment, the camera captures Angie turning around, opening her mouth wide, and dispensing inarticulable, though very much pointed, words toward a group of people walking behind her. She raises her index finger up to emphasize her point. Are they Xtravaganzas? Are they ball-goers from other houses? Is she reprimanding, offering advice? It remains unclear, though I rewind many times this second-long glimpsing of Angie. Each frame, each pause, she is but a bluish-black pixelated blur. Every pausing produces but a distortion of Angie. Many distortions I continue to pause over, linger over, longing for figural clarity, for a crystalline image. But in the trans of color archive, we must learn to work with the blurs and pixelation, the opacities and distortions, the many forms, styles, and matters trans of color life and history takes.

This moment of Angie is fast and fleeting, nearly indiscernible, surely forgettable, another mundane gesture and dialogue in the life of trans Boricua living in the eighties. The camera passes her by, as it passes many by throughout the many recordings comprising the *Paris Is Burning* filmic apparatus, on its forward march through the hallway of the ballroom lodge and out through the double doors into Harlem. The camera functions in this instance as a threshold between inside and outside, private and public, poor documentary subject on view and funding elite viewer, white and nonwhite. The camera's sustained attention of this threshold tellingly reminds us of what balls also were at the time: messy, uncoordinated dispersals into the early morning, mothers and children heading out to homes, to lovers, to the piers, satisfied exhaustion. Even in filmic ephemerality, in the camera recording her by happenstance as it pivots, we glimpse Angie, sensing her presence so palpably. There she is among the many crowded trans and queer of color dispersals, part of these many scenes throughout the years, now cinematically compressed into a few seconds one can view anywhere in the world. Angie's second-long distortion is a dispersal of unimaginable scalar dimensions. She can be viewed on a DVD-playing device, or she can be streamed. She can be viewed on the couch in one's apartment, on a train or bus, in a classroom. She can be viewed in 2025, or years from now. She can be viewed across the globe. Such distortional dispersal gives Angie many afterlives. Angie's afterlives remind us how trans Latinx quotidian histories inventively and insurgently take shape against all the odds. Angie's afterlives show us how trans Latinx quotidian lifeworlds emerge in the unlikeliest of places, and through innovative and transformative methods. Viewing Angie's finger-pointing pixelated figure moving across time and space is another way of being with her, of not letting white-centric cisnormative logics and rubrics of historicity brush her aside.

THE LITERARY AND DIGITAL AFTERLIVES OF ANGIE XTRAVAGANZA

Angie Xtravaganza ushers the children of her house onto the bus that will transport them to the US capital. "¡Arriba! ¡Montate! Pa'tra, entre," she says, lobbing commands in a Spanish distinctly Puerto Rican. Her hands flop in the air, affectionately, motioning them forward into the bus. She's a quintessential Boricua mother in these seconds, a unique blend of bossy, nagging, and loving. This glimpsing of Angie corresponds with Angie glimpsed in the fundraising trailer.

These various glimpsings of Angie's mothering parallel those of a fictionalized accounting of her in Joseph Cassara's novel *The House of Impossible Beauties* (2018). Told in multiperspective, first-person narration, the novel focuses in on the members of the House of Xtravaganza before, during, and after the filming of *Paris Is Burning*. The novel tells a fictionalized narrative about the life and times of Angie, Venus, and Hector, founding father of the Xtravaganzas, posthumously glimpsed in a photo shown in the film, which also includes the two young, unidentified kids hanging around outside on the street, named in the book Juanito and Daniel. We witness how Angie meets Hector, how she falls in love with him, befriends Venus, and, after Hector's passing, becomes the mother of the Xtravaganzas. "This is how a house becomes a home. This is how a house becomes a family. It had been Hector's idea from the start to form a community of runaway Boricua queens," notes the text when Angie acquires a bigger apartment to house her growing family.[34] Various facets of Angie's characterization in the novel seem to derive from writer Michael Cunningham's 1995 profile of Angie, "The Slap of Love," which relied exclusively on Dorian Corey and Angie's children to provide posthumous anecdotes about her and her all-too-brief life.[35] The novel depicts Angie as a fiercely caring and devoted mother, and envisages scenes of quotidian life, familial intimacy, and communal care in places besides the ballroom: ordinary scenes of trans Boricua living, like Angie, for instance, "dancing herself in circles in the middle of the sala, feeling the beat within her heart, that beat in her heart, that beat, as Lisa Lisa sang her anthem on the radio—and nena, every time that tune came on, her heart did double-beats and triple-booms and she wanted to shout out, Yes I can, Yes I *can* feel that beat in my heart."[36] Or, after a rough day, respite and conviviality with a trans and queer Latinx family: "She [Angie] went back into her room, took out the lamé, and changed into it. She put a tape in the boom box and put some Whitney on blast and marched out with her arms up. 'Come on nenas,' she said to them all. 'Dance with me.'"[37] We see the Xtravganzas together in places like Angie's apartment and beachside boardwalks in New Jersey, contrasting significantly with the documentary's spatial attention on the ball spaces. The novel offers a different perspective into the lives portrayed in the documentary, de-emphasizing the spectacle of the balls in favor of intimate glances into interpersonal relationships.

The novel dramatizes the lives of the various characters, significantly upping the ante of spectacle and tragedy, for, presumably, novelistic effect. For instance, after a boyfriend breaks up with her, Venus takes on a coke addiction. This addiction leads her, as the novel takes time to illustrate, into seemingly dangerous actions of searching for drugs on the street, culminating in her eventual murder. The coke addiction reads as a narrative prop to push Venus's story along, a cause and effect helping to rationalize, and narrativize, her murder. Juanito, similarly, takes on a drug addiction, and responds in turn by doing sex work. The novel's penultimate turn is that Juanito contracts HIV from his rash behavior, as the novel suggests, and subsequently commits suicide. Angie follows this streak of death, dying of AIDS-related complications, which accords with her real-life death in 1993 due to the virus. Juanito's lover, Daniel, distraught and devastated by the many Xtravaganza deaths, carries on as the father of the House. Though the novel may obviate from the spectacle of the balls and theatricalized performance vital to the documentary, it traffics in another spectacular currency: the spectacle of tragedy. Tragedy as spectacle abounds, structuring the cohesiveness of the narrative, and precipitating its forward progression to the end. Certainly, the novel takes creative license in narrating a fictional story inspired by the people featured in the film, and in no way claims biographical or historical veracity.[38] Moreover, there is no doubt tragedy was present in the real, historical lives of the Xtravaganzas represented in the documentary, defined as they were by transphobia, homophobia, poverty, homelessness, and mass deaths caused by HIV/AIDS.

However, I wonder how else might portraits of the Xtravaganzas, of historical trans and queer Latinx people, dynamically materialize if spectacular tragedy is not the sole or defining rubric of intelligibility? How else might we enmesh ourselves in the constructing of historical portraits without resorting to, or heeding, novelistic techniques that often demand plot spectacle, high stakes, and prescriptive narratives? Do the genre conventions and audience expectations over what constitutes a novel constrain what trans and queer Latinx stories are tellable and thinkable? I am not making the case the novel should have abstained from representing addiction, poverty, illness, or death, because it does not adhere to some notion of respectability or "positive" representations. Rather, I am interested in robustly considering what other aesthetic, affective, and sensorial strategies are available for imagining historical trans and queer of color life and community, ones that do not readily or predominately traffic in spectacle, tragedy, or representational schemas bound to neoliberal capitalist conceptions of respectability, bootstrapping, and profitable cultural producers. Homing in on an analytic of critical otiosity, as I've been articulating, evidences ways of figuring historical trans Latinx life that attends to the complex, polyvalent, capacious, and indolent quotidian lifeworlds trans and queer people have lived, and imagined, through time.

Angie not only finds an afterlife in novels, but also finds her way onto social media. On the social media platform Facebook, there is a page dedicated to Angie.[39] With over a thousand followers, the page serves predominately as a repository for photos, many of which seem to have been sent directly to the administrator by people who knew her. The comments under the photos are loving and elegiac, by people who have come to know her through the film, some Xtravaganzas, and even biological nieces and family. There are various sepia-hued photos of her in domestic spaces, suggestive of the late seventies or early eighties, glimpses of Angie in her teenage years. Many are of her participating in balls, eclectic dresses and sky-high wigs, side by side with friends and family. The photo album functions as a scrapbook collecting and displaying fragments of historical trans Boricua life, "trouble[ing] the line between public and private, official and unofficial narratives, by indexing those fault lines as organizing constraints on many trans lives."[40] This social media scrapbook serves as a memorializing nexus, bringing together those who knew Angie and those who never did into the same digital space, allowing for intergenerational contact and conviviality through public comments and even direct messaging.

In two black-and-white photos included in the album, taken by John Simone, who photographed scenes of New York City eighties nightlife, Angie poses with a big cheesy grin. The caption for both reads, "Angi Xtravaganza and Friends at The World, 1988," both taken presumably on the same night and right after one another. She wears a striped dress and black tights in what appears to be some back room of the club. Each photo depicts her striking a pose with a group of friends, most notable of whom is Danny Xtravaganza, who makes brief appearances

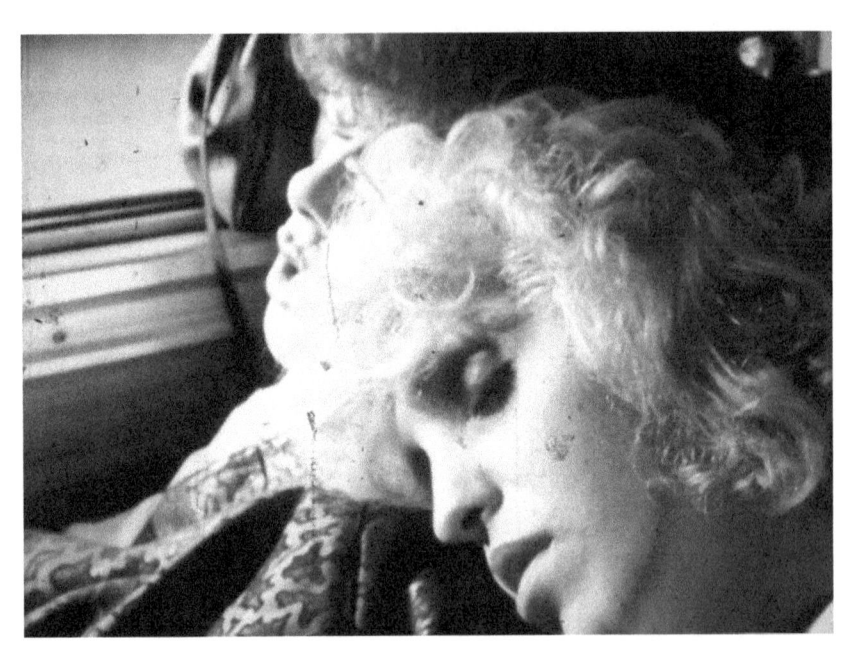

Figure 1.4 Angie laying her head on a friend. *Paris Is Burning*, Criterion Collection edition outtakes.

throughout *Paris Is Burning* and its outtake footage, as well as becoming the father of the House of Xtravaganza after Angie's passing in 1993. The World was a popular nightclub in New York City's East Village, frequented by the likes of RuPaul and permanently closed in 1991 due to the murder of the owner. In one of the photos, Angie tenderly holds Danny's forearm, leaning in toward him, the brightest of cheesy smiles. In the other, she leans back, her right knee raised to waist-level with the foot curled around the calf of the left leg, left hand holding what appears to be lipliner and the right arm gently draping another's shoulder, projecting the widest of toothy grins. Her pose in this latter photo resembles that of a model in a magazine ad, cute and corny, perhaps modeling the lipliner in hand. These photos of Angie grinning prove a striking contrast to the other photographs of her in the album, most of which show her serious and focused, or with a toothless smirk. These photos differ from her general cinematic presence in *Paris Is Burning*.

Here we glimpse Angie with friends and family in the throes of joviality. We glimpse Angie as a model in a magazine ad. We glimpse her as the trans Boricua ancestor enjoying herself on a night out on the town. This cheesy glimpse of Angie becomes a digital intimacy and being-with across time and space that many may now have with her. This digital glimpsing of Angie stages a "complex crisscrossing of time" that veers from "teleological continuities and intimate reconciliations between AIDS generations, sexual geographies, and viral legacies," as Robb Hernández poignantly elucidates on the trans and queer Latinx speculative intergenerational art practice of Olivero Rodriguez, which, nonetheless, "dares to imagine queer and trans Latinx futurity where there wasn't one."[41] Glimpsing Angie on social media becomes a practice of trans Latinx memorializing and futurity-making, a glimpse of trans Latinx joy and freedom in digital dimensions.

CODA

The outtake footage concludes with the Xtravaganzas returning to New York City from Washington, DC. It is twilight hours, and the camera roams about the bus. Venus Xtravaganza lies sprawled out, thick blond hair cascading on her partner seated beside her. An unidentified blond woman rests her head on Angie's shoulder, fast asleep, as Angie leans her head upon the top of the other, also asleep, a second-long glimpsing of femme-to-femme intimacy (see fig. 1.4). The camera cuts to the window, tracking the world outside: the sun an orange creamsicle hue, rising; trees without a single leaf on them, signaling deep winter; farmhouses. Before the credits roll, one final shot of everyone from the front of the bus. Early morning light washes over their faces. Soon, they will transition into wakefulness and get off the bus. Dozily heading out the doors and off into time, away from the camera's gaze, and away from us. They will head into the elsewhere we can only fantasize knowing.

But for now, they are asleep. Heads on top of one another, hands enfolded. Angie asleep, dreaming beside a friend, the sun not yet fully on the horizon. Another day about to begin.

2 | Lounge Lizard Aesthetics

LOS ANGELES NIGHTLIFE VISUALITIES

PORTRAITS OF LOUNGING: REYNALDO RIVERA'S *PROVISIONAL NOTES FOR A DISAPPEARED CITY*

"How does one stage utopia?" asks José Esteban Muñoz in the opening of a chapter on Kevin McCarty's photographs of Los Angeles queer club stages in *Cruising Utopia: The Then and There of Queer Futurity*.[1] For Muñoz, the queer utopian impulse—"that thing that lets us feel that this world is not enough"—can be witnessed in the quotidian practices of queer living, a privileged site for the expression of a queer aesthetic that "frequently contains blueprints and schemata of a forward-dawning futurity."[2] Muñoz examines how McCarty's photographs of empty Los Angeles bars and nightclubs, like those of Spaceland or Catch One, reflect stagings of queer utopianism that are "both temporal and spatial, one in which potentiality, hope, and the future could be, should be, and would be enacted."[3] It is in the quotidian aesthetic, Muñoz claims, that we find utopia and craft queer futurities that the present may not realize. The ordinary is where it's at.

Whereas McCarty's photographs of Los Angeles bars show the

emptied stages of queer nightlife, the work of Mexican American photographer Reynaldo Rivera peoples them with the everyday performers and patrons that make them what they are. Rivera's photographs of Los Angeles queer and trans nightlife, house parties, and underground fashion are collected in *Provisional Notes for a Disappeared City*. The volume contains almost two hundred photographs, an opening essay by Chris Kraus combined with Rivera's memories of the people and places he photographed, an email correspondence with legendary performance artist Vaginal Davis, and a feature story on performer Tatiana Volty by Luis Bauz. The black-and-white photos, and Rivera's accompanying memories throughout, chronicle the photographer's early career, a period defined by familial instability and journeying between Mexico and California. "I got to choose the people I wanted, and I would photograph them however I wanted," Rivera recalls of those early years. "They looked like art photos, as opposed to commercial photography. Maybe it's because I wasn't thinking, oh, I'm doing this for my career, to put on my resume, so I can sell it—I'm doing this for myself. Photography, for me, was that space between reality and make believe."[4] What emerges from these years of casual photography is a picture of the queer and trans Latinx Los Angeles community and culture in the last decades of the twentieth century.

This chapter further schematizes the scope of my critical reading for indolent liberatory practices and does so by pivoting to queer and trans Latinx Los Angeles nightlife visualities. I examine the Los Angeles nightlife photography of gay Chicano photographer Reynaldo Rivera, and the collaborative mural project undertaken by queer Chicanx artists rafa esparza and Gabriela Ruiz. Unlike the moving image of film, like in *Paris Is Burning*, the photograph and the mural of the lounger or partygoer presents *lazy* as a hypervisible, dynamically still, and unavoidably ostentatious encounter that hails the viewer to engage with it on its own terms. The queer and trans Latinx visualities staged by these artists proffer moments of queer and trans Latinx indolent lounging, which becomes a relational intensification of indolence, an intensifying procedure produced in and because of the still image, challenging the normative rubrics of aesthetic valuation and sensorial experience. The intensified attention on the mundanity of these lazy lounging scenes is precisely what propositions sensorial rearranging that encourages unexpected aesthetic responses, affective attachments, and modes of attention.

Tina M. Campt's theory of "listening to images" is formative for further developing my sense of reading for indolent liberatory practices. Through close examinations of photographs of Black subjects overlooked yet contained in colonial archives, Campt elaborates upon a method of apprehending photography that is a "practice of looking beyond what we see and attuning our sense to the other affective frequencies through which photographs register." The Black feminist method outlined by Campt is one prioritizing the haptic, and the sensory, experience of photographs and images, an analytic connection to the image that examines the event of the photo, the conditions surrounding its moment of instantiation, and its ongoingness across time and space. Listening to images is a method fostering a "quotidian practice of refusal" that is "defined less by opposition or 'resistance,' and more by a refusal of the very premises that have reduced the lived experience of blackness to pathology and irreconcilability in the logic of white supremacy."[5] This method takes into account the seen and unseen, the past, present, and future of what constitutes the image. The photo becomes an interpretive event in and of itself, working against the capture of anti-Blackness and coloniality.

These nightlife scenes of queer and trans Latinx indolent lounging demand an interpretive framework that identifies, describes, and amplifies the radical energies indolence possesses. Reading for indolent liberatory practices functions by observing in these scenes of lounging a specific queer and trans Latinx orientation, an orientation requiring the reader to attune oneself to the sensibilities, space-times, and worlds the images compose. If one takes seriously the premise of the indolent invitation, these visual imaginaries constructed by queer and trans people of color lounging call into question hegemonic systems tied to capitalist work ethics, productivism, bourgeois respectability, minority uplift, assimilationist mandates, bootstrapping, and other logics bound to neoliberalist modernity. This occurs through the intensification and extension of indolence's presence by mapping it along axes of race, gender, sexuality, nationality, and class and then telescoping out how such indolent ways strategize against and imagine elsewhere from oppressive logics and structures. The lounging visualities I trace in the following are charged with queer and trans Latinx indolence, that is, photographic and muralistic scenes evincing lax and lounging bodies, slowed temporalities, pleasurable intimacies like drinking with friends, and hanging about. Reading these photographs for the nonwhite queer and indolent potential they carry requires a close critical attention and sensorial adjustment that does not fall back on for legitimacy nor rely upon for legibility neoliberal capitalist paradigms like bootstrapping, respectability, representational visibility, or minoritarian uplift. Orienting oneself to reading for indolent liberatory practices meets these loungers where they are: there and then in the nightlife scene, there and then for all that they are in that lazing moment. By doing so, sensing out indolent lounging and reading critically for indolence challenges normative modes of valuation tied to minoritized peoples. Instead, sensing and reading for indolent lounging redirects pathways for how we value queer and trans of color cultural production, and how such valuing reimagines structures built on inequity and exploitation.

Queer nightlife studies provides an important framework for examining the lounging in this chapter, particularly in the attention given to how queer nightlife spaces stage queer of color world-making practices. In their coedited anthology on Latinx dance practices, *Everynight Life*, Celeste Fraser Delgado and José Esteban Muñoz remark how "dance incites rebellions of everynight life," and their introduction to the volume and the collected essays attest to the radical energies inherent in racialized dance forms circulating across the Americas.[6] Following in the footsteps of this landmark anthology, *Queer Nightlife*, edited by Kemi Adeyemi, Kareem Khubchandani, and Ramón H. Rivera-Servera, anthologizes an expansive and robust set of writings examining the importance of performance for queer of color theorizings on nightlife, where "performance has been a critical optic to studies of nightlife that depend on the aesthetics and sensorial data of the night—from the music played to the lighting to the ways that people move together and apart, reading bodies as they perform against visual, sonic, and kinesthetic landscapes that surround them—to make sense of the ways that individual and collective identities are felt and negotiated."[7] The writings in *Queer Nightlife* importantly expand upon our understandings of the politics of nightlife: what goes on before one heads out for the evening, where nightlife spaces happen (clubs, apartments, the internet), the various forms nightlife takes in different locales across the globe, and what happens after the night is done. Nightlife spaces, like all spaces, the anthology surmises, are constantly changing and contested, not a portrait of facile utopia or nonhierarchical entanglements.

The critical focus in queer nightlife studies predominately rests upon the importance of dance, which makes sense given dance's eminent role in fostering pleasurable and enticing nightlife scenes. However, my intellective pursuits wander elsewhere to contemplate the following: What other modes already present within queer nightlife make possible queer and trans of color liberatory practices that are not dependent upon formulations of high energy or kinetic speed? What other frequencies are available for theorizing upon queer and trans nightlife's potential for the production of radical social transformation, corporeal pleasure, belonging, and imagining elsewhere from oppressive frameworks? My attention is less on dance and rather on the sensorial, affective, and kinetic forms of slowing down that occur in queer nightlife spaces and aesthetic manifestations of lounging. Through an examination into the performance strategies of trans Latina Chicago club performer Ketty Teanga, also known by her stage name as Miss Ketty, whose performances contrast with that of the neoliberal, gentrifying club's aesthetic incentivizing of speed, consumption, and immediacy, Ramón H. Rivera-Servera outlines how her performances "mak[e] the past, even the recent past, available for contemplation in a performatively intensified deceleration, and thus, extended present."[8] Miss Ketty's pause-riddled and temporally slowed performances incite queer and trans Latinx collectivity, the belonging in the club's space-time through shared knowledge of songs and dances, whose performances "demanded that we just pay attention, that we simply stop time to spend time with one another."[9] Richard Rodríguez also reminds us how suburban queer Latinx nightlife in places like Berwyn, Illinois, outside Chicago, "functions as a refuge from, simultaneously, urban exclusivity and the normative tenets of suburban life," with such nightlife spaces providing slower-paced environments that traffic in different relations to space.[10] Kemi Adeyemi's study of queer Black women's nightlife practices in Chicago's Logan Square is likewise instructive for what it teaches us about queer of color nightlife and slowness. Adeyemi analyses how queer Black women attend a party called Slo 'Mo, which is kinetically and sonically structured around slower energies and calmer sensibilities rather than the higher-energy and predominately white clientele of the majority of other nightclub spaces. Slo 'Mo, and the people who attend it, according to Adeyemi, fosters a mode of slowness that navigates and challenges gentrification and the neoliberal city, while also significantly serving as a space that nourishes Black queer pleasure, joy, and community. The right to slowness, as Adeyemi insightfully points out, is political, especially so within the parameters of coloniality and capitalism, where "the sense of rapidity that neoliberalism conditions is deeply racialized and territorialized and depends on the exploitation of those who *cannot* afford to take time."[11] These various cases of nightlife slowness as queer of color world-making practice productively situate my own sense of indolent lounging. Plugging in to a slowed, leisurely nightlife temporality, indulging in the tempos and flows of an intensified attunement to taking one's time and taking up space under strobe lights or sonic vibes, is one aesthetic-political strategy for sensing, knowing, and creating nonoppressive worlds delinked from capitalist spatiotemporalities and rationalities. The nightlife scenes of queer and trans Latinx lounging, as evidenced in Rivera's photographs and esparza and Ruiz's mural, disturb the spatiotemporal rationalities governing US contemporaneity. The Los Angeles visualities in these works luxuriate in an aesthetics of lounging, which activates possibilities for minoritized, liberatory imaginaries to flourish.

Many of the photos in Reynaldo Rivera's *Provisional Notes for a Disappeared City* are of the everyday performers and patrons that moved through Los Angeles's Latinx and multi-ethnic queer bars and clubs such as Silverlake Lounge, La Plaza, and Mugi's. Other photos in the collection were taken at house parties in pregentrified Echo Park, featuring up-and-coming local artists, performers, and singers—including Francesco Siqueiros, Alicia Armendariz, and Roberto Gil de Montes, among others—whom Rivera met through his cousin Trizia. These were people and places familiar to Rivera. As Elizabeth Ferrer summarizes in her overview of Chicanx photography in Los Angeles, many were "devoted to documentary modes and to chronicling the local scene, but by the 1980s, Chicanx photographers were working with a multiplicity of approaches to communicate concerns both political and personal."[12] Like his Chicanx contemporaries, Rivera, too, demonstrated interests and approaches outlined by Ferrer, using his insider perspective to capture the metropolitan nightlife scenes he frequented. Scenes of urban nightlife made possible Rivera's aesthetic inclinations, like many other Chicanx photographers who were drawn to city barrios across the US Southwest.[13] The documentary drive is especially salient for Rivera, as he confirms throughout the accompanying writings in the photobook, because it challenges the historical and ongoing erasure of queer and trans of color lifeworlds. "So many of us died without a trace, due to AIDS and other acts of violence," Rivera explains in an email to performance artist Vaginal Davis, the text of which is included in *Provisional Notes for a Disappeared City*. "I've chosen to leave a trace. Recording their images as they re-imagined themselves and their stories in the '80s and '90s in Los Angeles, the city of dreams. Mrs Alex, Olga, Yoshi and all the rest of us were here, and we mattered."[14]

Many of Rivera's subjects are trans and, as he points out in his notes, no longer with us. Rivera recalls that, at his first exhibition in 1995, he chose not to use the word "transvestite" in descriptions, in order to refuse "the sensationalism" the term signaled. "They were beautiful photos of performers, who were performing. There's a whole social layer going on, behind this," Rivera remarks,[15] demonstrating an attentiveness and sensitivity to the ways in which the visual images of trans people are often exploited. "When I photographed these people, I was just documenting a moment that I found beautiful and interesting."[16] Rivera's photographic aesthetic shies away from the sensational, and even high theatricality, of his subjects, opting instead for the more muted, subdued, and banal moments he witnessed: performers lounging backstage, patrons waiting in line to use the bathroom, partygoers drinking in cramped apartment hallways. These aesthetic foci reflect Rivera's view of these photographs as documenting a working-class, multi-ethnic, and Latinx Los Angeles. "All these neighborhoods were ethnically diverse," Rivera recalls, adding that "most of us were poor, but then again we were living in a different time, where you could live with a minimum wage job."[17] According to Rivera, this archive performs a future tense recalling "one big movie" composed of an amalgam of black-and-white photos, the monochromatic color scheme suggesting a time gone by, something old-school. This work is especially pertinent for Latinx people in Los Angeles, as Rivera emphasizes, because it rewrites that common script of feeling like "we just got here," mapping and restoring the presence of Latinx life in the story of the US Southwest.

This is why Rivera's positing of these photos as a "document" is a compelling way to view them. They are evidence of past lives and places. "I was determined to find beauty in places deemed ugly," Rivera explains, "or maybe I was just documenting the way that beauty can live side by side with violence and the ugliness of life, society and this country, a country that let millions of us die in the most inhumane way."[18] Yet Rivera's documentary photographs and the tone of the essays and correspondence included in the book are not overtly elegiac, the typical approach for many accounts of queer and trans of color life as AIDS and gentrification displaced communities. Rivera's photos are not sensationalized or ethnographic depictions for an imagined cisgender, heterosexual, or white audience. Rivera's photographs embark upon a different kind of quotidian work for aesthetically rendering queer and trans Latinx life, one that elucidates "an infinity of fleeting profiles like dream images, in order to capture absolutely unique moments of the reciprocal situation of things."[19] They document a performative, affective, and sensorial register of the impressively unimpressive: hanging out with a friend at the queer bar, performers backstage lounging, drunken posing for the camera at a house party, a sibling photo shoot. These are the images of everyday nightlife and indolence, commonplace Polaroids, the ordinary and leisurely of queer and trans Latinx Los Angeles imaged by Rivera.

Take, for instance, the photograph of two women sitting at a bar (see fig. 2.1). One smiles grandly, joyously, her legs crossed and left hand falling elegantly back at the wrist, while the other looks on with a rouged smirk, hand up to the side. They pose for the camera, surely, seated there as they are with beer bottles, cigarettes, and an ashtray on the small wooden table between them, after finding themselves prompted by the roving eye of the photographer. They seem so carefree, so at ease, unencumbered by the world outside the photo's frame. What about this setup catches Rivera's attention that night at the bar? What makes him decide these two will be his photographic subjects? This shot captures a quotidian moment and a world in a single image. A photograph that urges the viewer to dwell in the luxuriant lag of hanging out at the bar, the pleasurable laxity of spending time however one wants, in good company, in familiar spaces. Indolent lounging is the center of this nightlife gravity.

The various portraits in *Provisional Notes for a Disappeared City* of a queer and trans Latinx time gone by shuttle the viewer between past, present, and future, undertaking what John Berger postulates as the "instant photographed," which takes on "meaning insofar as the viewer can read into it a duration extending beyond itself. When we find a photograph meaningful, we are lending it a past and a future."[20]

Figure 2.1 Reynaldo Rivera, *Untitled, Downtown*, 1993. Courtesy of the artist and Semiotext(e).

Though I am in agreement with Berger's notion of the critic's need to imbue interpretative meaning into a photo, in order that it may be described, explained, and theorized for critical engagement, I depart from the maxim in that the hermeneutical project I find worthwhile is an extension into the world presented by the photo, rather than a departure beyond it. This is not to advance a necessarily historicist or exhaustively contextualized reading of photos. As Eduardo Cadava reminds us, "when we respond to a photograph by trying to establish only the historical contexts in which it was produced, we risk forgetting the disappearance of context—the essential decontextualization—that is staged by every photograph."[21] Rather, what I am suggesting aligns most pertinently in what I am theorizing as reading for indolent liberatory practices. The interpretive stance this ordains is about not leaving the queer and trans nonwhite person behind for a beyond, but rather for the hanging out with, the potentially perverse desire to dawdle too long with the photo, to ease into its world, to lounge about wantonly in what it might propose if we stay awhile. This modification of prepositional phrasing might seem minor, or superfluous, but I, nonetheless, find it imperative for orchestrating the sense of liberatory indolence I am outlining. For reading indolent lounging entails the extended and extensive lingering with an image, inside its universe, that constellates unpredictably, nonlinearly, through spatiotemporalities, through aesthetic-political possibilities hitherto acknowledged. A reading of indolence into the visual field lets us feel an image for an alternative politics besides one bound to criteria of objectivity, mimetic faithfulness, representational authenticity, and minority uplift.[22] The sensorial errancy enables liberatory narratives unforetold.

Two photographs of unidentified performers at the Silverlake Lounge taken in 1995 further encapsulate Rivera's lounging aesthetic (see figs. 2.2 and 2.3). In these two shots, like so many of the others, Rivera seemingly impresses upon his subjects an added layer of quotidian sparkle, as if his lens is predisposed to heighten the everydayness of the subject and the environment in which they find themselves. In the first, a performer smirks brightly at the camera. She's slightly hunched over, her hair tied back in a ponytail, adorned with modest necklace and earrings. Looking closely, one notices how an earring appears to be in movement as if the photographer has hailed her attention. Over here, Rivera must say, as the performer turns quickly to look at him with her piqued curiosity, her lips smacked together as if readying a quip, preparing to reprimand Rivera for distracting her from getting ready or bothering her after a long night performing. The second performer dons a blond wig, dark lipstick, and a simple monochromatic dress. She is plainness itself, really, seated in what appears to be the backstage area, waiting her turn to perform, waiting for her moment to shine. She knows the camera is there, certainly, its lens fixed on her awaiting a pose, asserting her contemplative countenance, looking afar and aside of the photographer. There is no doubt she is posing. There is no doubt she wants her photographic immortality. Yet she, the entertainer, the illusionist, presents it with a demure naturalism: I see you seeing me, so here I am. These photos render entrancing a lounging aesthetic, a visuality to stay awhile in.

In her treatise on photography, Susan Sontag, writing on the work of Diane Arbus, describes the function of frontality in portraiture thusly: "In the normal rhetoric of the photographic portrait, facing the camera signifies solemnity, frankness, the disclosure of the subject's essence."[23] However, Arbus's photographic interest in socially abject subjects, according to Sontag, evidences how her use of frontality "implies in the most vivid way the subject's cooperation. To get these people to

Figure 2.2 Reynaldo Rivera, *Performer, Silverlake Lounge*, 1995. Courtesy of the artist and Semiotext(e).

Figure 2.3 Reynaldo Rivera, *Performer, Silverlake Lounge*, 1995. Courtesy of the artist and Semiotext(e).

pose, the photographer has had to gain their confidence, has to become 'friends' with them."[24] Sontag imbues Arbus's camera with a magical quality, able, even in spite of her outsider status from the outcast milieu she photographs, to have her subjects expose themselves to her, to perform for her camera. For Sontag, Arbus's portraits result in a deviation from the norms of aesthetic reception typical (or what she deems typical) of portraiture. Frontality conventionally aestheticizes the subject as Art, whereas Arbus's work elicits alternative outcomes.

Rivera's deployment of frontality, in contrast, messages to the reader a relation of familiar intimacy. "We're completely different," comments Rivera on how critics compared him to Arbus. "When you look at her shit, I don't know . . . it felt like you were excluded. Like you're not invited to that party. My work is not like that at all. She took people that were normal and made them look freaky. I took people that were ordinarily considered freaky and made them look amazing, or cool, or normal. My gig was to have people look the way they wanted to look."[25] He is not outsider to the groups he photographs, some of whom are friends of his, nor does he seek to elicit reactions from them that confirm some preconceived essentialist notion. There are no countenances of shock, fear, or overt theatricalized posing within the portraits. Nor are there any semblances of elaborately staged or intricately mediated shots instigated by the photographer in order to "elevate" the pictures into the realm of "high art." Rivera, as he makes well enough clear throughout the writings in the photobook, aims to document, to track the beautiful found in nightlife. The portraits catalogue an array of broad smiles, coy smirks, cheesy grins, bored gazes, and the other embodied countenances and comportments that encompass queer and trans Latinx nightlife. The expressive banality and simplicity of these photographed instances aestheticize queer and trans Latinx nightlife, sensorially orienting the reader into the frame, which further supplies the necessary resources for establishing an indolent lounging reading practice. The quotidian countenances of an ordinary night out at the queer bar exampled in Rivera's portraits equip the reader to question the protocols of valuation within capitalist modernity, and, most importantly, how we work to value otherwise our relations to time, space, aesthetics, and one another according to indolently liberatory strategies.

The elegant drabness and stridently relaxed comportment of these two photographed subjects reminds us of the allure of documentary photography and its ability to transport us to a past never lived, a past we can only experience as a projected fantasy, as an entanglement with fiction. These photos of a fantastical past slow us down and ease us into the indolent lounging spatiotemporality they proffer, reminding us that there were connoisseurs of indolent nightlife before us, those bar-hoppers and partygoers who modeled modes of reorganizing space-time according to minoritarian desires. These indolent scenes rehearse what Kareem Khubchandani recognizes as the possibilities between nightlife-goers and queer activism, where "nightlife traffics in a different set of political tools, relying less on the didactic verbiage of systematic and social change, instead orienting its subjects and patrons through a variety of sensorial instruments."[26] Sensing out indolence in nightlife scenes of aesthetic lounging, and how that recalibrates relations to self, others, and space, broadens the horizons of what counts as activism and what activism can look like in queer nightlife spaces. The two backstage performers above are akin to McCarty's unpeopled stages in that they are moments when the high theatricality and liveliness expected from a stage performance are undercut by the offstage nightlife ordinariness: images of various performers getting ready backstage, fooling around with one another, posing, or just hanging out in between sets. Many are identified by name—Olga, Miss Alex, Tina, Yoshi (the owner of Mugi's bar)—yet many are not. We can read through Rivera's brief reminiscences on the identified ones, or simply Google to get a few hits on a few of them. Even if identified, most are bound to a name in a caption—an "Angela" or "Melissa." They are photographic evidence of quotidian queer and trans Latinx nightlife torqued to the frequencies of indolent lounging, a record of those nights out relishing in boredom, flirtatiousness, euphoria, revelry, erotics, and the various other affect-dispositions locatable in such undercharged scenarios. The documentary function of these photographs, as Rivera puts it, offers a way to forge queer and trans of color futurities from a past that provides an example for thriving: "We made this city our city, if only for a brief time. And then we disappeared as quickly as we appeared. Still, our stories are woven into the story of this city—every alley and shitty bar, every empty lot where a rent-controlled building once stood."[27] Rivera's work testifies to the fact that queer and trans Latinx life does not have to be just tragedies, nor theatricalized sensations, nor martyrs to a cause. Instead, queer and trans of color aesthetics and worlds can frolic in the pleasurable possibilities of indolent lounging aesthetics, of cavorting and comporting a spatiotemporality otherwise.

LOUNGING IN THE DEEP: *SILVERLAKE LOUNGE* (1995)

Rivera's photographs in *Provisional Notes for a Disappeared City* are comprised primarily of portraits. Throughout the collection are intense close-ups and medium shots of patrons, partygoers, and performers. Rivera is interested in the human figure, how a queer and trans Latinx person occupies a nightlife space, photographically documenting the many types carousing through lounges, bars, and house parties. There is one photo, however, in the collection which stands markedly distinct from this general stylistic inclination: a wide shot of the Silverlake Lounge itself. Taken from a distance (as if shot from the entryway), with no clearly delineated or focalized human subject for the viewer, *Silverlake Lounge* (1995) is centralized around the negative space of the lounge floor (see fig. 2.4).

The foreground of the photo is the main lounge floor area, where one would presumably dance or cluster together on a busy night, except on this night the area is thick in darkness and relatively empty of people. The background of the photo is the lit-up stage, absent of any show or performers, with a few people congregating at the far end of the bar and at a set of tables. There is a light emanating from the bar itself, another on the stage, but the majority of the shot is doused in a textured darkness. We see people talking at the bar, others across the way at a set of tables, a woman riffling through her purse, and one person blurred and in movement toward the tables. The lounge floor is devoid of the hubbub of patrons. Foreground and background unite in the photo through a sense of ascending depth, an impression of one moving from darkness to lightness, spatial emptiness to spatial congestion. Perhaps Rivera takes the shot before a show begins, or perhaps after the performance has ended, or perhaps this is merely a moment in between sets. Or, maybe, it's just a casual weekday evening with no drag performances to be had, a slow Monday or Wednesday night, when patrons go for a drink after work with a friend, or by oneself, to hang out, chill, and relax. The photo narrates an ordinary evening at a lounge, and the photo's distancing effect, unlike the majority of Rivera's oeuvre, which

Figure 2.4 Reynaldo Rivera, *Silverlake Lounge*, 1995. Courtesy of the artist and Semiotext(e).

favor portraits and proximity to photographed subjects, materializes lounging as an abstracted spaciousness.

The abstracted spaciousness on display in this photo of the Silverlake Lounge is an antiportrait: no frontality, no close shots of bodies performing or posing, no emotions to be read in the contortions of a face or gesture. There is no definitive, represented person as is the hallmark of portraiture. How does a faraway, wide shot of a lounge landscape manifest queer and trans Latinx indolent lounging? In the absence of the portrait, the most popular format for portraying the embodied social subject, for giving presence and substance to the minoritized person perpetually consigned to absence and erasure, how do queer and trans of color liberatory aesthetics and emancipatory practices emerge? The abstracted spaciousness of the lounge antiportrait, I contend, further enhances the scope of reading for indolent liberatory practices by proffering queer and trans Latinx indolence as irreducible to a representable body or intelligible identity. Instead, the lounge antiportrait grafts the aesthetic and political possibilities of indolence onto scenic abstraction and atmospheric moods exuding nonwhite queerness and transness even in the absence of the performing, affecting, and embodying minoritized subject. The photo of the Silverlake Lounge allows us to sense out the space-time of Latinx indolence beyond the portrait, as well as beyond the representative minoritized subject. This, in turn, conceptualizes a notion of Latinx indolent practice according to a different aesthetic, social, and political rubric, where "the visual is an enframed visibility" that "lock[s] the visible into a determined perspective . . . in which a relational matrix foregrounds the visuality of specific elements."[28] The milky darkness of the near-empty lounge floor of the queer and trans Latinx space coordinates the viewer into sensing liberatory spatiotemporal possibilities as a relaxed, slowed, and a durational aesthetic experience. The formal properties of *Silverlake Lounge* (1995) allow for an identity-informed understanding even in the absence of normatively construed representative human subjects.[29]

"The burden of frontality," writes John Tagg on the history of portraiture, "was passed on down the social hierarchy, as the middle classes secured their cultural hegemony."[30] Tagg locates the originary function of the photographic portrait as one administered by the bourgeoisie to fashion a sense of social distinction, but portraiture also doubles as an apparatus consolidating regulatory state power over the proletariat, which produced "photographic documents like prison records and social surveys in which this code of social inferiority framed the meaning of representations of the objects of supervision or reform."[31] Portraiture, therefore, in its role of capturing the human face and silhouette for photographic representation, "is both the description of an individual and the inscriptions of social identity." The frontal exposure signature of the portrait abets the ability to surveil and manage minoritized subjectivity, the portrait serving a truth-claim function, which Eduardo Cadava and Paola Cortés Rocca caution is "the policing use of photographic technology." "The confidence that what we call the referent or subject of an image is an entity that is stable and identical to itself," they contend, "[of] which the camera (or language) gives us a 'faithful' or 'true' representation, corresponds not to a characteristic proper to photography."[32] The photograph, Cadava and Cortés Rocca advance, cannot make an evidentiary claim, because it is a mediated framing of the photographed object, not the thing in and of itself.

Positing Rivera's *Siverlake Lounge* (1995) as an antiportrait, then, is to postulate a conception of Latinx indolent lounging that is not aesthetically fixed or predetermined by representational realism. Minoritized aesthetics and cultural production, particularly those by queer and trans people of color, are often evaluated according to rubrics of representational veracity, respectability, and uplift. Such evaluative assumptions depend upon the belief that realism—and the attendant drive to represent marginalized peoples, to render representable as face, voice, body, and other markers of legibility agreeable to the capitalist, majoritarian sphere—is the most politically salient, expedient, and efficient aesthetic mode. However, as I hope my expansive sense of reading for liberatory indolence attests, there are other aesthetic strategies and evaluative criteria available in which to facilitate a politics of resistance and critical reimagining of oppressive systems. Rivera's portraits of loungers are merely one iteration, among other possibilities, for how to operationalize a sense of indolent liberatory practice. The spatiotemporality framed by a photo like *Silverlake Lounge* (1995) challenges the commonsense and standardized notions of what it means to theorize queer and trans Latinx presence, politics, and aesthetics. The wide-shot photograph of an environment like the gay bar renders sensible and perceptible queer and trans Latinxness as a distinctive, and abstract, spatiotemporality, if, that is, we attune ourselves to what it means to read space-time, to read queerness, transness, and Latinxness, as categories that emerge in nonrepresentational modes.

Let us take, for instance, the backgrounded lit-up stage in the photo, which serves as a focalizing point. Its luminous rectangularity saturates the photo with light, as a bulb fixture hovers like an otherworldly orb at the topmost of the image, prominently contrasting with the thickly textured darkness of the photo's foreground. Though a focalizing point for the photo, the lit-up stage finds itself empty of performers. The gleaming, incandescent orb directs the viewer toward the absence on the stage: the absence that is the lip-synch performances, the wigged and gowned queens twirling and shimmying, the bawdy theatrics and campy impersonations entertaining a packed bar. Yet the stage is haunted by the presence of performance: balloons on the floor. The balloons signal a show has transpired or is about to transpire, their helium-filled bodies accentuating the spectacle at hand, garnishing a performance with the over-the-top ridiculousness that is the bread and butter of drag. The abstracted spaciousness of the photo, and its human-less stage festooned with balloons, narrates an indeterminate temporal zone: it could be the time before the show begins, after the show concludes, between sets, or the remainder of a performance from some other day and time that, for some reason or another, no one cleaned up. The spatiotemporality exhibited in Rivera's *Silverlake Lounge* (1995) lags and loafs about in the light/dark contrast, unimpeded by the demand for representational coherence of minoritized countenances and bodies, projecting, instead, the sluggish broodiness of the bar interior, the pleasure of hanging out, just lounging with oneself and others.

Though the image may not be a portrait, nevertheless, there are people in this photo of the Silverlake Lounge. However, many, if not all, of their faces are visually indistinct, and most of them have their backs toward the camera, projecting to the viewer figural inscrutability. None even look at the photographer taking his shot, none seem to really care, probably because the photographer, like them, is also a patron of the Silverlake Lounge. One figure on the right near the stage is blurred, an effect of spontaneous movement while the camera takes the shot, a distortion of the human shape, making forever unknowable the details of the person there in the photographic moment. What these various effacements of human distinctiveness, individuality, and singularity attest to is the everyday reality of moving through the urban sphere and the queer and trans nightlife spaces therein. When we go to the bar, there are people there we will only know as indistinct faces, as backs turned, as blurs in the far background or in the corner of our vision, all never cognized because our minds cannot process that many stimuli, all going, by the end of the evening, unremembered. When there is engagement at the bar with that other we don't know who comes into relation with us, those one-off conversations, those desiring gazes, those brushings up against another, these, too, tend to fade from our consciousness, our memories, as quickly as they came. The photo of Silverlake Lounge, more than any other in Rivera's oeuvre, addresses most powerfully the quotidian condition of the queer bar: there we transform into beings who share in the intimacy of queerness and transness with familiar strangers. We may never know everyone around us at the queer bar, we may never be able to fully account for all the other lives in our midst, yet that is what precisely composes the spatiotemporality of the queer bar, what makes it tick. Each person contributes to the sense of the space, allowing everyone to immerse themselves into the bar in order to slow down, ease up, and luxuriate in the universe created. An alchemy truly divine.

Conceptualizing the photo in this manner prompts the proposal, then: What does it mean to imagine an indolent lounging commons like that which *Silverlake Lounge* (1995) proffers? A commons motivated by the pleasure of idleness, doing nothing, laziness, taking one's time, hanging out, easing up, all of which are so contrary, plainly appalling, to contemporary US neoliberal capitalism. The indolent liberatory schema on proposal here is one that jams commonsense rationalities near and dear to capitalist mandates.

The photo primes the viewer for sensing a queer, trans, and Latinx lifeworld via the abstracted wide shot of the lounge. We know the photo is of a lounge frequented by queer and trans Latinx people, who may very well be some of the figures in the shot. We know this photo is taken by a gay Chicano photographer, a photo side by side with other photographs by the photographer documenting queer and trans Latinx life at the close of the twentieth century. These facts layer into the photograph's abstracted qualities, into how we look upon it, into how we sense out what it has to offer, letting us not forget, as the caption does well too, that this is a photo of a specific location at a specific calendrical point in time (1995). This context-specific dimension of the photo does not cede to representational dictums but rather signals, alludes, in decontextualized abstraction, to the nonwhite queer and trans specificity that provides the atmosphere for the photo, that equips us to sense out another politics. The quotidian photo of queer and trans Latinx nightlife, in this way, becomes another kind of world, "a movie," as Rivera explains of his photographic practice, where "I was constantly creating the movie I wanted to be in, as opposed to the one I was born into."[33] For Rivera, his photographs in *Provisional Notes for a Disappeared City*, photographs of bygone queer nightlife cultures and ethnic enclaves displaced by gentrification, photographs documentary in nature, still can generate fantasy, movie-making possibilities for the formation of alternative kinds of being, knowing, sensing, and worlding. The nightlife banal transmogrifies us across time and space.

Indolent lounging is the nothing extraordinary happening in spacetime: the people chatting at the bar, the stage empty, the riffling through a purse. Indolent lounging is atmospheric, which the photo relays in its drowsy and gauzy darkness. What are we being asked to view exactly? What does the photo want us to see? The photo precisely calls into question our processes of aesthetic attention and valuation, one which prompts us to dwell upon the significance of space. If we are to perceive an indolent mode, the photo suggests, it has to be according to a different aesthetic rubric, one which holds the space of the queer and trans Latinx lounge, where ordinary conviviality and pleasurable indolence occur, as a site meaningfully important, as critically reorienting us. The photo propositions a different indolent schema, one that is about space itself. In the absence of focalized human subjects, indolent lounging still thrives and is still perceivable as something that is very much there. We can sense indolence's radical force even in the distant shot, the abstracted human shapes, and the atmospheric lull of the lounge. Indolent lounging vibrates with the potential to remake the world as we know it.

THE STYLISTICS OF FRIVOLOUS LOUNGING: ON RAFA ESPARZA AND GABRIELA RUIZ'S *NOSTRA FIESTA* (2019) MURAL AT THE NEW JALISCO BAR

In downtown Los Angeles, there stands the New Jalisco Bar. Opened in 2005 in order to address the need for a gay bar in downtown Los Angeles after the closing of the only other one in the area, Score, the New Jalisco Bar caters to a multilingual, transnational queer and trans Latinx demographic, featuring Latinx drag queens, music, food, and drinks. The New Jalisco Bar has much in common with the older Los Angeles queer bar Silver Platter, opened in 1963 in the MacArthur Park area. Silver Platter, catering to a trans Latinx population, was the focus of artist and filmmaker Wu Tsang's 2012 film *Wildness* about the Tuesday night parties she threw at the bar. Bars like the Silver Platter and the New Jalisco serve as sanctuaries for a multiply marginalized group, especially considering that the majority of US queer bars cater to an imagined white, monolingual audience. Overall, these bars are like any other bar, but the queer and trans Latinx-specific focus make them uniquely stand out.

From the street perspective, the New Jalisco Bar is a relatively unassuming one-story edifice. Next door to the bar, there is a parking lot, and across the street from it, a multilevel parking garage, all of which combines to add an aura of urban shabbiness to the bar. However, there is one standout aspect of the bar's exterior that draws attention: murals. There are two distinct murals on the street-facing side of the building. On the left side, a white mural with multicolored squiggly lines and lettering reading "Not Our President," a popular slogan lobbed against former president Donald Trump during his presidential tenure from 2017 to 2021. Underneath the words, and encircling a set of doors, are drawings of various people holding up signs like "Black Lives Matter," "Defund the Police," "Trans Rights," and "Siempre Unidos." On the right side of the building, we see a purplish-pink mural of Latinx patrons, types, and popular singers like Celia Cruz, all of whom merrily carouse and dance around the name of the bar prominently written in Pride, trans, and Mexican flag colors. This mural, titled *Nostra Fiesta* (2019) (roughly translating into English as "our party"), a collaborative labor by queer Chicanx artists rafa esparza and Gabriela Ruiz, boldly and proudly affirms the historical and contemporary significance of queer and trans Latinx nightlife spaces (see fig. 2.5). Latinx indolent practices materialize in the public sphere as a visual horizon all can experience in esparza and Ruiz's *Nostra Fiesta*.

Since the 1970s, murals have been a medium for Chicanx social critique and political consciousness-raising in Los Angeles. The Chicanx movement empowered Mexican-descendent peoples to transform their sense of selves, history, community, and politics within the United States, critiquing prior hegemonic conceptions of Chicanx cultural backwardness and social criminality, which were, according to the nation-state, desperately in need of state-based reform and uplift. Murals functioned as "public genres" that were "recognized as the essential visual expression of the activism and social demands associated with the Chicano movement."[34] Though many mural projects were funded by governmental agencies in efforts to sanitize buildings of gang graffiti and to provide sources of employment for working-class Chicanx people, many artists, including the gang youth such artistic efforts were made to reform, subverted hegemonic mandates by either overtly or slyly incorporating imagery that critiqued state power and policing.[35] Muralism, then, functioned as a public art practice reflecting cultural pride and political transformations, allowing a "subject denigrated in the popular consciousness to become an actor, a creator of language, and a shaper of space. The platform of the mural provided a physical space in which to materialize counternarratives that questioned and reimagined existing political

Figure 2.5 The New Jalisco Bar front. Photo taken by the author.

and social structures."[36] Esparza and Ruiz's *Nostra Fiesta* follows in this Chicanx Los Angeles mural tradition yet deviates from the implicitly cis-gender-heterosexual foci inherent in Chicanx muralism across the years by prioritizing a patently queer and trans visuality. Their explicitly non-white queer and trans mural coincides with murals like *Por Vida* (2015), commissioned by Galería de la Raza and created by Manuel Paul, a member of the queer artist and DJ group Maricón Collective invited to oversee the mural's construction. Displayed in the Mission District of San Francisco, the mural, a triptych of homeboy-homegirl lowrider culture figural types, defiantly depicts same-sex intimacies between cholas, as well as a shirtless transmasculine person displaying scars under the pecs (suggesting top surgery), overlaid by thorn tattoos. The mural was the subject of vitriol on social media, defaced several times, and, ultimately, was subjected to a firebombing.[37] The story *Por Vida* narrates is one over the fraught and precarious place of queer and trans Chicanx murals, where their public nature leaves them susceptible to scrutiny and defacement from hostile cisgender, heterosexual, and white populations. "Queer visual artists confront the limits of barrio publics, test the cutting edge of queer ethnic visibility, and challenge an oppressive regime of heterosexual sight," acknowledges Robb Hernández of the significance of murals like *Por Vida*.[38]

Nostra Fiesta is informed by the Mexican artist José Guadalupe Posada's drawing of a 1901 Mexico City raid of a queer ball held in a private home, what came to be known in the popular press as the Dance of the Forty-One. The raid was particularly scandalous because it involved the Mexican bourgeoisie, entailing a plethora of media scrutiny and satire, making the raid one of the first publicly discussed events in Mexico over homosexuality and cross-dressing. The mural's stylistic allusion to the Mexican artist's 1901 satirizing of the Dance of the Forty-One constructs a queer Latinx artistic genealogy through a Muñozian disidentificatory practice: esparza and Ruiz reconceive the anti-queer and anti-trans image at the dawn of the twentieth century into a twenty-first-century queer and trans Latinx aesthetic of revelry. Through stylistic adoption, the mural visually cites Posada's artistic ridiculing of the queer and gender-variant people in the Mexico City ball, disidentifying with it, which allows for a promiscuous rearticulation of transnational and transhistorical queer and trans affiliations. The queer Chicanx artists rework earlier iterations of Latin American queerness as visually rendered by the cisgender-heterosexual press into a mural made by and for queer and trans Latinx peoples within the contemporary United States. By doing so, they trace a queer and trans geohistorical trajectory from Mexico City to Los Angeles, one that affirms the importance of a mural like *Nostra Fiesta* in the Los Angeles landscape, indexing the transnational circuits constituting a working-class, multi-ethnic metropolis like Los Angeles. More pressingly, the mural's citational genealogy implicitly highlights the ongoing carceral policies, xenophobic ideologies, anti-queer and anti-trans violence, and rabid gentrification measures enacted against nonwhite, immigrant, poor, and LGBTQ+ communities by state power.[39]

Though *Nostra Fiesta* indexes these social, historical, and political dimensions through the genealogy set up via stylistic citation, the mural's visual-surface schema staggeringly contrasts with the overtly political referential apparatus underlying the mural. *Nostra Fiesta* is a vibrant, vividly colored, and tonally joyous mural honoring queer and trans Latinx nightlife lifeworlds. The mural's surface is painted in a popping purplish-pink color, with the letters of the bar's name, the New Jalisco Bar, colored in with the Pride, trans, and Mexican flag colors. Rendered in a cartoon like caricatured manner, the mural features an assortment of Latinx people, types, and icons: a masculine-presenting pair in cowboy hats dancing entwined; a femme-presenting pair exuberantly twirling together; iconic Latinx performers like the flamboyant Mexican singer Juan Gabriel and the fabulous Afro-Cuban songstress Celia Cruz, both of whose music is widely played and enjoyed in queer and trans Latinx spaces. On the far left of the mural, above the dancing masculine pair, is a bearded figure, Nacho Nava, an homage to the queer Latinx DJ and producer of the Los Angeles queer nightlife scene, who passed away in 2019. Altogether, the mural's compositional structure confidently flaunts a queer and trans Latinx nightlife visuality in the public sphere of downtown Los Angeles.

Esparza and Ruiz's collaboration draws together local and global, masculine and feminine, queer and trans, past and present—all under the banner of Latinx nightlife space. This is a bar, and these are the people and icons circulating through it, the mural narrates to passersby, where Latinx revelry, leisure, intimacy, erotics, euphoria, and joy can flourish. These formal and thematic elements of the mural combine to facilitate what I am calling a stylistics of frivolity: the laminating of queer and trans Latinx life, sociality, and politics to a notion of nightlife silliness, lightheartedness, and pleasurable unseriousness, adding another strategy to the toolbox of an indolent liberating practice. The sense of indolent liberatory practice I am delineating locates in *frivolity*, that is, in the pejorative associations linked to the term by majoritarian rationalities, an accusatory and disciplining term deployed to denote triviality, unseriousness, unproductivity, wastefulness, and inconsequence, a crucial capacity to expand the parameters of queer and trans Latinx indolence's critical scope. Stylistic frivolity, torqued to a queer and trans of color indolent mode, is revolting to bourgeois capitalist logics, because it disturbs ideologies of bootstrapping, respectability, uplift, professionalism, and the overall neoliberal capitalist obsession with positing the social good and intrinsic value of work for the exploited proletariat. An aesthetic centering on queer and trans Latinx frivolousness, as I propose *Nostra Fiesta* does, supercharges the category for social critique and liberatory world-making. The stylistic frivolity I attach to the mural bolsters a queer, trans, and Latinx counterpublic and countervisuality through the silly, playful, and unserious, contesting xenophobic white supremacist bourgeois capitalist drives to discipline unruly, and unproductive, minoritized subjects. Mounting a defense of stylistic frivolity in this way incentivizes the need to analyze thoroughly, and capaciously, those castigated, overlooked, or deemed-irrelevant categories like frivolity, or indolence for that matter, which neoliberal capitalist modernity has dictated "detrimental" for the wellness and prosperity of civilization itself.

Nostra Fiesta eschews representational realism of the queer and trans Latinx subject in favor of the cartoon-inflected figurative caricature, transforming the patrons and partyers into a kitschy, adorable, stylized group of revelers. Whereas *Silverlake Lounge* (1995) exudes an abstracted serious spaciousness devoid of close-up human singularity, the mural depicts a caricatured figurative rendering of queer and trans Latinx nightlife-goers and performers frivolously frolicking up close to us, which aesthetically contrasts with Rivera's realist, documentary nightlife scenes. By stylizing Latinx types and nightlife publics in this way, the mural images a world that is both here and not here, real and surreal, exuberantly banal and fantastic. Above all else, the mural, contra Rivera, stages frivolity as consequential to how we apprehend queer and trans Latinx artistic practice and liberatory world-making.

The stylistics of frivolity, for instance, take intriguing shape in the nonhuman ornaments and details of *Nostra Fiesta*. The mural is festooned with twinkling comic book–like stars, musical notes, and bubbles. Besides these decorative fixtures, there are two items that stand distinct from the human figures as well: clinking pitchers and glass bottles of beer in an ice bucket. Both the pitchers and the beers in the ice bucket float in the mural's landscape, unhandled by human hands, drawn in a whimsical mode suggesting they are, like their human counterparts beside them, shimmying. These objects of quotidian nightlife, ordinary accoutrements that synecdochically comprise any sense of being at a bar, club, or party, come alive, as if dancing, as if jovial, as if animate, rollicking in the frivolity the mural advances. The clinking pitchers appear to be entwined lovers, one seemingly wearing a sombrero and the other a crown of flowers with a cascading ponytail, a brewed Romeo and Juliet. The whimsicality of these nightlife objects, and their personified frolicking, underscores the stylistics of frivolity palpable in *Nostra Fiesta* by asserting how even nonhuman objects are vitalized by Latinx nightlife energies. Venues like the New Jalisco Bar, which the mural asserts as a space championing queer and trans Latinx life, makes such places and publics tantalizing for all, a world anyone, or anything, would want to shimmy in, want to be a part of. Nightlife objects vibrate with the romping energies of queer and trans Latinx frivolity and, by doing so, let us experience a different order of sensing, knowing, and worlding.

The mural depicts a world where nightlife frivolity, quite literally, transforms both humans and nonhumans, where such playful transmogrifications of form produce a life-affirming minoritized practice that can unsettle the exploitative and violent rationalities constituting anti-queer and anti-trans white supremacist neoliberal capitalist modernity. This transformative potential aesthetically recalibrates how we conceive of the nightlife space, of all spaces, and what it might mean to propose queer and trans Latinx nightlife frivolity as the means of social, corporeal, and political transformation. The visual composition of the mural espouses a stylistics of frivolity, a concentrated playfulness, unseriousness, and revelry that is the queer and trans of color nightlife space, that can be all spatiotemporalities if we just work to imagine, create, and sustain it.

3 | The Poetics of Latin Night

THE LITERATURES OF THE PULSE NIGHTCLUB SHOOTING

"Today they killed more lorcas than yesterday," announces the narrator in trans Puerto Rican poet Roque Raquel Salas Rivera's award-winning poetry collection, *the tertiary / lo terciario*.[1] The today of the poem's temporality is the day of the Pulse nightclub shooting, "today june twelfth / today june 12," and the narrator lyricizes concurrently to the Orlando shooting's immediate unfolding and aftermath. The poem yokes together the threat of anti-queer and anti-trans violence emblematized by the shooting with the collection's overall critical concern in addressing Puerto Rico's colonial condition and imagining decolonial futures, all of which is informed by Pedro Scaron's Spanish translation of Karl Marx's *Capital*. The aftermath of anti-queer and anti-trans violence in Orlando becomes for the narrator an injunction to queer and trans communal revelry as anti-imperialist political action: "i wait for the living to get here, / to cluster us, to arm us / (against the state)":

> i will bless this night with (jello)shots.
> i will arrive at the thirteenth of june,

without june 13, dirty, and burn
the confederate flags,
the american flag burn
your programing.[2]

The poem envisions queer and trans people getting together in the post-Pulse moment, in mourning, in care, in resistance, operationalizing a hemispheric anti-colonial imaginary that spans the physical and the digital: "my loves arrive and arrive. / *also on twitter and whatsapp*, / *we swear to the water we'll be unclean*, / *go to bars and dance*."[3] Orlando is Puerto Rico is social media is the global waters connecting continents and archipelagos is the bar and dance floors where all are space-times where queer and trans life reside.[4] Partying after Pulse with the "(jello)shots" and exchanges on "*twitter and whatsapp*" contributes to the building of anti-colonial and revolutionary sensibilities.

In this chapter, I turn my attention to literary representations and ruminations on the mass shooting that occurred in June of 2016 at the Pulse nightclub in Orlando, Florida. I set out to outline what makes the literatures focusing on Pulse a unique literary canon, and, most importantly, I enumerate how indolence as nightlife experience manifests throughout this corpus of texts, further developing upon what I am postulating as reading for indolent liberatory practices. On June 12, forty-nine people were killed and fifty-eight injured by mass shooter Omar Mateen. Pulse was hosting its Latin night that evening, and most of the people there were Latinx and queer and trans people of color. Twenty-three of the people murdered that night were Puerto Rican, unsurprising given the significant presence of diasporic Puerto Ricans living and traveling through Orlando, making life for queer and trans colonial subjects like LGBTQ+ Puerto Ricans "strange and at times profoundly dangerous," as Lawrence La Fountain–Stokes urgently expresses it.[5] Pulse numbers among many mass shootings in the twenty-first-century United States, a nation-state mired by a normalized culture of gun violence and white supremacist terror, and contained as it is within the larger North American continent constituted by a long history of settler colonial dispossession and mass killings of Indigenous peoples.[6] Popular media responses to the shooting reified homonationalist narratives,[7] flattening the social-historical-political complexities encompassing the people there that night and what had happened, and it became the work of scholars, writers, and activists to counter these broadly disseminated narratives with more nuanced and intersectional responses.[8] The downplaying or outright overlooking of the queer and trans nonwhite specificity of the victims and the evening allowed for the reproduction of a racially unmarked (read: white) homogenous LGBTQ+ citizen-subject threatened by anti-gay radical Islamic terrorism, which the Afghan American Mateen was made to emblematize.[9]

There is a growing body of literature on or related to the Pulse nightclub shooting. At the current juncture of this writing, the literatures of Pulse are comprised primarily of poetry, with autobiographical responses and theoretical essays following closely behind. Published a day after the massacre on June 13, 2016, Justin Torres's essay "In Praise of Latin Night" is a lyrical meditation on the beauties of a night like Latin night for queer and trans people of color, and an incendiary polemic on the abhorrent tyrannies that perpetuate anti-queer and anti-trans violence, xenophobic nationalism, and gun violence.[10] *Glass: A Journal of Poetry*, two months after the shooting, published an online volume of poetic responses, featuring over forty LGBTQ+ poets. Edited by Miguel M. Morales and Roy G. Guzmán, the anthology *Pulse/Pulso: In Remembrance of Orlando* highlights an array of poems by poets of color on Pulse. *Love Is Love* is a comic anthology published by IDW Publishing in collaboration with DC Comics that raised money for the victims of the shooting. Anthologies arranged around crises, like *Pulse/Pulso* and *Love Is Love*, according to Amanda Torres and William Orchard, mount a collective "action and a speculation about the future," which "mobiliz[es] bodies into new coalitions."[11] *GLQ: A Journal of Lesbian and Gay Studies* and *QED: A Journal in GLBTQ Worldmaking* organized special dossiers with scholars and writers responding to and theorizing upon the massacre. Queer nonbinary Nicaraguan–Puerto Rican memoirist Edgar Gomez attends to Pulse in a chapter of their memoir, *High-Risk Homosexual*, and Driftpile Cree poet Billy-Ray Belcourt in his essay collection *A History of My Brief Body* discusses how the mediatized aftermath of Pulse produced a "negation of queer-of-color life."[12]

What I am outlining as the literatures of Pulse are organized according to a rubric that charts how writers and texts thematically, aesthetically, rhetorically, and semantically respond to or represent the shootings at Pulse nightclub. There are five thematic criteria encompassing the literatures of Pulse, summarized as follows: (1) addressing the violence that occurred that night, (2) the aftermaths of trauma, (3) the nature of mourning, (4) the ongoing trials and tribulations queer and trans people of color face in cisheterosexist white supremacist patriarchal settler colonial nations, and (5), what is the primary theme analyzed in the chapter below, the joys, pleasures, and indolent indulgences of a night like Latin night for queer and trans of color communities. For instance, Julia Leslie Guarch's poem "Shh. Shh. Be Quiet," anthologized in *Pulse/Pulso*, incorporates the text messages of one of the victims of Pulse, Eddie Jamoldroy Justice, and imagines what transpired during the shooting and what it must have been like for those who were there: "Joshua McGill helps another man, / riddled in gunshot wounds, / limp to safety. / They embrace."[13] Many of the writings document heightened anxieties and fears over anti-queer and anti-trans hatred and gun violence, like Baruch Porras-Hernandez's "Ceremonias De La Superviviencia," which focuses on the everyday psychic terrors a mass shooting induces: "my eyes focus on the exit sign / then the door   the front lobby / then back to the exit sign / the door."[14] "I have crossed a continent / to cast forty-nine names into the sea / cuarenta y nueve nombres mangled," details the solemn narrator in Caridad Moro-Gronlier's "Pulse: A Memorial in Driftwood, Cannon Beach, OR," where the primary theme of the poem is mourning, a common thematic interest the literatures of Pulse share.[15] Included in the *GLQ* dossier on Pulse, queer of color theorist Juana María Rodríguez's poem "Pulse" undertakes a poetics of naming the victims of the shooting. "Shot down, erased, disappeared / Akyra, Alejandro, Amanda, y Ángel / Disappeared . . . / Like the immigrant sent packing,"[16] where naming imagines a singular person as part of a larger web of queer and trans of color histories and socialities: "And we remember Xavier and Yilmary / Like we remember Venus Xtravaganza and Gwen Araujo."[17] Trans-hemispheric and trans-local sociopolitical commentaries on topics like Latinx and Latin American social justice movements, US borders and immigration, urban poverty, and anti-queer and anti-trans violence spill out across the poem vis-à-vis the practice of naming. Christopher Soto's "All the Dead Boys Look Like Me" performs a poetic procedure of identification through tracing out other instances of queer and trans death due to violence and the enduring impacts of the trauma resulting from anti-queer and anti-trans of color violence. "Last time I saw myself die is when police killed Jessie Hernandez," begins the first line of the poem by the queer nonbinary Salvadoran poet, citing the 2015 death of a seventeen-year-old in Denver, Colorado, and then moves to the event of Pulse: "Yesterday, I saw myself die again. Fifty times I died in / Orlando."[18] Soto's poem engages in several of the criteria related to the literatures of Pulse, especially concentrated around the aftermaths of trauma and the ongoing struggles queer and trans people of color experience. Overall, most of what I am identifying as the literatures of Pulse overwhelmingly contains all five thematic criteria, while other works only some, and each emphasizes certain criteria more than others.

The Pulse nightclub shooting brings into sharp relief the axes of race, sexuality, nationality, and gender. We cannot not think these categories together when thinking the event that is Pulse.[19] Moreover, the fact it was Latin night, and a predominately queer and trans Puerto Rican and Latinx audience was present,[20] further focalizes the shooting's sociopolitical dimensions. I propose, then, that what I am terming the literatures of Pulse constitute their own burgeoning literary canon located under the larger umbrella of Latinx literature and queer and trans literature, while most especially residing as a subset of queer and trans Latinx literature. In "Queering Latina/o Literature," Lawrence La Fountain–Stokes incisively queries the historical trajectories, aesthetic dimensions, and interpretative frameworks available for determining what constitutes queer Latinx literary production.[21] Establishing a queer Latinx literary canon, as La Fountain–Stokes posits, raises a set of concerns over discerning earlier historical iterations of Latinx queerness, cultivating reading practices that locate Latinx queerness in texts by both queer and nonqueer authors, and, most practically, advocating for the work of queer and trans Latinx authors. Alicia Gaspar de Alba moves in similar critical strides as La Fountain–Stokes by providing an in-depth bibliography of Chicana and Latina lesbian literary production since 1991.[22] Gaspar de Alba chronologically formulates a Chicana and Latina lesbian literary canon through the past three decades, while also elucidating upon the diversity of themes, genres, and publishing routes Chicana and Latina lesbian production has taken. One could look to earlier periods for Chicana and Latina lesbianness, but Gaspar de Alba limits her historical scope and, by doing so, asserts a subcanon that highlights and champions overt expressions of Chicana and Latina lesbian themes and analytics at the turn of the twentieth century. La Fountain–Stokes's and Gaspar de Alba's explorations into what constitutes and how to formulate a canon like queer and lesbian Latinx literature, and the subsequent instability over author identification and periodization, echoes an earlier critique made by Kirsten Silva Gruesz of *The Norton Anthology of Latino Literature*. "Canonicity happens here without a clear sense of its relation to periodicity," writes Gruesz of *The Norton Anthology of Latino Literature*'s inability to conceptualize a firm idea of literary historicity.[23] What is the historical narrative and genealogy constituting Latinx literature, Gruesz argues, when the anthology posits it as both transnational yet US-based, as English yet Spanish, identities hundreds of years old yet still somehow new in relation to the US nation-state? As Gruesz's review makes clear, debates over canon formation bear political import, mattering for how we contextualize and narrate the place of ethnic literary production in classrooms and beyond. For minoritized literatures, especially those doubly peripheralized like queer and trans of color literary production, literary canonization matters for how it ascribes value to a compilation of insufficiently studied texts according to particular criterion, and for the ways it promulgates practices of reading those texts while attendant to their historical, aesthetic, and sociopolitical specificity. Canons produce readerships.[24] Stressing the significance of minoritized canon formation, as I do in relation to the literatures of Pulse, challenges the constraining and unmarked majoritarian biases entrenched in what is read in academia and by the broader reading public.

These debates over what constitutes canonicity and how to determine the US Latinx literary canon frame my conceptualizing of the literatures of Pulse. The literatures of Pulse propagate a subcanon around both the event of violence and the subject of nightlife, and not necessarily a historical period or aesthetic movement, which is de rigueur for the formation of canons. Nor, for that matter, does my mapping of the literatures of Pulse "conform to the time of the nation" or the "longue durée of the ethnos," as María Josefina Saldaña-Portillo succinctly puts it in regard to the geographical and ethnic-nationalist scope of US Latinx literary studies.[25] What does it mean, then, to formulate a queer and trans Latinx canon around an event of violence and a subject like nightlife? What aesthetic dimensions, thematic inclinations, and political concerns arise that nightlife especially allows us to investigate? The literatures of Pulse share much in common with the literatures concerning the 9/11 attacks,[26] though there are various scalar differences between the two events: the 9/11 attacks had global ramifications and world-reorganizing repercussions, while Pulse is much more local though no less consequential in raising intersectional and transcontinental politics and concerns; the 9/11 attacks had more mortalities than Pulse (both on the day of the event itself, as well as the overall global mortality rate due to US war and invasions across the Middle East); there is now a vast body of literature engaging with 9/11, while Pulse is far more limited.[27] The violent event for both is the locus around which their canons form. However, the literatures of Pulse differ from much of the 9/11 literature by the pronounced interest the literatures of Pulse share in forwarding anti-nationalist, anti-imperialist, and anti-assimilationist politics.[28] This set of politics arises in large part because the event of Pulse catalyzes attention toward nonwhite queer and trans subjectivities and, most importantly, forefronts aesthetic, affective, political, and world-making practices that seek to challenge oppressive structures that perpetuate violence against queer and trans people of color. Key to understanding the formulation I am setting up is that the violent event occurred in a space for queer and trans of color nightlife, which many consider special and sacred because such spaces center leisure, pleasure, desire, joy, and spatiotemporalities distinct from cisheteronormativity and whiteness. This convergence of anti-queer and anti-trans of color violence and the pleasures of nightlife, this disturbingly jarring pairing of violence and joy, I propose, is the primary matrix configuring the literatures of Pulse, which, in turn, mobilizes a radical literary imaginary for critiquing and transforming oppressive structures. This coupling of violence and leisure operationalizes an analytic standpoint that draws out the liberatory potentials of indolence.

The literatures of Pulse I closely analyze below contribute to mapping out the importance of nightlife for queer and trans of color indolence, pleasure, joy, and world-making. More specifically, the literatures of Pulse stress how the racialized dimensions of an evening like Latin night are of consequence for how we understand liberatory spaces. Latin night hails a nonwhite demographic of queer and trans peoples, and that is significant for articulating why these spaces matter. My critical intention, however, is not to fixate upon the site of violence, whether thematically or narratively, though unavoidable it may seem at times. Rather, my focus aims at tracing the nodes of indolent clubbing coursing through the various literary engagements with the violent event that we now know as the Pulse nightclub shooting. The scenes of literary lazing and the indolent undercurrents running through the literature attune us to indolent sensoriums and modes of reading, to space-times that yearn to value pleasure, joy, euphoria, desire, and other affective-embodied modes distinct from pain, labor, trauma, respectability, and suffering. This mode of reading for indolence engages in what Ralph. E. Rodriguez posits as "unbinding" for the study of Latinx literature, the analyzing away "from the preconceived, unquestioned notion that there is something called 'Latinx literature' and from the identity and thematic expectations attendant to that formulation."[29] Reading for indolent liberatory practices likewise borrows from Sandra K. Soto's prescient work on reading queerly Chican@ literatures against the routinized critical protocols and argumentative conclusions that tautologically evidence queer nonwhite experience from queer nonwhite literatures. Undertaking a provocative rereading of shame and enactments of racialization through sexuality in Cherríe Moraga's writings, Soto enumerates various "critical departures" from how Moraga's work has been analyzed, by "dislodging her work from the register of evidence; de-homogenizing it by noting the ways in which her meaning-making speech acts perform radically different functions at various moments; disrupting the teleological narratives and analyses that her work so easily invites."[30] Ricardo L. Ortiz's insightful inquiry into the parameters of what counts as US Latinx literature and the associated protocols governing how scholars and critics study such literatures is also of consequence for nourishing indolent reading practices. The scholar "interacts with creative work not exclusively in some relationship of irreducible alterity, where criticism and scholarship only appear 'outside' and 'after' the literary objects and acts to which they can only respond," Ortiz details, interrogating the upholding of impersonalized distance in literary criticism and the widely enforced distinctions between the literary text and the interpretive practice of the text, "but in ways that activate in modes of productive simultaneity new processes of creating and transformation in collaboration with the artistic work."[31] Christopher González similarly queries, "What is permissible in narrative form?" for Latinx literary production, explicating how formalist reading strategies offer alternative routes for how readers and publishers can interact with Latinx literature: "[an identity-oriented approach] largely ignores how both formal features of a particular narrative and its built-in relationship to an ideal audience radically complicate any dual-identity model."[32] Using formalist methods as a means of differently orienting ourselves to Latinx literature, according to González, frees up both authors and readers from reductive identitarian tropes or prescribed narrative schemas (magical realism, bilingualism, barrio bildungsroman), which have long held dominance over what kinds of Latinx authors get published and how we read Latinx literary production. For these scholars, the task at hand is to expand how we engage with US Latinx literature, to center ethnic literary-critical practice in and of itself for the robust and innovative work that it can do, rather than exclusively or predominately using literary study to evidence or prove theses related to US latinidad; gendered, sexual, or racialized essentialism; or cultural authenticity.

I move in similar theoretical strides by pondering, How can we study the literatures of Pulse, in particular, and queer and trans Latinx literatures, in general, and affix our critical interests and scholarly inquiries upon other primary sites without needing to incentivize or foreground anti-queer and anti-trans violence and death? What other interpretative frameworks and evaluative criteria are available for the study of queer and trans Latinx literature besides the overdetermined and overrepresentative narratives of pain, trauma, and tragedy? How does reading for indolent liberatory practices unlock other avenues for scholarly inquiry, artistic creation, and liberatory imagining? Such a theoretical wager depends upon another order of queer and trans of color intelligibility,[33] one not dependent upon appearing properly legible, respectable, or victimized according to the scripts of neoliberal settler nation-states. Nightlife scenes of queer and trans Latinx lazing depicted in the writings of Maya Chinchilla, Edgar Gomez, Roy G. Guzmán, and Justin Torres form a literary repository for enacting sociopolitical transformation that imagines other interpretive schemas for the study of queer and trans Latinx literary and aesthetic production.

THE PULSE OF LITERARY LAZE: CHINCHILLA, GOMEZ, GUZMÁN, TORRES

Appearing first in the *GLQ* special issue on Pulse, and later anthologized in *Pulse/Pulso: In Remembrance of Orlando*, Maya Chinchilla's poem in honor of Pulse, "Church at Night," enacts what Gloria Anzaldúa and

Cherríe Moraga have termed, in their landmark anthology *This Bridge Called My Back*, "theory in the flesh." "A theory in the flesh," according to the two lesbian Chicana feminists, "means one where the physical realities of our lives—our skin color, the land or concrete we grew up on, our sexual longings—all fuse to create a politic born of necessity."[34] The queer femme Guatemalan American poet's poem for Pulse does just that by bringing in the names, the bodies, and the human everydayness of those forty-nine lost and the many others who were injured, all the while mounting a fierce critique against US neocolonial imperialism and carcerality. The poem is broken into eight sections, which read predominately as elegy, as memorializing of the people at Pulse that evening, and maintain a present-tense anguish characteristic of reckoning with such profound loss: "I'm still not ready to be coherent or make connections / I will never be ready to wake up to this news."[35] Mourning permeates the poetic voice, but the poem also operates as a paean to queer and trans Latinx nightlife, to the joys and pleasures of going out and having fun. There is revelry, too, among tragedy in the nightclub. "Do you remember the names," the poem's narrator apostrophizes:

> of your first gay bars,
> early afternoon tea dances,
> house parties and special
> POC or Latinx nights?
> How we'd meet to get ready,
> a few drinks before entry,
> to save our dollars for tacos
> to soak up the night life in our belly[36]

The poem's second-person address, and list of nightlife spaces, imagines a queer, trans, *and* nonwhite reader. Stanzas like the one above function as a sanctuary in language for the people who were the direct targets of the violence that occurred at Pulse. The poem's salvific hailing materializes in and as a spatiality of indolence shaped by queerness, racialization, and latinidad: the pregaming with friends before the bar or house party, the special dance parties and Latinx nights, and the delight of tacos after a night out. The poem illustrates the pleasurable banality of queer and trans of color living, and the ordinary evenings out, which are so crucial for forging space-times different from the overwhelmingly cisgender, heterosexual, and white ones outside. It is not that Latin night or the special house party for people of color escapes from the majoritarian world outside, or is devoid of intra-communal exclusions, biases, or discrimination.[37] The atrocity that occurred at Pulse shows that anti-queer and anti-trans white supremacist violence is potentially always around the corner. Rather, Latin nights, and poems like Chinchilla's, demonstrate how forms of queer and trans Latinx lazing carve out spaces that operate according to alternative logics and grammars, ones where dancing under a disco light or sitting at the bar are an instant of freedom imagining, of sensing and being in another kind of world.

Listing serves as a prominent poetic tactic across "Church at Night" that asserts at once the queer, trans, and nonwhite qualities that make an event like Latin night so special. Noting the once-a-month Latin night most gay and lesbian bars host, the narrator follows with a substantial list of parties:

> the Noche de Queer Cumbias,
> las Placitas, the Pan Dulces,
> las Escuelitas, the Mangos,
> las Botas Locas, the Buttas,
> Circus and Arenas, Wet,
> Coochielicious, Splashes, . . .[38]

The playful and humorous Spanish-derived names of the various Latin nights testify to the joyous and revelrous bounty that is queer and trans Latinx nightlife. These are spatialities coming together as the accrual of lines, "some decorated like a year round / quinceañera" and others "small like dancing / in someone's living room," their exquisitely tacky aesthetics on display no matter where or when or however great the odds. These spaces exist on the page, named and noted, but also, importantly, out in spaces across settler colonial nations like the United States, shaping queer and trans Latinx worlds and possibilities. They may come, and go, in living rooms and dance halls, provisional and happenstance, but their many names are crucial: "Executive Suites, Esta Noche, / Chuparosa, Papi Chulo, the Boss / Pulse and, and, and . . . " We need to keep naming, keep on listing, the poem suggests, as Richard Blanco also urges in his poem for Pulse, "One Pulse—One Poem": "find details for the love / of the lives lost, still alive in photos."[39]

To amass the names of parties and clubs and details of lives lived that foster the radicality of queer and trans Latinx lazing, which nourishes the desperate need to kick back, have fun, slow down—that is the work at hand.

The listing and naming contributes to the overall interest Chinchilla's poem has in poetic typology, that is, how classification of types aesthetically renders the queer and trans of color plurality at Pulse that evening as well as a more generalized image of Latinx nightlife scenes: those plenty who go out at night, like the "proud sissy boys, beefcakes, bears, butches, and fabulous femmes" and the "trans girls, maricones, drag queens, club kids lightning on the dance floor."[40] This plurality of types present at a night like Latin night speaks to what T. Jackie Cuevas formulates for the study of Chicana lesbian literature as "gender variant critique," which "works to unsettle the dominant sex/gender binaries by demanding a feminist response that does not always assume 'women' as the primary signifier through which to demand gender justice."[41] The poem also nominally conjures those killed at the Pulse shooting and pluralizes their names, making them many at once: "The Simons, the Gilbertos, the Javiers, / The Oscars, The Miguel Angels, The Jorges, The Joels." This practice of naming the dead multiplies them into a multiplicity that transcends the singular person or singular identity, "Puerto Ricans, Mexicans, Salvadorans, Afro-Latinos,"[42] or even merely the singular event that is Pulse, opting instead for a Latinx assemblage that defies spatiotemporality and geohistories, "our story stretched across bloodlines, backrooms, and borderlines."[43] Chinchilla's classificatory impulse across the poem attends to the many types of people, histories, and nightlife scenes that cohere around a night like Latin night. In this way, the various and disparate types hang out all at once on the page, partying together as words, lines, and stanzas, where the space of the poem becomes the space of queer and trans Latinx nightlife, the literary and the sensory and the corporeal intimately linking for new imaginings.

Queer and trans Latinx spatiality is key to Chinchilla's poem. Being together, indulging in the embodied and sensorial proximity to other queer and trans people, which the space of the nightclub allows, engenders a politic for queer and trans of color world-making and liberation. Space matters for indolent revelry. For instance, section five of the poem, written as a prose poem the length of a paragraph, begins this way: "With each precious face passing on the screen I am right back in every club near every small town and big city where I loved and Li*iiii*ved and made out with dates and lovers."[44] This prose section presents itself as one long and singular sentence interspersed by clauses documenting ordinary goings-on at clubs, like flirting, seeing former lovers who transitioned, grinding on another person, sipping a drink in the corner, and other such banal nightlife occurrences. The paragraph-length sentence begins with the narrator recounting a scene of watching the Pulse nightclub victims stream across a screen, and then quickly pivots to a spatial memory: they are now right back in every club in every small town and big city they have been to. This activated memory also operates as a kind of fantasy work, where the scene of queer and trans of color suffering and death transmogrifies into pleasure, desire, belonging, and everyday living that the queer nightclub champions. This fantastical pivot and transformation of very real violence seems necessary for the narrator, the fantasying a means of coping with the faces flashing across the screen, the faces that metonymically demand the viewer to confront the pervasive culture of US gun violence and cisheterosexist white supremacist terror. This act of coping doubles as a world-making practice forged through memory and fantasy. The queer and trans of color socialities the nightclub invites materialize on the page.

"Church at Night" features all the criteria outlined earlier in the chapter over what constitutes the literatures of Pulse. The poem weaves in and out of accounting for the event itself, the trauma, mourning, and the ongoing trials and tribulations facing queer and trans of color communities, and it spotlights the quotidian joy and pleasures of the queer nightclub. Yet the poem mediates the intensity of the first four criteria by returning to one of the poem's central preoccupations: the pleasures and indolent indulgences of Latinx nightlife. Through the poem's various poetic techniques, Chinchilla prompts the reader to imagine the ordinary pleasures, intimacies, erotics, and joys of Latin night, even still, and in spite of unfathomable violence and loss. For "Church at Night," it always goes back to the dance floor, to the bar, to the house party, to the lovers and friends and strangers encountered on a night like Latin night.

"Pulse already had a place in my memories, where it firmly existed cloaked in the nighttime," writes Edgar Gomez in the aftermath of the shooting, the narrator electing to remember the good times in the club before the event of violence.[45] The narrator recalls a scene when they are in the car with their brother passing by the club during the daytime, mourners and vigils outside as the club remains in a post-shooting limbo "between crime scene and memorial."[46] For the narrator, "if it wasn't going to be *that* Pulse anymore, what was the point?" The narrator insists upon Pulse signifying queer and trans nightlife revelry and pleasure, spending an "eighteenth birthday, my twenty-first, buying an all-you-can-drink wristband," and its daytime form, its post-shooting temporality, only serves to perpetually cite the scene of mourning, trauma, and death.[47] This significance of Pulse in the nighttime attends to María DeGuzmán's formulation that "night is a living condition . . . where the basic moorings of one's identity (defined in relation to what one has been taught to believe and/or what one has convinced oneself about oneself and others) have become unmoored, when the scripts of the daytime existence have been suspended."[48] The aftermath of violence both physically and psychically transforms the space of the nightclub. One cannot think of Pulse in its post-shooting moment and not think of the referential apparatus at play, which perpetually invokes queer and trans violence, tragedy, and death. Yet the narrator chooses an alternative memorializing practice by refusing the overcharged significations and prescribed logics of linear mourning and moving on. The reader witnesses the incentivizing of the nightclub's indolent spatiotemporalities of yesterday. The narrator indulges in the pleasures of Latin nights past, frolicking in the what-was in the here-and-now of queer and trans embodied reminiscing, enacting a practice of queer and trans world-making that does not jettison the past's spatiotemporal pleasures.

This rejection of the norms of mourning properly and memorializing conventionally enacts what Che Gossett theorizes in relation to neoliberal whitewashing of historical sites of queer and trans resistance as a "refus[al] to be contained within neoliberal packaging or sanitized by homonormative narratives of progress."[49] Gossett saliently elaborates how the nation-state's procedures of memorialization and construction of historical narratives of sites like Stonewall and Compton's Cafeteria scrub out the role played by queer and trans people of color, as well as diminish and invisibilize other locales and histories of queer and trans resistance. Unruly historical and present queer and trans people of color, those acts and bodies that do not fit the bill of white cis-homonormativity and classed respectability, the nation-state must eject in order to dispel the notion that "the trauma and violence queer and transgender people of color face on a quotidian level" is merely "a vestige of an unfortunate past."[50] Gossett's formative inquiry leads me to my own set of questions: What other modes of historicizing, narrativizing, and knowing the event of Pulse and the post-Pulse moment are possible distinct from those sanctioned by the neoliberal nation-state? What possibilities emerge when the unbearable site of trauma and violence is spatiotemporally negotiated through situating oneself in the pleasures, euphorias, and joys of the nightclub of before? Lingering unapologetically in the indolent Latinx past is one strategy that reorients relations to the historical event and the memorializing function. What was, what is, and what may be can be rejiggered according to alternative indolent practices, ones that mobilize scenes and pasts of queer and trans of color nightlife for radical world-reimagining ends.

"Restored Mural for Orlando" is a poem by queer nonbinary Honduran American poet Roy G. Guzmán, dedicated to Pulse. Included in Guzmán's debut collection of poems, *Catrachos*, the poem circulates around the Pulse shootings, how the murders produce shockwaves of fear and mourning for queer and trans nonwhite people, and the acts of care between partners working through the trauma of the massacre. The narrator of the poem speaks in what amounts to the immediate aftermath of the Pulse shooting, adding a present-tense immediacy and angst to the voice.[51] For the narrator, who grew up poor and in another locale in Florida, Orlando signifies a particular class connotation and is associated with access to leisure time. The central Florida city is known for housing Disney World and Universal Studios, which the narrator notes only some can afford—"You visit Orlando to fantasize about the childhood you didn't have"—and the narrator can partake in what Orlando symbolizes only as an adult: "when I finally could afford it I took my parents to Universal / Studios." The narrator's parents have "worked themselves sick" and "the debt collectors still call," so the association of Orlando with leisure is telling for how it represents both the exclusionary protocols of capitalism prohibiting poor people from relaxation and the need for places like Orlando, because they signify much-needed time away from wage labor.[52] The contradiction is not settled by a simple demand of inclusion into capitalist consumerism, which places like Disney World and Universal Studios signify. Rather, the poem points out how leisure is denied working-class nonwhite people and that the representational power of Orlando is that it draws out the critique of why leisure is needed: a time-space away from capitalist labor and systems. Being able to rest and relax is a privilege only some can afford, the poem affirms, but it matters that we rethink who can attain it and how one goes about attaining it in and elsewhere from oppressive systems.

The mentioning of Orlando's classed barriers to leisure occurs early on in the poem and serves as backdrop for the narrator's reflective segue into the leisure value of nightclubs and queer nonwhite mortality. Going out with friends for drag night is a way "to escape / my schedule & relive my adolescence" but comes with the reasonable caveat of "I am afraid of attending places / that celebrate our bodies because that's also where our bodies / have been cancelled."[53] The queer bar and club provides refuge from what the narrator terms "my schedule," alluding certainly to routine forms of labor and necessary involvement in capitalism's machinations, but also to the everyday worries of living as queer and nonwhite. In addition to the referencing of gun violence in nightlife spaces, the narrator, for example, documents how "my mother might never approve / of me pressing my lips against another man's," and "even our fathers have prayed at least once for us to be gone."[54] Queer and trans of color nightlife as an indolent mode is respite from these devastating realities. Yet, as the poem articulates throughout, this refuge is psychically, and even sometimes physically, interrupted by the perpetual threat of soul-crushing, body-mind-traumatizing, and life-ending violence due to cisheteronormative white supremacist patriarchal violence.

Near the conclusion of the poem, the narrator details how they are back home in Minnesota, and in the arms of a partner. Even then, in a lover's embrace and protection, miles away from Pulse nightclub, the narrator can't help but "stay awake out of need & continue to whisper their names / as they are added to the list."[55] Here the listing function recalls Chinchilla's "Church at Night," and the nominal act incites a contemplative revelry about the goings-on at Pulse nightclub before the shooting. The opening line of the poem situates the reader in the "seconds before the shooter sprays bullets on my brothers' & sisters' / bodies," as the narrator tries to know, to sense, what it is like at Pulse before the act of violence, and once again at this concluding point the narrator attempts to imagine what it's like before. "I forgive / the earth for not turning its neck further," the narrator ruminates,

> for not allowing those pink lights
> to keep flashing / for the cackles to remain intact no matter how boisterous.
> In those seconds when their skin has never beamed so bright / so self-
> assured / the bartender is shaking a piña colada / goose bumps flower
> on someone's arms / the streets are humming from delight / a pair of lovers[56]

What was Latin night at Pulse before the shooting? How did bodies move, sense, desire, love, relax, fuck, and vibe under the strobe lights before the spray of life-ending bullets? The reverie fabulates the pleasures of queer and trans Latinx nightlife before the scene of violence, before the event becomes the event, which parallels Gomez's insistence in their memoir on remembering Pulse for what it was rather than what it had become post-shooting. These sensuous and sensory descriptions bookend the poem, hailing the reader to think of queer and trans of color life not exclusively as a narrative of violence or the event we will come to know as Pulse. Rather, the bookended reveries compel the reader to imagine the quotidian pleasures encompassing a night out, the banal beauty of whiling away the hours with those like you on Latin night. The reader is brought into the world of the poem trying to know what a world free from anti-queer and anti-trans white supremacist violence feels like, a world where Pulse has not yet happened, though we know it will, and the reader leaves in the same way as they began. What was it like to feel the pink lights on skin? To hear the boisterous laughs around you? The goosebumps of anticipation at a kiss? To rework one's relation to the historical record, and to resolutely affix oneself to the temporality of the not-yet-happened, prioritizes queer and trans of color life-affirming worlds. Fantasying the details of an ordinary night out at the queer club becomes the site where such worlding is not only possible, but realizable.

Justin Torres's essay "In Praise of Latin Night at the Queer Club," published the day after the shooting in the *Washington Post*, likewise seeks to detach the violence of Pulse, and its concomitant politicizations, from that of the quotidian pleasures and communal belonging of nights like Latin night.[57] The essay is brief and tonally bursting with a mix of fury and elegy, reflective of the moment of its writing and the attendant urgencies, and roves between lyrical assays on the importance of a night like Latin night for queer and trans Latinx people and scathing sociopolitical commentary on anti-queer and anti-trans bigotry, xenophobia, the colonial status of Puerto Rico, and the US media's campaign of vilifying Islam and brown peoples. Written in the second person,[58] the essay is similarly skeptical of the promises of rights-based discourses for liberation: "People talk about liberation as if it's some kind of permanent state, as if you get liberated and that's it, you get some rights and that's it, you get some acknowledgment and that's it, happy now?"[59] The essay fiercely politicizes queer and trans Latinx nightlife in order to critique US imperial hegemony and the myriad ways it effectuates violence. Torres's critique aligns with Chandan Reddy's notion of "freedom with violence," where even if the neoliberal nation-state "produces the source of a grievance, injury, or horrific exposure to arbitrary violence"—which the United States has culpability for its perpetuating in the normalizing of gun violence, rampant Islamophobia, and unceasing wars in places like Afghanistan, which is where Mateen's family originates—"its epistemological assumptions ultimately affirm the value of that very state formation."[60] The queer Puerto Rican author writes on the plurality of peoples who frequent Latin nights and the differences among those who occupy the category of Latinx: the fluent Spanish speakers and those who only speak English, the muscle gays and the femme queens, the out and the not out, the undocumented, the documented, and the condition of the Puerto Rican on the US mainland. The narrator voice expresses itself not just as a distant, impersonal observer but as fully embodied with them, producing a lyrical and theoretical embrace where words become a manifesto, a rallying cry for queer and trans of color safety, joy, pleasure, and community.

The essay hinges upon a structural paradigm of inside the queer club versus outside the club. Inside the club is where one encounters queer safety, belonging, erotics, pleasure, and plurality, whereas outside the club is queer- and transphobia, homogeneity and conformity, US imperialism and white supremacy, and an overall cultural ethos that seeks to extinguish queer joy and pleasure. The prose toggles between contemplating these two registers. "Outside, there's a world that politicizes every aspect of your identity," notes the narrator.

Outside, they call you an abomination. Outside, there is a news media that acts as if there are two sides to debate over trans people using public bathrooms. Outside, there is a presidential candidate who has built a platform on erecting a wall between the United States and Mexico—and not only do people believe that crap is possible, they believe it is necessary. Outside, Puerto Rico is still a colony, being allowed to drown in debt, to suffer, without the right to file for bankruptcy, to protect itself. Outside, there are more than 100 bills targeting you, your choices, your people, pending in various states.[61]

The refrain of "outside" establishes for the reader that external to the club is a world hostile to queer and trans people. These passages utilizing the language of what is "outside" directly address the ever-ongoing threats of anti-queer and anti-trans violence and the urgencies of queer survival. The gravity of what occurred at Pulse nightclub, the narrator suggests through the referencing of "outside," cannot be brushed off or diminished. The essay wants the reader to have to confront it. However, "In Praise of Latin Night at the Queer Club" strives not to make anti-queer and anti-trans violence and bigotry the principal focus for the reader by continuously offsetting what happens "outside" with that of what pleasurably goes on "inside" the club. The subsequent paragraph begins in this way: "But inside, it is loud and sexy and on. If you're lucky, it's a mixed crowd, muscle Marys and bois and femme fags and butch dykes and genderqueers."[62] Inside, a sonic world apart, and crucially so. Inside, it is a plurality of queer and trans types, much like Chinchilla illustrates it in her attention to typologies in "Church at Night," the "But" significantly accenting the "inside" in that one can hear the full-throated knowingness and sassy tone implicit in that prefatory pivoting: "But inside." The worded combination signals the urgent need for Latinx nightlife and leisure, the prioritizing of what those spaces allow for, so as not only to affirm the lives and communities of queer and trans people of color but also to organize alternative publics and worlds away from oppressive and injurious systems.

Inside symbolically functions within the essay as a critical spatiotemporality delinked from violence, wage labor, and expectations of minoritized visibility, while *outside*, on the other hand, signifies the burdens of having to navigate, negotiate, and survive in cisheteronormative white supremacist capitalist systems. *Outside* also represents the site of various forms of labor demanded of queer and trans people of color. "Outside, tomorrow, hangovers, regrets, the grind," the narrator expresses of the everyday encumbrances of existing within capitalism, and then pivots to the work of activism and social change: "outside, tomorrow, the struggle to effect change." Yet, once again, in the following sentence the essay swerves the reader back to the pleasures of Latin night, the indulgences of lazy comportment:

> But inside, tonight, none of that matters. Inside, tonight, the only imperative is to love. Lap the bar, out for a smoke, back inside, the ammonia and sweat and the floor slightly tacky, another drink, the imperative is to get loose, get down, find religion, lose it, find your hips locked into another's, break, dance on your own for a while—but you didn't come here to be a nun—find your lips pressed against another's, break, find your friends, dance. The only imperative is to be transformed, transfigured in the disco light.[63]

Latin night, according to the essay's rhetorical posturing, is not about needing to go protest, needing to worry about identity-based forms of violence, or even death. Rather, the point of Latin night, of being inside of it, is for leisure and revelry, for the transformative impact nightlife brings about in its own unique way. Tonight, not tomorrow; inside, not outside, is the spatiotemporality the prose wants the reader to relish. The sensorial buffet of a night like Latin night, as Torres renders it, transforms the club-goer, but it depends upon staying present, staying there inside the queer club: "But for a moment, I want to talk about the sacredness of Latin Night at the Queer Club. Amid all the noise, I want to close my eyes and see you all there, dancing, inviolable, free."[64] Liberation can be sensed and experienced in the rush of Latin night immediacy, the here and now of sonic, kinetic, affective, and sensorial Latinx queerness and transness, the savoring of every moment while inside the club. Outside, that's for later. Outside, that's for another day. Inside, on Latin night, that's where it's at. Inside, on Latin night, another world is already happening. All we have to do is sense the Pulse of it.

4 | Slacking Off on the Main Stage

RUPAUL'S DRAG RACE AND THE PERFORMANCE OF SPECTACULAR OBFUSCATION

In a profile video uploaded to YouTube for *Vogue México y Latinoamérica*, a *RuPaul's Drag Race* (season 9, 2017) contestant, Valentina, opens her monologue this way: "I felt I was born into a world that was not made for me. Therefore, I have to close my eyes and dream, and involve myself in the biggest fantasy until it becomes my reality."[1] This notion of operating in a fantasy of one's devising—the "biggest" one, at that—is frequently noted in the nonbinary Mexican American drag performer's appearance in season 4 of *RuPaul's Drag Race All Stars* (2018–2019). Her own fantasy world becomes a way of negating the harshness of the judges' critiques, a way of affirming her own self-worth and value in the midst of reality competition television. Following the judges' critiques in various episodes of *All Stars*, Valentina remarks on how their critiques don't fit the vision of her fantasy, and, therefore, she takes them with a grain of salt. The other queens read her fantasying as delusional. Throughout her appearances on *RuPaul's Drag Race*, on the many offshoots of the *Drag Race* franchise, and in other unrelated media appearances, her fantasying is often depicted as laziness, dallying, or ridiculousness. For instance, instead of "properly" preparing for the lip-synch performance to save herself from elimination in her premiere (season 9), she lounged on the couch while her competitor rehearsed. Her vocalized fantasies of being in her own world, and her unusual methods of glamorous femme being-performing on the show, obfuscate the logics of a show like *RuPaul's Drag Race* that readily peddles neoliberal, feel-good, pick-yourself-up-by-the-bootstraps sentiments and rhetoric.[2] Valentina's persona and performances are spectacularly over-the-top, fantastical, and defiant.

Valentina provides another indolent liberatory schema to the arsenal of strategies theorized thus far through the medium of television. The slackerly aesthetic of Valentina's televisual performances take shape in what I am identifying as queer and trans of color spectacular obfuscation. Valentina speaks to instances in which trans and queer of color performers and people spectacularly display obfuscation that puts into disarray colonial-capitalist logics, confounding the cisheteronormative white supremacist rubrics that demand productivity, professionalism, exceptionality, positivity, and compliance. Whether intentional or not, as Valentina's persona and performances attest, these spectacularized obfuscations happen. These spectacles of trans and queer Latinx spectacularity sometimes go under the radar within the televisual schema of *Drag Race*, other times not, and yet they abound nonetheless.[3] My critical sense of obfuscation resonates with that of Caribbeanist thinker Édouard Glissant's formulation of opacity. For Glissant, opacity is the right not to be intelligible or comprehended according to the imperatives of Enlightenment rationality, in which difference, contradiction, and multiplicity must be made to fit into a universalizing totality. The refusal of one's opacity, in which the other (read: nonwhite) must be made intelligible in order to be conquered, has allowed for the propagation of colonialism and imperialism across the centuries.[4] Glissant's opacity informs my sense of spectacular obfuscation in that the latter is characterized by abstruse and unintelligible modes of being-thinking that resist colonial-capitalist impositions. However, my sense of obfuscation differs by the way it intentionally prioritizes performative tactics and strategies that absurdly refuse colonial-capitalist imperatives, mobilizing stupefyingly spectacular performances that recalibrate the world to trans and queer of color sensibilities and possibilities. The term *obfuscation* and its verb counterpart, *to obfuscate*—meaning "to confuse, bewilder, or stupefy" and "to make (a subject, etc.) unclear, obscure, confused, or difficult to understand"[5]—precisely capture Valentina's glamorously ridiculous and quirkily over-the-top performances and monologues, which stupefy judges, contestants, and audiences alike, leaving all in her wake entertained, charmed, and perplexed at why she did what she did. Through her appearances in various media—television, magazines, YouTube, Reddit forums, and social media—we quickly learn what Valentina's fantasy is. To trace the fantasy's multiplatform, multifaceted dimensionality, I utilize what Amy Villarejo identifies as "a mode of analysis of television that traverses various levels, including textual analysis, industrial infrastructure, processes of spectatorship and reception, and both formal and informal networks of creators/artists/producers,"[6] as well as Nick Salvato's call for scalar thinking in television studies.[7] I use this multiscalar televisual approach to apprehend Valentina in tracking her appearances on *RuPaul's Drag Race* (season 9), *RuPaul's Drag Race: Untucked!* (season 8), and *RuPaul's Drag Race All Stars* (season 4) as well as in promotional videos, magazine profiles, and Reddit discussions about her.

I critically situate Valentina's televisual spectacle in a trans and queer paradigm. As the opening quote from her interview for *Vogue México y Latinoamérica* attests, Valentina is the drag persona of James Andrew Leyva. The two identities (Valentina and Leyva) converge through the mass media modes in which we encounter the two (television streaming platforms, YouTube, magazines, social media), making it hard to decipher where one ends and the other begins. Yet we are more so experiencing Valentina than Leyva; that is, audiences are intended to interface with the persona and performance of Valentina, and less so the autobiographically inflected person that is Leyva. The audience, nevertheless, experiences both the sexualized variance and gendered nonconformity that is Valentina-Leyva, who conducts the slippages of self/performance, fact/fiction, and authentic/inauthentic that reality television promulgates.[8] Valentina's drag presentation and performances are glamorously transfemme, luxuriating in high-femme modes of theatricality, zaniness, and joy. Her transfemme performances display a Latinx transness that forces the viewer to contend with her gendered variance in all its glory, and thereby queerly "trans-shapes" televisual reality. I find value in a trans and queer paradigm, because her drag performances move in various registers of queerness and transness, with her femme Latinx transness both challenging the norms of respectability and propriety and queering the space-time of *Drag Race* and its audiences, all of which propose different strategies for gendered and sexual dissidence. This calls for a robust analytic framework that does not adhere to rigid boundaries between sexuality and gender, persona and person, performance and performer, and queer and trans studies. I understand the disciplinary need for and the distinctive analytic foci provided by trans studies,[9] as well as the backgrounding queer theory has done on forms of trans embodiment and gendered variance in attempts to fuel the authority of the category of queer.[10] And these two areas of inquiry have always stressed the need to simultaneously think multiple vectors of social difference. Yet a well-documented whiteness has long pervaded queer and trans studies writ large, and so I have opted for a trans and queer paradigm that is informed by the contributions made by queer and trans of color theory.

Trans of color theory has most ardently elaborated how we must make unthinkable the assumption that race, sexuality, nationality, and gender can be categorically separated, especially since these axes interanimate and configure the social-cultural-political realities governing the world. C. Riley Snorton, for instance, convincingly argues the ways in which sexuality and gender are constituted by chattel slavery, by the ungendering and fungibility of Black women and femmes, which, in turn, conditions the stability and reproducibility of binaries like female/male, man/woman, and heterosexual/homosexual.[11] Critiquing the universalizing protocols of trans historiography that render white trans subjectivity abstract and make white normativity intuitively align with trans experience, Jules Gill-Peterson notes that "trans of color historicity from the early twentieth century plays a particularly important role in destabilizing the racial innocence of transsexuality," which can articulate "the many disavowed racial histories of transness that precede it."[12] Jian Neo Chen persuasively narrates how trans of color social movements and activism, which helped mobilize transgender identity as we know it, were effectively "sidelined by the more linear and one-dimensional gender identity–focused narratives of white-dominant transgender movements and communities."[13] Trans of color theory pivotally intervenes in conceptions of transness that hinge on single issues or a universal trans subject, by pointing out how race and gender have always been mutually entangled.

The field of trans Latinx studies is especially generative in schematizing the trans and queer of color obfuscation that I locate in the drag performer and persona Valentina. In his important study of trans Chicanx representation, *Brown Trans Figurations*, Francisco J. Galarte contributes to how we analyze race, ethnicity, and gender, positing an analytic strategy for knowing trans Latinx life otherwise, called figuration, a "critical tool to illuminate the material, discursive, and affective conditions that are often left out of brown trans narratives because they are framed by existing tropes that predominately cast brown trans subjects and their narratives as exploitable and sensational."[14] Cherokee scholar Joseph M. Pierce looks to trans and travesti artists and performers in Latin America who enact forms of monstering that counteract neoliberal regimes of inclusion, producing ways of "undermin[ing] the normative orientations of the neoliberal state" by proffering a "politico-poetics of monstrosity" that "depends on techniques of bodily experimentation and on relishing the dangerousness of desire."[15] Examining the work of Peruvian scholar-artist Giuseppe Campuzano, Malú Machuca Rose theorizes how Campuzano retools a category like travesti, particular to and localized across Latin America, as "not an identity but as a methodology and epistemology," enabling *travesti*'s context-specific particularity to counter the use of terms imported from the Global North like *transgender* or *trans*, which are often assumed to be universally applicable.[16] Machuca Rose emphasizes, "Travesti is not woman and is not trans. Travesti is classed and raced: it means you do not present femininely all of the time because you cannot afford to."[17] This reminds us that terms do matter, and terms help articulate the experiential differences and uneven access to resources constituting gendered variance and embodiment in situated contexts. Trans Latinx studies, crucially, activates hemispheric and transnational modes of thinking *trans*, which allows me to explicate the performative strategies Valentina deploys that are informed by hemispheric transfemme Latinxness.

Valentina works hard for her fantasy—fantasy that is multiplied by the televisual encounter. We, in turn, ooh and aah at the fantasies of trans and queer of color joy, pleasure, and thriving that her performances and persona make happen, applauding and snapping fingers for a fantasy that becomes, there on the living room couch, or at the bar, or on the bus to work, our reality, our possibilities. And we can't turn away.

VALENTINA'S MASK, VALENTINA'S CLAWS

It is an iconic moment in *RuPaul's Drag Race* herstory: Valentina's botched lip-synch. "I'd like to keep it on, please," Valentina states in episode 9 of season 9, first aired on May 19, 2017, through a bejeweled red mask to the panel of judges, donning a matador-like outfit that is supposed to be a club kid–inspired look.[18] Her request to keep the mask on only furthers the anger of the eponymous show host, RuPaul, who is already frustrated by her insolence of not showing her mouth for the performance. In the era of the COVID-19 pandemic, fans humorized Valentina's pre-COVID insistence on mask wearing, particularly apt, given the antimasking backlash that now defines US society and culture. This supercharged Valentina's already iconic elimination with another layer of pop culture iconicity. Ultimately, RuPaul denies her request to keep the mask on, demanding that she remove it. She does, and the viewer then finds out why she wore the mask: she does not know the lyrics. She dances across the main stage, unenthusiastic, defeated. What went wrong? Why did she not know the lyrics to the song? Why did she not properly prepare and adhere to the conventions of the competition?

 RuPaul's Drag Race (2009–) is a competition reality television show. The show follows in the footsteps of other contest reality television that centers fashion, glamour, and weekly challenges like *America's Next Top Model* and *Project Runway*. *RuPaul's Drag Race* has become a massively successful global franchise and phenomenon, with many country-specific spin-offs, variety show–styled world tours, conventions, song releases and book publications, and related programming across many networks and streaming platforms. The US-based show now has a codified episodic structure and mise-en-scène. The hour-long episodes feature three challenges: a mini challenge, a maxi challenge, and a runway presentation. The mini challenge is a low-stakes challenge that tests contestants' drag acumen and skill and, if won, comes with added advantages like setting the lineup order for comedy roasts or selecting teams for the high-stakes maxi challenge. The maxi challenge varies week to week and encompasses challenges that require contestants to act, dance, sew, impersonate, sing, write sketches or stand-up routines. The episode concludes with a themed runway walk in which contestants must show off garments that fit the theme. The contestants are evaluated on their runway looks and maxi challenge performances by RuPaul, staple judges like Michelle Visage and Carson Kressley, and a rotation of guest celebrity judges each week. There is a winner for each episode, with the reward varying week to week, and the two queens who are judged to have done the worst must face off in a lip-synch. Each episode is interspersed with direct-to-camera commentary by the contestants, done in the present tense and in a confessional style, as is de rigueur of reality television, and many of these moments are transformed into GIFs and memes that circulate across social media.[19] Another staple of the show is the extensive and passionate engagement by the fans, taking place across social media and discussion forums, where fans stan, praise, debate, and joke about contestants, judges, and overall *Drag Race*–related content.[20]

Prompted by continual fan interest, as well as a fellow queen discussing it elsewhere, Valentina addresses what fans have dubbed "maskgate" by stating, "I don't remember!"[21] It is hard to believe she doesn't know why she couldn't recall the words. Rather than scrutinize why she didn't know, let's inquire into what such not knowing, and the televisual spectacle it generates, does. Valentina's masked spectacle exposes the logics of neoliberalism's dependence on capitalist productivity, respectability, professionalism, and compliance. More importantly, Valentina's seemingly inexplicable televisual blunder obfuscates such commonsense rationalities and, by doing so, ushers in queer and trans Latinx indolent performance strategies and world-making practices. I relish Valentina's explanatory obfuscations over why exactly she wasn't ready for the lip-synch, and I take it as an invitation to critically fabulate on what such obfuscation opens up for us.

The incriminating evidence of Valentina's faux pas of not knowing the words also appears in the spin-off show *RuPaul's Drag Race: Untucked!* (2010–). Airing immediately after the elimination episode, this companion show to the headline competition films the queens "untucking" backstage while the judges deliberate over the contestants' looks and performances for that week. *Untucked!* features the queens lounging backstage and sipping cocktails while commenting on runway looks, debating who they believe did the worst, bickering over grievances or tensions, and learning the words to the song of that week's lip-synch in case they need to lip-synch for their life. In stark contrast to the main show, *Untucked!*'s mise-en-scène has a behind-the-scenes aesthetic: cameras and crew visible; shaky, quick-paced camera shots; and a diversity of angles like extreme close-ups and low-angle shots. This produces the intended effect of making viewers believe *Untucked!* is less censored than *Drag Race*, raw, unscripted, and unmediated. *Untucked!* has become a staple of the *Drag Race* franchise and the viewing experience.

In the *Untucked!* episode aired immediately after Valentina's elimination, Valentina is seated next to the queen whom she will lip-synch against, Nina Bo'nina Brown. The two had been paired up for the challenge, to create an original TV pilot episode, but they attempted to do the pilot improvised, which, ultimately, backfired on them and put them both up for elimination. Backstage, the two competitors are sharing headphones, with one in Nina's ear and the other in Valentina's. The camera documents Nina mouthing the lyrics, getting the words down, as her eyes theatrically move about, preparing herself for the main stage show-off. Valentina, on the other hand, has her head slumped downward and eyes cast down sullenly, while the mask on her face obscures whether she is lipping the words or not. Then a production crew member announces that it's time to head to the main stage for the lip-synch performance. Nina hugs Valentina one last time, the footage abruptly cutting to the other queens heading back out, and then the camera returns once more to Valentina alone.

The camera provides an extreme close-up of Valentina's gloves (see fig. 4.1). They resemble claws, stunningly bejeweled with blood-red rubies. Her right hand hangs limp in the air, as the left sits on top of it, as if the left were wringing out the right, but without the pressure needed to perform such an action. It is an unusual pose, perhaps a suggestion of anxious contemplation or a means of fabulously and ferociously flaunting the gloves for the camera.[22] Her face is doubly obscured, covered by her bejeweled, clawed hands, and behind those hands, as the viewer knows, is her mask. The mask and infamous words spoken beneath it, "I would like to keep it on, please," have become an unforgettable, meme-ified, and iconic moment in *Drag Race* fandom history. The camera then pans out, quickly moving backward and away from her, as if it is trying to obtain more information from the queen, more interiority, more melodrama, more content for the reality television

Figure 4.1 Valentina's bejeweled claws obscuring her face. *RuPaul's Drag Race: Untucked!*, season 8, episode 9 (2017).

show to consume. As the camera moves, so do Valentina's hands. She moves them upward to her face, clawed fingers fanning out, shielding her from visibility and from the scrutiny of televisual commodification. It is almost as if she knows the original double-obscuring is happening, and, to make up for the hypervisibility and surveillance the camera is trying to initiate, she moves her hands to cover her face fully. It is reality television, after all, so the camera moves to expose interiority and reveal emotion and strife, to record what sells, and to generate memes and hashtags, clickbait articles, fan-based recap videos, discussion forums, and other potentially documentable aural-visualities that can snag the attention economy. Valentina's clawed obfuscation denies the hypervisibility, hyperexposure, and hyperknowability that the televisual places on queer and trans people of color. She denies the conventions of the format that she signed on the dotted line to participate in, refuting how "reality programming asks audiences to believe in the form, i.e., the use of documentary techniques . . . to symbolize realism, even when the content is obviously staged or fake."[23]

Valentina sitting backstage on the couch is another instance of what I have termed critical otiosity. The behind-the-scenes-style footage offers another vantage point into theorizing the minoritized performer and schematizing minoritarian aesthetics against the grain of the dominant televisual apparatus. This televised moment is only several seconds long. It is not part of the main show. There are no highly theatricalized actions that the camera loves to catch, no catty phrases or dramatic dialogue to spin into narrative drama. It is merely spectacular banality, the Mexican American nonbinary queen vividly red and glitteringly magnificent, unspeaking and in a bad mood, trampling on the camera's incessant desire for commodifiable televisual instances. The camera's extreme close-up and subsequent rapid panning out into a long shot is an attempt at capturing the queen of color, but she has her coy tactics. She counters the televisual medium and the form of reality television through a visual obfuscation, what Eliza Steinbock terms, in relation to trans cinema and an aesthetics of change, "shimmering," "a suspension of being either really there or not there, of being fully graspable."[24] Those glamorous claws obscure whatever depressive emotion she is expected to perform to show her humility and penitence at not knowing the words, and to hide whatever demonstration of preparedness she is expected to give in order to prove her worth. Her claws strike at the core of the neoliberal tenets underlying *Drag Race*.

Her form of blasé leisureliness, as documented in the incriminatory footage of her sitting on the couch, is rendered as inappropriate, ungrateful, and rude (see fig. 4.2). She should be more appreciative of the opportunity, and RuPaul says to her on the main stage after her elimination, "I thought you had the stuff to go all the way." RuPaul positions herself in the show as a mother figure to the queens, doling out advice and expertise in a tone, as occurs with Valentina's elimination, that can fluctuate between that of a disciplinarian and a disappointed parent. *RuPaul's Drag Race* shares much in common with makeover reality television, presenting a "collection of attitudes and techniques that take the production of the self as their central, vexed concern,"[25] and inviting viewers "to recognize—and reinvent—ourselves in the image of ready-made consumer 'types,' even as [lifestyle and makeover television] promises to facilitate active (and ongoing) processes of self-making."[26] The transformation of the self to do and be better, a guiding principle of makeover television and self-help culture, permeates the stage of *RuPaul's Drag Race*, imposing a neoliberal, capitalist schema fueled by uplift narratives and fantasies of meritocracy. Makeover television expects participants, particularly Black and non-Black Latinx working-class queens, to adhere to aspirational forms of normativity associated with white, upper-class culture: requiring money for more

Figure 4.2 Valentina lounging on the couch before her lip-synch. *RuPaul's Drag Race: Untucked!*, season 8, episode 9 (2017).

expensive wardrobes, maintaining "positive" attitudes, keeping sociopolitical commentary to a minimum, demonstrating working hard to be a better queen, fitting into Western European styles of fashion, and other white-coded and classed markers.[27]

Alongside the filming of the queens rehearsing the lip-synch song backstage, another convention of the *Untucked!* series is a concluding segment dedicated to watching the eliminated queen pack up her suitcases, reflect on regrets or feelings about the time on the show, and head out to the vehicle that will drive them away. During her *Untucked!* send-off, Valentina notes that it was an "out-of body experience" when RuPaul told her to take off the mask, and that she was in a dark place prior to the performance. She mentions multiple times that she wasn't prepared for the lip-synch: "This was never supposed to happen. I was going to win. I wasn't prepared."[28] Her lack of preparedness did her in, she concludes, and she has to live with that: "It was so unlike me to have gone out that way. Because I'm the type of person that if I was in that situation, I wouldn't go out without a fight. But I was just so unprepared. That is something that I'm going to have to live with."[29] Valentina frames her unpreparedness in a regretful manner. She wishes she had rehearsed those words. She wishes she had nailed that lip-synch. She could have won the competition.

The filming and production pressures of the show surely got to

Valentina.[30] Her unpreparedness was more than likely a result of the demands the show places on the queens week to week. There was also considerable anti-Black backlash on social media from the fans toward Nina Bo'nina Brown for continuing in the competition, which Valentina failed to condemn. The show's production conventions, editing techniques, and fandom have overwhelmingly vilified Black queens through the years, while also ostracizing Latinx queens who have accents or speak Spanish. Valentina's unpreparedness speaks to the high-stakes, labor-intensive, and body-mind-draining pressures of living in cisheteronormative and white supremacist structures. In a comprehensive assessment of Valentina's mask fiasco and departure from season 9, poet and cultural critic Vanessa Angélica Villarreal incisively articulates Valentina's racialized particularity on the show and the neoliberal tenets underlying her "failed" lip-synch this way: "All our lives we've heard 'You can have it all if you just work hard for it.' But hard work and a smile can never prepare us for cultural alienation, illegibility, racism, loneliness, burnout."[31] I extrapolate this singular account of a now famous, and well-paid, Latinx drag performer for how her experiences, and her unpreparedness, allow us to contour a different mode of being-knowing. I don't locate Valentina's unpreparedness as a failing.[32] For queer and trans people of color in general, whose lives are conditioned by colonial-capitalist regimes that produce and proliferate poverty, displacement, precarity, exploitation, violence, and unequal access to medical and gender-affirming services, failure is an untenable option. Valentina, on the main stage not knowing the words and backstage lounging on the couch, diverges from the trajectory of queer and trans of color exceptionalism. She opts for a path that makes her motivations and aspirations unclear, even in the face of seemingly clear-cut rationality. Her unpreparedness stupefies. Her insolent loafing astounds. She embodies racialized stereotype, becoming the Latinx spitfire: a ferocious femme, full of nonwhite racialized flair and phrasing, a seductress slacker wanting all the attention and rewards of society.

Much of the scholarship on Latinx people in US television is centered around the politics of representation.[33] Mary C. Beltrán's formative study on various US film and television Latinx stars across the twentieth century and the turn of the millennium examines the representational routines and portrayals of Latinx people, noting "the stereotypical representation of Latina/os as highly sexual, comic, subservient, and/or criminal."[34] Focusing on the post–9/11 era of Latinx representation in sitcoms, Isabel Molina-Guzmán assesses television shows like *Modern Family* and storylines including Latinx people, which often skew toward post-racial fantasies that are unthreatening to white audiences. For Molina-Guzmán, "happiness" becomes the governing affect appealing to white and nonwhite audiences, "characterized by the norms and values of whiteness and white civility that demand the erasure of overt signs of social conflict on the screen."[35] A key analysis of Latinx representation in *RuPaul's Drag Race* is Larry La Fountain-Stokes's examination of the depiction of the Puerto Rican drag queen from season 1, Nina Flowers. "Her inclusion and exclusion," La Fountain-Stokes explains, outlining how the show staged Flowers's racialized difference and drag nonconformity in a disparaging light, "was determined as much by her unusual gender presentation as by her limited command of the English language and generous use of the exclamation '¡Loca!' in a predominately monolingual American TV program."[36] Flowers commits a linguistic blunder in her season, as La Fountain-Stokes elaborates: instead of saying "hit TV show" from the cue card, she says, "Tell me about your HIV." This blunder draws out her Puerto Rican and Latinx difference, akin to Valentina's own in season 9. La Fountain-Stokes's study of Flowers importantly documents how Puerto Rican and Latinx drag queens are perceived and mediated on the show, especially when it comes to how they present themselves linguistically and aesthetically. Valentina shares much in the way of this Latinx racialized difference, in her use of Spanglish and referencing Mexican iconography and culture, but monolinguistic bias has been predominately deployed against many of the Puerto Rican queens throughout the show's run.

As important as these inquiries into the representational regimes of Latinx identity in television and film are, my critical interest is not in determining how positive, negative, or representative is Valentina's televisual presentation. Valentina's avowedly queer and trans Latinx aesthetic unsettles prevailing representational discourses premised on a good-versus-bad paradigm that has historically governed much ethnic studies scholarship and our overall cultural criticism landscape. The remixing of stereotypes for nonwhite queer and trans peoples can be a politically liberating practice, qualifying as a disidentificatory procedure in the Muñozian sense. I am intellectually stimulated by what Valentina's stereotypically charged queer and trans Latinxness does as she gives it to us,[37] especially since television has historically been a crucial "site where ideas about Latinas/os have been enacted on a national scale."[38] From the get-go of her introduction into the *Drag Race* franchise, Valentina utilizes stereotyping to her advantage and, as I contend, fosters queer and trans Latinx spectacular obfuscation that obstructs the neoliberal schemas of a show like *RuPaul's Drag Race* and imagines trans and queer of color worlds otherwise. Key to her success as a queen of color on *Drag Race* has been the strategic deployment of stereotyping. Valentina exudes racialized excess and Mexican and Latinx stereotype, torquing it in the queerest and transest of tunes. She dons, for instance, a scandalously skin-exposing queer mariachi-inspired outfit on episode 1 of her first season on the show,[39] and she dresses in the signature red jumpsuit of Chicana pop star Selena, for a group challenge in episode 2 of *All Stars*.[40]

In another instance, Valentina shows fellow contestants her Virgen de Guadalupe candle, a bedrock of Mexican religious devotion and cultural iconography, identifying the Virgen as her drag mother and frequently mentioning throughout the season that she prays to the Virgen to guide her through the drag competition.[41] The inspiration for her drag encompasses a far-ranging scope of pan-ethnic and hemispheric Latinxness: from Mexican starlets like María Félix, to entertainers like Thalía and Selena, to telenovelas, to the aesthetics of Latin American Miss Universes. She unabashedly speaks Spanglish on *Drag Race* shows and in other appearances. Valentina collates together these various styles, traditions, and icons with multilingualism to produce her own trans and queer Latinx aesthetic: quirky, glamorous, campy, eccentric, and an all-around joy to experience. She has made such slacker performances televisual spectacle and entertainment. Her Latinx slackerliness and collage of Latinx styles sashays into existence queer and trans of color worlds, ones not determined by capitalist imperatives and aspirational normalcy that constrain minoritized peoples from flourishing.

TELENOVELA REALNESS, DELUSIONS OF DRAG GRANDEUR, AND SERVING SPECTACULAR OBFUSCATION

Not too long after her debut in the *Drag Race* universe, Valentina returned in *RuPaul's Drag Race All Stars*, season 4 (2018–2019), for her redemption. A spin-off series of the original *Drag Race* competition, *All Stars* brings back queens from prior seasons who didn't win a chance to compete for the all-stars crown. Many return to redeem themselves, demonstrating how they have grown in their drag, and to rectify any errors or flaws that might have cost them the crown the first time around. The makeover reality ethos is in full swing in the spin-off. The structure of the show is a bit different from that of the primary show; instead of the bottom two queens lip-synching to save themselves, the top two all-stars of the week must lip-synch to determine who is eliminated. Prior to the lip-synch, the top two queens sit down and talk with the bottom two queens, as the bottom queens plead their case why they should stay.

Valentina fits neatly into the category of those who qualify to return to the show to seek redemption. She makes this clear in her remarks about *All Stars* being a form of redemption for the lip-synch blunder.[42] Ultimately, Valentina does not win in season 4 of *All Stars* and finds herself eliminated in episode 7. What we find in Valentina's appearance in season 4 is a queen who is much more certain of herself. She exudes confidence. She embodies the glamour and poise of telenovela actors and beauty pageant queens. In this more seasoned version of Valentina, she presents the persona of a diva, someone who knows what she wants and is assured she can get it. The other queens notice this more self-assured Valentina, and they frequently shade her for it, consistently describing her as "delusional." However, she is not one to shy away from this label, and plays it up by fitting it into the larger project she identifies as her fantasy.

Even before the all-stars season begins, Valentina sets the stage for her fantasy in a promotional profile video made by the show, "Meet Valentina: All About the Fantasy": "I feel like *Drag Race* was the pivotal moment that put me in my fantasy, finally."[43] She doesn't define what the fantasy is, or what exactly it means to be put in it, nor does the video explain what precisely constitutes this fantasy. Not knowing how her fantasy operates makes sense, given it is a promotional video intended to create preseason buzz and not meant to be comprehensive. Whatever this fantasy is, it is uniquely her own. As the season progresses, we will come to hear more about this fantasy and understand it as a particular kind of attitudinal ridiculousness that shields Valentina from the judges' critiques, allowing her not to heavily internalize negative feedback. In the promotional video, this fantasy is vague to the viewers, and what this fantasy will look like is uncertain. Yet, even as Valentina's fantasy is referenced throughout the season, and in many spin-offs and additional appearances where she makes note of it, it lives in abstraction, and the abstraction might very well be the point for enacting queer and trans of color worlds.

Well on her way to redemption, Valentina is one of the top two contestants of the week in episode 2 of *All Stars*, "Super Girl Groups, Henny!" After exiting the main stage and gathering backstage with the other queens to deliberate, Valentina, along with the other top contender of the week, Monét X Change, must hear the bottom two queens explain why they deserve to stay. Monique Heart, one of the queens up for elimination, asks Valentina if they can talk so she can convince her of her worthiness to be on the show. Valentina responds that she first needs to share something with everyone. This cues one of the iconic sound effects of the show, the shade sound, which signals to the viewer versed in *Drag Race* conventions that a conflict or tension has arisen. Valentina tells the other contestants, much to their disapproval, that she is more worried about successfully pulling off the lip-synch, especially since she spectacularly failed her last one. She comes across as more interested in recovering her image, and proving she can lip-synch, than properly vetting the other queens for who gets to stay. Though no extended conflict emerges between Monique Heart and Valentina, this editorially mediated tension speaks to the ability of the show's editors and producers to manipulate dialogue and footage to produce drama and conflict for the audience that may or may not be felt or experienced by the queens.

The minimally tense moment of Valentina looking selfish is followed by a direct-to-camera confessional by Trinity the Tuck, a contestant who will ultimately win the season 4 crown along with Monét X Change. She remarks, "Girl, Valentina is a diva. She seriously thinks that she is like a telenovela star."[44] The scene immediately cuts to Valentina in a slow-motion montage of various poses accompanied by a Spanish guitar score and a subtle, glitzy bronze filter: splayed hands rising to the chest with a face expressing awe; Valentina laughing boisterously; a flat, open-palmed hand pointing to another queen; and fists clenched as she stares stoically toward an imaginary horizon. The editing here denotes telenovela aesthetics like theatrical gestures, clichéd guitar instrumentals, dramatic faces, dreamy filters, and general gusto.[45] The show is once again playing off the fact that Valentina is Mexican and Latinx, a hamming-up that Valentina herself instantiates and welcomes. She also elsewhere comments on how telenovelas, particularly their villains, inspire her drag.[46] The montage segues back into the show's standard pacing, sound, and filtering, with Valentina saying, "It's just so hard, girls," and Trinity the Tuck groans in annoyance.

This seconds-long telenovela-inspired montage is surely meant only to be a campy, tongue-in-cheek moment, one of many in an episode, in a season, immediately forgettable as the viewer televisually tramps on in pursuit of the next rush of laughs and scandal. The production techniques of *Drag Race* are set up to amplify campiness, thereby normalizing it to the viewers.[47] But this montage, special in that it is not the standard mode or aesthetic within an episode of *Drag Race*, also enchantingly intrudes on the normative televisual experience. It is a spectacle within a spectacle, yet a spectacle that speaks to the trans and queer racialized particularity Valentina traffics in the show. The montage contributes to Valentina's fantasy. In fact, it realizes, through televisual fantasy, the spatiotemporality that is the televised edit, what Valentina has conjured primarily as words thus far in her *All Stars* debut. Here the fantasy becomes montaged spectacularity operating akin to telenovela fantasy, in which life is lived more theatrically, ridiculously, dramatically, and raucously. What if life were like a telenovela, the montage seems to suggest, a life full of posed thrills, days populated by arched brows and wayward gazes into the heavens, where in the end you get your man, the house, the economic security, that happily-ever-after. What if life were like that montaged fantasy, edited into its regularly scheduled programming, that fantasy constructed from Latinx televisual mundanity, in which queer and trans Latinx peoples can fantasy into existence fulfilling lives for ourselves, fabulously edited on our terms, wondrously fantasied according to our wishes? The telenovela montage lets us relish in the what if.

In the following episode, Valentina has a fall from grace, again: she is in the bottom two. The tides turn quickly on contest reality television. The maxi challenge in this episode calls on the queens to conduct an impersonation of a celebrity or famous person. Valentina chooses Eartha Kitt and spectacularly flops at being as funny as the diva. No matter, Valentina suggests, when the queens convene backstage to deliberate who should and shouldn't go home. Backstage, her fellow competitors ask how she is feeling, and she responds, ever coy, ever in character, "I just feel . . . gorgeous right now."[48] After several laughs and shady looks by her fellow competitors, she goes on: "I have my head held high. I handle everything with grace 'cause I'm a pageant girl. I've never done a pageant, but in my mind, I am Miss Venezuela, bitch."[49] The other queens laugh at this fantastical absurdity. The humor of it also fits into the schema of the fantasy Valentina has been building for herself. Though she may very well go home, in her mind, in her fantasy, she is a winner, baby. Her fantasy of being Miss Venezuela extends so far as to becoming Miss Venezuela (adorned in pageant sash and crown) for her runway look on episode 7, "Queen of Clubs," which is the episode of her *All Stars* elimination. Valentina also impersonates—for the staple challenge, Snatch Game, in episode 6 of her debut season—the now infamously incorrectly crowned Miss Universe 2015, Miss Colombia, Ariadna Gutiérrez.[50] Latinidad becomes high-femme, campy glamour through Valentina's drag and performances. This, in turn, transes and queers notions of latinidad, in which latinidad becomes a collaged queer and trans femme aesthetic deployed through drag, a latinidad hailing many types of audiences throughout the world.

Marcia Ochoa's groundbreaking ethnographic study, *Queen for a Day*, on Venezuelan nationalism and the production of femininity in beauty pageants and transformista communities, is instructive for mapping out Valentina's referential and aesthetic interests in Latin American pageantry. Beauty pageants have been fundamental to Venezuela's project of forging a national and transnational identity, as Ochoa illustrates, and have relied on concretizing particular gendered notions of bodily comportment and performance. For instance, they propagate a sense of beauty that is "colorblind," which only furthers national anti-Blackness and myths of racial mestizaje, or they encourage feminizing body modification, especially for ciswomen, which is unevenly accessible for transformistas. Describing her approach to thinking glamour and femininity within Venezuela "as a set of practices that can and do produce specific effects in the negotiation of power," Ochoa situates glamour as something that enables agency and social movement for both cisfemme and transfemme peoples, because "glamour, beauty, and femininity are technologies with specific practices that result in social legibility, intimate power, and, potentially, physical survival in a hostile environment."[51] The pursuits and deployments of glamour are not apolitical, nor merely simple vanity; rather, they foster the means for femme people to navigate and negotiate cissexist patriarchal systems.

Valentina embodies high-femme glamour. She collates various Latin American traditions and genres of glamour like that of telenovelas, beauty pageants, and pop stars. She is Miss Venezuela, even though she has never even done a pageant. She is Miss Colombia moaning and crying on Snatch Game. Her glamour is a queer and trans Latinx slacker strategy that thrives off ridiculousness and obfuscation and deviates from the neoliberal capitalist productivism of US culture. This slacker glamour is key to activating her fantasy, to living in it. The insistence on living in the fantasy, as she asserts when making the Miss Venezuela comment, is foundational for constructing indolent liberatory lifeworlds.

The viewer often hears about Valentina's fantasy in her *All Stars* appearance as a way to lessen the harshness of, or outright nullify, the judges' critiques. "In my world, in my fantasy, I won," she says, after stating that the judges overlooked her.[52] After RuPaul temporarily suspends the rules of the game, Valentina emphasizes that she doesn't care what the judges say, even though she was selected to go home by both top queens of that night. She declares, "When it comes to me and living in my world, and this little coconut head that I've got, it's a lot of fantasies. And when I feel the fantasy, it is my reality, and nobody can change that."[53] The other queens playfully ridicule Valentina for using fantasy as a defense mechanism, but, oddly enough, we never see the judges comment on this behavior, either on the main stage or backstage. In a show in which judges are fed behind-the-scenes gossip in order to bring it up later for the sake of generating tensions and drama, it is remarkable that there is never any mention of Valentina's fantasies, which openly dismiss the judges' critiques. Valentina's fantasying work, even though it undermines the evaluative authority of the judges and contestants, is too ridiculous, too comic, for the televisual production mill that thrives off manufacturing drama and scandal where it can.

Valentina and her fantasies are of especial interest for *Drag Race* fans. In particular, sites like Reddit are fascinatingly generative spaces in which to witness how Valentina—the persona, the image, the fantasy—is debated and interpreted by a general audience. A Reddit post from May 2020 proves to be an intriguing case study for further examining Valentina's fantasy.[54] After bingeing all of season 9, and disapproving of Valentina's appearance on the reunion episode and her being crowned Miss Congeniality, the Reddit user u/avp_1309 asks, "Why do people like [Valentina] so much?" The user clarifies further: "I know she is in all stars 4 and maybe she did something there but I haven't seen that all stars season yet." By this point in 2020, when the question is posed, Valentina is one of the most popular and beloved *Drag Race* queens, with over a million Instagram followers, acquiring cameos in films like *In the Heights* and full-on roles in the disastrous TV musical event *Rent: Live*. In a reply to the inquiry, u/Diredr provides an answer: "There's nothing wrong with knowing what you're worth, with being 100% confident in who you are, and with acting like a character when you go on a competition about drag. I'd rather see a queen be delusional than see one be miserable." Here we see the recurrence of the label *delusional*, which the queens on the show used, except now it has entered the sphere of fandom, which evacuates it of the playful and relatively affectionate tones the fellow queens use. U/Diredr finds entertainment value in Valentina's delusion and juxtaposes it to queens who position themselves in more depressive idioms. Presumably, those queens are not as entertaining. In another reply, by the user u/wyattmallard, the tone of the post pivots to meanness: "In AS4 she comes out as this self aware delusional weirdo." *Delusion* now becomes an epithet, and it refers to a delusion deserving of criticism from audiences. "Like her or not, Valentina has *so* much star quality," user u/annievaxxer writes, feeling similarly to u/Diredr. "She's mesmerizing. And as others have pointed out, she's delusional yet she's self aware, which makes her extremely entertaining and likeable." "During the reunion and on AS4 she was living her french vanilla fantasy and it was very endearing and made her pretty likable during AS4," writes u/Lucia_97, and we see Valentina's purposeful introduction of her fantasy in the season 9 reunion and then how she will further develop it in *All Stars*.

Other Reddit discussions centered on Valentina are likewise structured around debating her likeability and entertainment value. Most of the posts are sympathetic to Valentina's idiosyncratic ways. Many find the peculiar qualities of her persona appealing. What does it mean, then, for fans and audiences to dwell in the slacker fantasy that Valentina conjures? To like and find entertainment in Valentina on television, in interviews, makeup tutorials, on social media? To take to forums and social media to discuss with others, be with others, in the slacker fantasy, the fantasy that fandom helps articulate and expand? The fantasying Valentina does, and that audiences engage with, is, at its core, a spectacular abstraction. Whatever this fantasy world is, exactly, however it may operate, it expresses itself in vague terms, and yet we still somehow know. We know it is a means of shielding her from the judges' critiques, like her red, bejeweled glove claws obscure her from the penetrating gaze of the camera. It is a haphazard patchwork of Latin American traditions and aesthetics that both Valentina and the production crew and editors play up. It is endearingly quirky zingers and actions that fans discuss on Reddit. We can nod our head when she names her fantasy, we can point to the screen when we think it is happening, yet, nevertheless, it revels in slackerly abstraction—one that is adamantly here and now. We experience its commonness most mundanely: on the couch in the living room with a partner, at the bar with friends, in our bed in the middle of the night, on a packed train or bus on the way to work. This confounding slacker abstraction hails us in different ways. The hailing is sometimes legible and at other times illegible, sometimes named and at other times unnamed, identifying it in uncannily myriad ways: guttural laughter, the post on social media, a recap of an episode with others, a smile, a debate on an online forum. What the many potential responses and scenarios in which we engage with this fantasied stupefaction demonstrate is that we watch because it is pleasurable. The hinting, alluding, and gesturing to the fantasy are the promise of another sense of the world, one full of flamboyantly raucous laughter and joyous smiles. It is the promise of glamorously quirky gendered comportments, and of not having to exist in anti-queer and anti-trans worlds.

Valentina's drag persona continues to evolve. In 2023, she cohosted the premiere season of *Drag Race México* with Lolita Banana, a Mexican queen who competed on the first season of *Drag Race France*. She primarily speaks Spanish on the show, while peppering in English here or there. The use of Spanglish circulates her East Los Angeles, Mexican American subjectivity to Latin American viewers. Her popularity keeps growing, with over 1.5 million followers on the social media platform Instagram. In these various appearances and mediums, she asserts a pride in her Mexican American and US Latinx identity, presenting a sensibility that celebrates Latinx fashion, Spanglish, and cultural iconography. In general, her mature public persona is now staunchly consolidated around glamour, sophistication, and a heightened degree of seriousness, though maintaining a kind of blasé comportment that signals back to her more pronounced slacker persona from her initial televisual debut. The slacker proves difficult to exorcise. One can only hope that future iterations of her public persona will develop upon her slacker origins, not forsaking the indolent thrall many fans found iconic.

In a makeup tutorial posted in 2019 on the *RuPaul's Drag Race* YouTube channel, "Valentina's Signature Look," the queen demos how she puts on her drag makeup. She reveals that applying makeup is but another ordinary, everyday practice of labor on behalf of the fantasy: "These are my little tricks that I like to do that maybe no one's really gonna tell, but it makes me feel fish, girl, makes me feel my fantasy. It makes me look like I just came from vacation."[55] Even the most subtle of distinctions—the brush-stroked difference no one else can see—contributes to the fantasy work. The smallest touch makes a difference toward feeling oneself on vacation, feeling oneself away from the stultifying humdrum of capitalist space-time. Attending to the minutest gradations of makeup application becomes, in Valentina's fantasy, a process of worlding queer and trans relaxation right there on the tip of a brush: "[A white highlight is] gonna give it that cartoony vibe that I like with my drag makeup, because I'm not necessarily trying to look like a real woman, ya'll. Let's make that clear. It's really a fantasy that I'm creating." The application of makeup is not an attempt to pass as a ciswoman, to pass into normativity and legibility. Rather, her makeup and drag are about bringing out the ridiculous, the over-the-top, "that cartoony vibe" that astounds and confounds all at once. Valentina's slacker fantasy is in the enticingly unreal, the tantalizingly bizarre, the splendorously absurd that is practicing a life that unmakes cisheteronormative constraints. The fantasy is a process one does time and time again, like putting on makeup, remaking yourself and the world around you—no matter how spectacularly fantastical it may be.

5 | The Textures of Our Daydreaming

JUSTIN TORRES'S *WE THE ANIMALS* AND THE ART OF SARAH ZAPATA

In the mud is where indolent daydreaming finds a home in the universe of Justin Torres's *We the Animals*. Similar in approach to Sandra Cisneros's vignette-based book *The House on Mango Street* or the earlier-twentieth-century poetry–short story sequence *Cane* by Jean Toomer, Torres's book, and the subsequent film adaptation directed by Jeremiah Zagar, is a story comprised of short scenes centered around a young queer white and Puerto Rican boy, his two older brothers, and his working-class parents. The novel follows the boy's coming-of-age story and, by book's end, his coming-out, along the way documenting the abuse toward the white mother by the Puerto Rican father, the adventures with his brothers, and his ultimate institutionalization after his family discovers his diaries depicting queer sexual fantasies. Published in 2011, the book has garnered much acclaim and success, and the film was equally well received upon its debut in 2018. In the book, the protagonist goes unnamed, and in the film version he is called Jonah, but otherwise the film adaptation corresponds closely to the book. Like the book, the film maintains a vignette-like and scene-oriented style to portray the child and his coming of age in his family.

My critical focus on *We the Animals* is premised on a particular scene in both the book and film where indolent daydreaming manifests in a peculiar juncture: the queer child of color lying in a mud trench in the yard. I will focus first upon the book's representation of the scene of the child bathing in the mud, aptly located in the chapter titled "Trench." I devote my attention to the syntactic and semantic composition in which the scene is narrated by the queer child of color lazing about in the mud, which orients our sensibilities to sense otherwise, to sense out in language other logics and modes of being and knowing the world. I will then turn to the cinematic adaptation's representation of the trench scene. Through a close reading of the surrealistic techniques and nonhuman sensuality deployed in the filmic rendering of the trench scene, I make the case that the film realizes a multispecies sensorial world-making possibility operationalized through an indolent daydreaming approach. The novelistic and cinematic counterparts further schematize what I have been identifying as reading for indolent liberatory practices, through the differing aesthetic approaches they take to depicting the trench scene. Both versions demonstrate how enacting a politics for queer of color liberation, for staging a means of critiquing and imagining elsewhere from oppressive paradigms that seek to discipline, exploit, and curtail minoritized life, can take shape through sensual, surreal, and multispecies sensitivities.

"Trench" opens with Paps, the Puerto Rican father, digging a hole in the backyard. The narrator and his brothers look on, without disturbing the father, and debate what exactly it is he is digging and for what purpose. Stupefied, they settle between calling it a grave and a trench. The father digs to exhaustion and collapses inside, and when the children come to assist him out, he says to them, "I'll never get out of here."[1] In the immediate sense, the father's statement refers most pointedly to his predicament of being stuck down in the trench. He cannot get out, because he has dug too far down into the earth. However, this is not the first instance in the book of the father making such ominous comments about never being able to escape, so the statement also reads as an ambiguously loaded provocation. Does the father suggest he will never be able to escape the constraints of fatherhood and heterosexual marriage? Maybe he refers to the unceasing frustrations of trying to achieve a cookie-cutter middle-class (white) respectability, which the parents' low-wage jobs and his nonwhite racialized status in a predominately white town prohibit. Or does he perhaps suggest he will never be able to escape the curious condition of being Puerto Rican in diaspora? The novel settles these uncertainties of meaning by leaving it up to the reader to determine whichever interpretative explanation suits them best.

Zorimar Rivera Montes poignantly articulates how Torres's lyrical and elliptical literary style and narrative voice in *We the Animals* addresses the novel's complex approach to queerness and latinidad through opacity, vis-à-vis Glissant. The novel's opaque style "eschew[s] facile representations of Latinidad," which, on the surface, the father summarily reproduces through his abusive machismo persona, easily lending to a reading of the father as antagonistic to his queer child. However, as Rivera Montes evidences by careful close readings of various instances where the father displays tenderness, affection, and affirmation, the portrait Torres paints of the father, through an opaquely lyrical language, is more complicated than any reductive accusation of stereotype would offer. "Torres stylizes an opaque form of cultural specificity that allows him to make his literary voice unique while still denouncing the structural inequality embedded in his difference," notes Rivera Montes, clarifying a dynamic method for reading this seemingly straightforward, though profoundly abstruse, novel in attentively queer, nonwhite, and Latinx ways.[2]

Later on in the day, the boy's mom also finds herself attracted to the trench in the backyard. She drops in, and right upon her descent a summer rain shower strikes, leaving the boys to remark how "she made it rain" and "that hole's magic."[3] This is followed by the older brothers' descent and then, finally, the youngest's. By the end of the short chapter, each family member takes their turn in the trench. There is something enticing down below in the mud. We do not know what makes the trench special for these other characters, nor the degree or intensity of specialness it precipitates in them, but we do learn of the particular uniqueness and significance of the trench for the narrator.

The unnamed protagonist of the novel, who is also the narrator, is the only family member for which the reader is given insight and perspective into what it's like being down in the mud-filled trench. "Paps had dug my grave," he thinks there in the trench. "Those were my first thoughts, and when I was fully horizontal, half submerged in puddle muck, stories about people being buried alive rushed into my mind—avalanches, mudslides, suffocation—but I had a wish, and so I stayed to wish it."[4] For the duration of a lengthy paragraph, the child narrates his thoughts and experience in the trench:

> I felt a great distance from the house, from Ma on the couch and my brothers and Paps. The clouds seemed to move faster than I had ever known them to, and if I concentrated, if I let go enough, an understanding would blur inside of me and I could trick my body into feeling that it was moving and the clouds were still—and then I was certain that I was moving, and the hole was magic. I closed my eyes and stayed quiet and motionless but felt movement, sometimes sinking, sometimes floating away, or stretching or shrinking. I allowed myself to lose all bearings, and a long, long time passed before I wished my wish.[5]

There as he is, horizontal, submerged in the mucky water, lazing about in the trench, the boy fantasizes. His corporeality and the world around him begin to transform. He feels movement, impossibly so, contradictory movements like simultaneous sinking and floating, stretching and sinking. He feels his body changing, inconceivably, letting time pass, easing into a temporality of his own liking. He waits for a precise moment to wish his wish. What are the conditions he establishes for himself for this perfectly timed wish? When is the right time? He doesn't specify. Yet it's less about what he wishes and more so the process he undertakes to wish it. The narrator transforms himself, transmogrifies the world around him, in accordance with the need to wish a wish. He sets the parameters for himself, he establishes the conditions needed for effective wish-making. In the end, he makes a wish the likes of which the reader never becomes privy to. That is his alone to know, and yearn for, because wishes are the lifelines of the disenfranchised, those hopes infinitesimal, and some grand, carried in consciousness manifesting in everyday actions and convictions. Wishes are the bricks forming another world.

Down in the muck and mire of the trench, the child narrates to the reader the labor of imagining an alternative embodiment, spatiotemporality, and sensorial apparatus. He feels a distance from the world as he knows it, below the earth, giving him the space and time to concentrate, to let go, all in order to allow the magic of the trench to activate. The magic that is inducing oneself into sensorial hallucinations: the being "motionless" yet still feeling movement; both sinking and floating, both stretching and shrinking, all somehow simultaneously; losing all bearings and not caring for what the world may think or do to you. All of it is magic. The mud incites this magic. There is something alluring, something magical about the trench, as the brothers and narrator continuously note. Something that is indescribable, otherworldly, and not located within language, the rational, the explainable. Gazing into the clouds, sinking deeper into the mud, lounging within it and losing track of time and space, the passing of time that can only be measured in the adjectival use of "long," allows the child to relax, to calm, from the highly volatile and unstable surroundings that are cishetero patriarchal white supremacist violence.

Marion Christina Rohrleitner, discussing the novel's conclusion, astutely pinpoints how, after the institutionalization of the protagonist and his subsequent disidentificatory embracing of the wildness ascribed to him by the nuclear family and the state, his queer breaking-down "refuses to participate in the rat race of US-American competition for material goods; instead, he chooses the zoo, an anarchic space that allows him to experiment with pleasure and desire without caring about the accumulation of material wealth or the norms set up by a society that rejects him."[6] By the end, the protagonist animalizes himself, and such a process counters anti-queer violence. However, it is not only in the end where such an experimentation of living otherwise occurs. Before he enters the zoo, he enters the trench. The trench does not operate in the same affective, stylistic, and spatiotemporal mode as the more electrified, sped-up, erratic, and as Rohrleitner remarks, anarchic, mode associated with the zoo and becoming animal. The trench induces an affective-sensorial slowing-down, a languorous bathing in the mucky water, a sinking into the muddy space-time that is getting free from what is above-ground, enacting muddied possibilities for minoritized flourishing. Such sensorial strangeness follows closely Leticia Alvarado's work on the aesthetic possibilities of abjection in the work of Latinx artists, where "abject performances reveal abjection not as a resource for empowerment fueled by normative inclusion but as a resource geared toward an ungraspable alternative social organization, a not-yet-here illuminated by the aesthetic."[7] The queer Latinx child lazily daydreaming in the mud is a performance in contrariness to cisheterosexual white respectability and productivity of any kind.

The cinematic version of this scene amplifies the magical aspects by implementing surreal filming techniques and nonhuman ecologies. In the film, the child goes by the name Jonah, and he hops into the trench—like his textual sibling, lying there horizontally. Unlike the textual version, the camera highlights the mucky waters, the writhing worms, and vegetal detritus accompanying the boy. We hear the squishiness of flesh in mud, and worms wriggling about in it. Human and nonhuman entanglements are markedly pronounced through the visual and the aural. Jonah then begins to rise out into the sky. He goes chest forward, legs and arms and neck limp, unburdened. Next is a panoramic shot of the surrounding forest and adjacent road. As the camera pans across the foliage, we then gain sight of the boy's shadow across the treetop canopy. His shadow looks like Christ on the cross, arms stiffly lateral and legs held tightly together. The camera becomes the midpoint between the treetops and the boy's actual body. We, as the viewers, do not have access to his flight, to his sky freedom. We are near, and we are close, yet the imagining is all his own. "The film," according to T. Jackie Cuevas, unlike the novel, "allow[s] the boy's desire for queer worldmaking to come across through his flights of fancy, as he pictures himself soaring above the trees, imagines erotic encounters through his drawings in his journal, and declares that he wants to escape to a big city."[8] The queer child's flight proves short, however. The scene cuts sharply from Jonah's fantasying to the intrusion of the brothers at the trench, who mock him from above. The abruptness is startling yet speaks to the urgency of the trench and what it affords: a space and time away from toxic masculinity, cisheteronormativity, and white supremacy.

In a reading of María Irene Fornés's short play *Mud*, José Esteban Muñoz explores how the symbolic registers of mud, rigging it as he does to his theorizing on the sense of brownness, must also hold failure as a condition of its possibility. Mae, the protagonist, unsatisfied with the state of her romantic life, wants the good life denied her, which she metaphorically links to whiteness and purity, while associating mud and brownness with being stuck. Muñoz describes Mae's sense of defeated stuckness through a mud-inflected lexicon: "Mae's main motivation to move out of the mud that surrounds her is the sense of constraint and limitations she feels while tethered to both these parasitical men"; "Mae imagines a life outside of the ramshackle muddy world of the play"; "When yelling at Lloyd, she makes sure to tell him that he will die in the mud while she will die wrapped in white, in a hospital, cared for"; "Mae wants out of the mud and squalor but meets a predictable and sad death as she attempts to flee, to turn her back on her problematic lovers."[9] Mud operates as the language of Mae's affective stuckness, its charged symbolical connotations (gross, impure, dirty) serving as a metaphorical armament for establishing Mae's muddied unhappiness. "To be lost in a brownness, to feel isolated and not in sync with the brownness of a vaster brown commons," Muñoz remarks, lamenting Mae's inability to sync up with and situate herself in relation to a broader array of minoritized affects and sensibilities, importantly highlights "the ways in which persistence can and does falter."[10] For Muñoz, mud, and its link to a racialized sense of brownness, requires an attunement to affect and disposition, a necessary modulation of valuation in worlds governed by stifling whiteness.

Mud is central to realizing the surreal space-time imagined in *We the Animals*, especially for the film adaptation (see fig. 5.1). Because of its consistency, colors, unpredictable nonhuman mixings and entanglements (worms, detritus, etc.), and overall symbolic association with dirtiness, grossness, and impurity, mud is overcharged with pejorative connotations. The stuckness mud signifies due to both its literal and metaphorical consistency suggests inactivity, immobility, and a stalled temporality, connotations strikingly resembling those of *indolence*. Mud is an indolent form. For Fornés's Mae, this is anathema to her flourishing, to a sense of self that is pure and happy. However, the stuckness of mud, the revulsive squishy consistency of mud's brownness, and its nonhuman interpenetrations of worms, vegetal detritus, and other kinds of organic and inorganic matter is, for the queer child of color lazily daydreaming, a form of liberation. Getting stuck in the mud, for the queer child of color, bears the promise of a sensorial, multispecies spatiotemporality unfettered from the cruel and unfair oppressions of cissexism, homophobia, and white supremacy. The muddy, nonhuman worlds of *We the Animals* radically resignify mud's stigmatized and demonized symbolic-material reputation.

The matter of mud, and its nonhuman ecology in *We the Animals*, extends further the horizons of indolent liberatory practices. The

Figure 5.1 Jonah daydreaming in the trench. *We the Animals* (2018).

nonhuman critical idiom I conceptualize allies with the work of those who have theorized the nonhuman in conversation with critical race studies, queer theory, disability studies, and other forms of minoritarian critique. Elsewhere, I have extensively formulated upon a notion of the queer nonhuman in the posthumously published work of Gloria Anzaldúa.[11] Mel Y. Chen's work on animacy proves formative in rethinking the relationship between animate and inanimate, subject and object, and human and nonhuman worlds, which the muddy scene in *We the Animals* addresses. Chen postulates the importance for cultural critique of studying a conceptual apparatus like animacy, where animacy's prevalence, though oft understated, "is relentlessly produced and policed and maps important political consequences."[12] Their critical interest in animacy is not merely diagnostic, deconstructing how metrics of animacy operate and structure human/nonhuman polities, but also ardently strives to "rewrite conditions of intimacy, engendering different communalisms and revising biopolitical spheres."[13] What Chen's evocative scholarship makes thinkable are broader, more dynamic, and daringly promiscuous analyses that can track the porous relations, intimacies, and becomings of human and nonhuman entities. More importantly, Chen's work does not evacuate the social differentials constituting the human in order to propose some universal human subject in opposition to the animal-nonhuman. Instead, they theorize how race, sexuality, ability, citizenship, gender, and other vectors of social difference and historical-political specificity condition the very frameworks of intelligibility for understanding human/nonhuman worlds. "The task remains," assert Chen and Dana Luciano, "how to forge connections between these divergent histories, how to think on more than one scale, how to remain responsive to the continuing historical urgency of particular or located crises at the same time as we face new universal or diffuse ones."[14] The matter of scale, and the ability to scale down in order to perceive the situatedness of nonhuman animals like worms and nonhuman matter like mud, will prove pivotal in my reading of the film's rendering of the trench scene.

Mud, like indolence, is revolting. Mud's peculiar form—the wet solidity, the propensity to thicken and clump up, the varying degrees of consistency and shades of brown that produce an uncanny resemblance to fecal matter—positions it as a matter contrary to popular sensibility and sensory perception. Not to mention the small organisms and inanimate detritus that call mud home, often going unnoticed because of their diminutiveness or overall imperceptibility to the human sensory apparatus (i.e., microscopic organisms), which all become a source of fear or anxiety over what "unsavory" things mud may hide. The revulsive qualities affixed to mud can be strategically revalorized and reworked to animate a queer and trans of color sensibility that galvanizes muddy possibilities for imagining indolent liberatory space-times and worlds. The unseemly consistency of mud allows for the queer subject to get stuck, to laze about with the worms and the vegetal detritus, in a spatiotemporality unmoored by the overwhelmingly encompassing oppressive structures of anti-queer and anti-trans white supremacist capitalist modernity. For the poor, queer kid of color, who must each day traverse uncaring, hostile, and violent worlds, getting stuck in the mud, stuck in the fantasies mud-lounging welcomes, offers much-needed hope, the potentiality of a much-needed elsewhere.

During the trench scene, the film conducts intensely intimate close-ups on the child lazing about in the mud. The clumpy wetness of the mud coats Jonah's body as he relaxes into it, accompanied by a range of squelching and slopping sounds of human body sinking into the muddy ecology, while the camera saunters across his body through a sequence of varied shots. The first shot pans across the feet where they are half-submerged in a pool of muddy water with vegetal detritus hanging on top of them. The next cut is of fingers submerged entirely in muddy water, with the exception of two, which stick out above the liquid, inserting themselves into a sticky solidity of mud. The camera then transitions to the face of the child, with his eyes shut, a meditative countenance, a drowsy contemplation, as mud splashed on the bottommost of the chin dries. The camera then undertakes a horizontal shot of Jonah's torso. His belly is fully coated in the dark muddy brownness, with numerous worms wriggling on top. The shot tracks movement through an aural fluctuation, the squelching sound of wet, sloppy earth sloshing and the worms' slithery bodies writhing due to Jonah's sudden levitation, magically, out from the trench. Another two shots follow of Jonah's hands and feet slinking out of the mud. The scene concludes its lackadaisical, muddy documentation of Jonah's body in the trench by showing the child floating into the air, then on across the sky. Mud and worms meet the open air of the skies.

The descriptive analysis of this scene accords with what Nathan Snaza theorizes as "bewilderment," "affective events" that "articulate bewilderment as a directly political phenomenon enabling dispersed, fugitive, and ephemeral dislocations and disorientations that move us away from Man."[15] Snaza's methodology of reading literature and literacy as bewilderment takes as its premise the work of Sylvia Wynter. This turn away from Western, Enlightenment Man demonstrated in this muddy scene notably emerges from the horizontal shot of the worms on Jonah's belly. Verticality defines the camera's overall perspective in the other shots of Jonah in the trench. The dominance of filmic verticality also serves as a synecdoche for the upright stature of the human, with such uprightness denoting the civilizational progress of humanity from ape to human, primitive to enlightened man, feudalism to capitalism, a mythic sequence operating as a staple of Western, European, and white Enlightenment thought. The horizontal plane of the shot unsettles the viewer from the conventional perspective of verticality, and the conventional standpoint of Man. The horizontality situates us on the same plane as the worms and the mud on Jonah's belly, cutting us off from the human face and any go-to interpretative efforts that rely on facial expressivity for surmising truth, effecting a lumpy, writhing brown planar expanse that puts "intimate and uncomfortable contact between human bodies and the nonhuman world."[16] The muddy, brown horizontality places into disarray commonly held hierarchies between human, nonhuman animal, and nonhuman matter. This cinematic depiction of multispecies intimacy "probes the limits of [species] distinction, the fuzziness of the borders between species, and the social and affective processes when barriers are breached and pays careful attention to moments when the hierarchical classificatory system is subverted or reworked."[17] Jonah and the worms in the trench index another type of worldly entanglement, where interspecies becomings instance an alternative plurality of relations, intimacies, and coimbrications, six feet into the earth.

The queer human child of color, the worms, and the mud generate an uncannily sensual conjunction of matters, making matter unlike, and unusual proximities that condition unforeseen intimacies for being, knowing, and sensing. "To dwell with worms, to kiss them and be friends, means to recognize oneself as constitutively enmeshed in unending cycles of appetite, while also making do in the time and matter we can claim as our own, inevitably shared with others," writes Karl Steel.[18] This unusual intimacy incisively demonstrates how "sexual agency and erotic resistance are possible," as Rosamond S. King theorizes, "among living, breathing, desiring Caribbean people, and that our understanding of both sexual transgressions and the structures being resisted can deepen our understanding of who Caribbean people are and who and how we desire."[19] This multispecies and multi-matter entanglement forms the crux of a world unfamiliar to the one outside the trench, where these various entities collude to unmake the world that so brutally waits above.

I loiter extensively over the faceless and limbless worms on Jonah's belly, and the emergent worlds their wriggling embodiment glimpses, because their presence evidences a multispecies politics that can challenge the oppressive logics governing colonial-capitalist modernity. Their filmic presence incites a series of questions: How do the worms get to the top of Jonah's belly to begin with? Does Jonah place them there, in tenderness, in an act of affectionate interspecies mingling? Does he lounge in the trench for such a long period of time that they wriggle their way up, a mountain of human flesh they travail? When Jonah levitates into the air, there is no indication the worms fall off. We can still see clumps of mud and other lumpy detritus clinging to his skyward-rising body. Presumably, the worms, too, are part of his fantastic flight, part of the wondrous journey into a queer of color elsewhere. I relish the thought that the worms accompany Jonah on his mystical flight. Worms as friendly companions for a little queer kid of color who is so terribly isolated, excluded, picked on, neglected, and, ultimately, violated, by both his family and his community. Worms, who are so vastly different from the human figure, become kin and kind for the queer kid of color, both cavorting through the muddy bowels of the earth and the sky, aliens in mutuality. "Tactful agents" like Jonah and the worms, "where each agent has an interest in seeing the other maintain its existence, are engendering livable futures."[20] The unusual, though far from unpleasant, entanglement between Jonah and the worms might find substance in Eva Hayward's incisive theorizations on transness and starfish. The embodiments of both the trans person and the starfish enact forms of regeneration, "imperiling static boundaries (subjective transformation)," that can "attend to desire, pathos, and trauma, but also to modes of corporeal intimacy, fleshy possibility, and most important, reembodiment," according to Hayward. Both types of embodiment "share a phenomenological experience of reshaping and reworking bodily boundaries," which scrambles Cartesian logics between mind/body, human/nonhuman, rational/irrational, as well as instantiating an overall contestation of binary logics in and of themselves.[21] Gender and transness are regeneration, cutting away and into and making anew, transformational embodied praxis that is consignable not to a binary of man/woman but to dynamic, nonlinear, spontaneous, and imbricated trajectories, all of which the starfish shares as well in its capacity for bodily regeneration. Hayward understands these interspecies likenesses and correspondences as indicative of the sensuality of embodied transformation, and of how these transformations effect pleasurable proximities, "reworking boundaries between subject and object, us and them, there and here, me and it."[22] In Hayward's formulation, starfish and human are pleasurably malleable entities, entities yearning for transing possibilities, cutting across species lines and possessive individualism for an alternative body-communal politic.

Worms, like starfish, are also capable of regeneration, capable of regenerating themselves into new forms, and new multiplicities. Jonah's indolent daydreaming in the trench, and the subsequent flight of queer of color fantasy he undertakes, is regenerative as well. His muddy undertakings regenerate his weary, and traumatized, mind-body. They regenerate that childhood curiosity and sensitivity toward all things wondrous, ineffable, and fantastic. In their brief appearance in the trench scene, the worms metonymically function in the film as a visual icon of regeneration, a symbol indexing the trench's role in Jonah's coming-of-age narrative and his coming-into-himself separate from his family, attesting to Mimi Sheller's observation that "embodied struggles come into focus as a key aspect of the making of freedom, and its historical narration" in Caribbean discourse and subjectivity, where "embodied agents may find ways to engage in transgressive, disruptive, or redemptive performances" that "infiltrate public space, exposing and possibly transforming assumptions about who is a free person, a citizen, or even a human being."[23] Yet I want to press the point of the significance of the worms' fleshy, and quite literal, materiality. They are beings in the film that wriggle, move, squirm, and slosh about on the muddy surface that is Jonah's belly. They are part of his experience in the trench, part of the queer Latinx transformative journey he undergoes in the mud, and he, in turn, is part of their worm existence, their squirming around in the earth below and their wriggling forays into the sky above. The uncanny corporeal intimacies between the worms and Jonah in *We the Animals* propose interspecies mingling that effectuates sensualities and sensibilities that organize reality differently. The spatiotemporality of the trench is one hospitable to nonhuman worm and human minoritized subject alike, their interspecies commingling demonstrative of reciprocal care, pleasure, belonging. In this muddy space-time, these differently constituted beings address the particulars of being-in and becoming-through difference, the careful and conscious attention to material differences, to sensuous materiality, in the construction of worlds rid of cruelty, exploitation, and premature death.

Both textual and cinematic versions of the trench scene share in what Ren Ellis Neyra posits as "sensorial errancy." Examining the work of Puerto Rican filmmaker Beatriz Santiago Muñoz, Ellis Neyra locates sensorial errancy within her filmmaking practice in sites across the Puerto Rican archipelago, tracing "sonic exorcisms that disrupt, slow down, swerve, and enact another audible arrangement" in order to compel "another way of being in places where invasion as status quo, structural disuse, thriving life, contamination, new growth, and art making happen in kaleidoscopic concurrence."[24] Ellis Neyra postulates the cinematic works of Santiago Muñoz as activating a poetics across sensorial axes, small-scale, and interspecies encounters, ones that reconfigure, untidily and unpredictably, the sensorium of how we know and experience our situatedness in the world. I likewise situate the queer child of color in the trench in this manner. Here is where the textual and the film counterparts come together to proffer an indolent daydreaming queer Latinx sensorium: the queer child of color bathing naked in the mud, worms wriggling among the soft flesh, the labor of imagining and contemplation as spatiotemporally distinct from the normative time outside the trench. I read this scene, in both the film and the book, not as escapist but rather as the sinking into another spatiotemporality, one whose governing logics and rubrics work differently than the stifling ones we all know so well. What is enticing in this passage is that imagining becomes a form of indolent labor, a sensorial provocation to labor on behalf of something else away from white supremacy and cisheteronormativity, and that also documents the process and methods involved in undertaking that pleasurably transformative work. We get in real time the thought process, the work involved, for activating the magic of the trench.

PLUSHY INTIMACIES, FUZZY AESTHETICS: ON SARAH ZAPATA'S INDOLENT HAPTIC WORLDS

In the winter of 2021, I travel from Manhattan to BRIC Brooklyn to see the exhibition *Latinx Abstract*. The group exhibition highlights abstractionist works of Latinx artists from various ethnic and generational backgrounds. I meander through the gallery, masked, delighting in the diversity of media used by the ten artists featured in the exhibition. In one corner of the exhibit, I notice a colorful, shaggy gathering of sculptures on the gallery floor, and a tufted, textile sculpture mounted on the corner of the wall. I approach the sculptures and take note of there being no tape on the floor to signal a barrier, the gallery and museum's way of saying, "Do Not Cross." Presumably, I can get as close as I want, and I do (see fig. 5.2).

The sculptures are vibrant multi-fabric amalgams, like a pile of dirty laundry heaped haphazardly into the corner of a room, where each sculpture leans precariously to a given side as if weighted unevenly on the gallery floor. Synthetic hair, in varying shades of blond and brunette, protrudes out from various points in the fibrous sculptures, titled *A Little Domestic Waste I* and *A Little Domestic Waste VII*. I loiter near them for a while, snapping photos up close, inspecting from various angles in efforts to account for all the fabrics, textures, and other odds and ends comprising the curiously hunched specimens. During my inquiry into the sculptures' composition, the most sudden urge overcomes me: to

Figure 5.2 Sarah Zapata, *A Little Domestic Waste I* and *A Little Domestic Waste VII*, 2017. Photo taken by the author.

reach out and touch, to caress, to nuzzle, to feel, to hug. I yearn to know how all the various fabrics and textures feel, gliding across them with a hand, their differences on skin, their hodgepodge unity all upon me in an embrace. I don't do any of this, of course. The walls of the art museum forbid such haptic intimacies and pleasures, unless otherwise stated by a nearby panel or guard. Yet I can't shake the haptic entrancement the sculptures induce in me. I can't shake the plushy allure tingling through my skin at the proximity.

These shaggy sculptures are the work of Sarah Zapata. Zapata is a queer Peruvian American artist originally from Texas and now based in Brooklyn. Her work employs the use of hand weaving, coiling yarn, rug making, tufting, and latch hooking, where she constructs vibrantly frenetic textiles and tapestries from a multitude of synthetic fibers, textures, and materials. "The shaggy environments can make the viewer feel ensconced in a 1970s rec room on acid or nurtured inside the womb of a Muppet," notes one critic.[25] Zapata's artistic approach gravitates toward abstraction, favoring wackily original patterns, boisterously clashing textures and materials, and otherworldly furniture-like arrangements, which draw from Peruvian, pre-Columbian Andean, and Christian biblical themes and iconography. Zapata has had several solo shows in both the United States and Latin America, as well as being included in many group shows, and her work has garnered considerable attention from the arts press.

The haptic entrancement I experienced at BRIC Brooklyn doesn't seem too far off from Zapata's artistic intentions behind her pieces. In her first solo show in 2017, *If I Could*, visitors were welcome to walk barefoot through the installation space, which was covered in a shaggy, synthetic rug utilizing her signature approaches to textile work and multitextural fabrics.[26] In *A Famine of Hearing* (2019), a later installation, visitors can sit or lean on the colorful yarn-sprawl across the floors, walls, and the rectangular structures protruding up into the gallery space. The installation "favors a mode of immersive abstraction," which activates through the haptic.[27] Zapata wants visitors to, quite literally, touch the installations, to experience haptically what they offer. Even bare feet are welcome to stroll across these lush landscapes.

In *In vastness of borrowed time (The taxing of a fruitful procession)* (2021), an installation first exhibited in the Crisis Galería in Lima, Peru, Zapata transitions from shaggy sculptural verticality to shaggy sculptural horizontality (see figs. 5.3 and 5.4). The installation features beanbag-looking, plushy-rock sculptures scattered across the gallery floor, with shaggy, colorful rugs that are situated either underneath or draped over the plushy rocks. Zapata's wall fixtures, which she identifies as "gargoyles," abstract figurations meant to resemble stone gargoyles perched atop a

Figure 5.3 Sarah Zapata, *In vastness of borrowed time (The taxing of a fruitful procession)*, 2020–2021. Courtesy of the artist and Crisis Galería, Lima, Peru.

building, adorn the wall corners. There are also smooth, painted rocks placed around the floor. The plushy rocks come in an assortment of patterns, shapes, and sizes, all of which are organized into various pile formations: some piles lean on one another, some are stacked one on top of the other, and some lay side by side without exerting much pressure on the others. The secondary color palette of the plushy rocks favors green and purple, which are the colors of the stripes of the gallery walls, and

147 | THE TEXTURES OF OUR DAYDREAMING

Figure 5.4 Sarah Zapata, *In vastness of borrowed time (The taxing of a fruitful procession)*, 2020–2021. Courtesy of the artist and Crisis Galería, Lima, Peru.

the overall effect telegraphs a swamp-like, cooky garishness. Faces adorn many of these plushy rocks, resembling pre-Colombian iconography and statues, with some of the faces baring teeth, others with puckered lips, and others indeterminable due to their highly abstracted nature. The variegated and mixed-material piles scattered about in the gallery space result in a kind of eccentric clutter the gallerygoer must navigate, like a child's playroom, beanbags and pillows and blankets and other items thrown into huddled heaps, in efforts to relay some semblance of tidying up, of getting the space into some kind of order.

Horizontality defines the plane of *In vastness of borrowed time (The taxing of a fruitful procession)*. There are none of Zapata's prolific vertical sculptures protruding out into the gallery space like in *If I Could*, nor any of the rectangular, shaggy tapestries hanging from the gallery wall like in *Siempre X* (2015–2016). The plushy rocks of the installation are low to the ground, requiring the viewer to look down, to double-check where they are walking, so as to not fall into one of the piles. But what the compositional scheme and kineticism demand from the gallerygoer of the installation—what its horizontal plane, its lowness, the clashing color palette, the cluttered floor space resembling a playroom demand—is precisely what makes it so alluring. What if the gallerygoer were to trip and stumble into the pile? What might such an impact feel like? What would be the haptic result of such a falling in to all those textures and fabrics? I linger over these hypothetical gallery accidents because their speculative nature conditions the possibility for what I propose the installation proffers: a queer and trans Latinx indolent haptic world. In this final section, I luxuriate intensely over the haptic for queer and trans of color liberation and world-making. I connect the sense of a queer and trans Latinx haptic to the plush and the cute; in the soft, the cushiony, and the pleasant that is plushiness, combined with the garish, cartoonish, and indulgently over-the-top that is the cute, I situate a politics of indolent liberatory haptics. Touch, texture, and style align in Zapata's work, providing an aesthetic of haptic unbecoming. Her plushy installations and sculptures ask us to reorient our relations to space, time, and embodiment: titillating us to loaf about as we desire in the cushiony and silly gallery-imaginings on offer, loafing into relaxed states of shaggy comfort, fantasy, and dreaming, where to loaf on and with her fuzzily goofy pieces is to broach intimacies that challenge neoliberal capitalist sensibilities. Her works invite the viewer to touch, where the act of touching, the convergence of human skin and nonhuman soft textures, results in the sensing of another space-time, one governed by slowness, relaxation, taking time, and slowing down. These installations and sculptures require indolent modes of aesthetic appreciation to engage them on their terms.

Zapata's plushy rocks recall a Latinx artist forebear who approached the rocky in uniquely queer ways: the Chicana lesbian feminist Laura Aguilar. Aguilar's body of work spanned over three decades, deploying a sensuously queer photographic approach centering Latinas and bodies of size. Before her death in April 2018, her first comprehensive retrospective, *Laura Aguilar: Show and Tell*, debuted at the Vincent Price Art Museum in Los Angeles, which helped to consolidate her place as a consequential visual artist and photographer. *Three Eagles Flying* (1990), her most well-known triptych, sets the precedent for displaying the nude women of color and bodies of size in her artistic oeuvre, which the *Grounded* series of photographs would come to expand upon in various ways. In the series, the bodies of Aguilar and other women are fully nude and placed in desert landscapes dotted with boulders, stones, mesas, and other desert landforms. The portraits are predominately of Aguilar in various positions, like sitting or lying on the earth, breasts and buttocks resplendently visible, the overall body, within the photographic setting, doubling as fleshy rock or smooth boulder. Aguilar's series of self-portraits in the mountains and deserts of New Mexico and California have been the subject of vast interest by scholars across the years. "Through images that eschew the formal qualities of studio as a white-settler aesthetic and its exotic lens," Macarena Gómez-Barris writes on the self-portraits, "Aguilar pushes against the colonial objectification of Native portraiture and the national archive."[28] Gómez-Barris highlights the shift in visuality Aguilar's portraits demand, a shift contextualized in relation to the colonial histories and Native dispossession defining the US Southwest, a shift that, as she formulates elsewhere, performs a decolonial queer eye.[29] The queer nonwhite body in the desert cites the troubling and complex histories constituting colonial-capitalist modernity.

In these series of fleshy-stone photographs, Aguilar transmogrifies into boulders and rocks. She is both part of the landscape and the landscape itself. Take, for instance, her photograph *Grounded #120 (Untitled)* (2006–2007). There are three tiers to the photographic composition.

There is a boulder resting at the topmost plane of the photograph, whose form in its entirety is contained within the frame. This boulder rests on top of a mesa, a prominent, zigzagging cleft running down its surface, as the mesa juts out horizontally past the boundaries of the photographic frame, past the boundaries of visibility and cognition. At the bottommost plane of the photograph, the viewer can discern another rock-life entity, rounded and smooth, with a much smaller, and linear, cleft running down. The beiges, umbers, and browns distributed across the three tiers of the photo contribute to an overall sense of unity, adding to the earthen complexion defining the desert landscape. Except, upon closer inspection, the rock at the bottom tier is not in fact a boulder, but Aguilar. This pseudo-rock is the human body bent over, the butt boldly out for all to see, stretch marks perceptible if one focuses hard enough, as the lower half of the legs are cut out of the shot. The cleft in the mesa and the cleft of Aguilar's butt, vertically juxtaposed as they are, form a visual field blurring the distinctions between animate and inanimate, soft flesh and hard rock, human and nonhuman. The rock's cleft could very well be that of their stony ass, and Aguilar's fleshy cleft could very well be part of the desert landscape. The erogenous becomes a site of stimulation and pleasure any entity may possess.

Aguilar's rocky portraits are uncanny for how easily the human can blend in as rock, how swiftly a human can pass over into the realm of the inanimate and nonhuman, how a portrait turns into landscape and vice versa. Aguilar's series of fleshy-stone portraits documents not merely a subject becoming an object, but rather the alchemical process of forms, perceptions, sensations, and matters transforming, eroding common-sense assumptions about what constitutes the human and the environment. The portraits clarify a way of being human that is about deep, boundary-defying entanglement with nonhuman ecologies. "Stone is a sympathetic companion, a source of knowledge and narrative," Jeffrey Jerome Cohen writes in his study on stone's role in Western philosophy and literature, "an invitation to an ethics of scale, the catalyst for humanist-scientist alliance, a disruption to everything we thought we knew."[30] Aguilar's photos extend Cohen's theorizing of stones by bringing into question what stony becomings do, politically and ethically, in human-nonhuman worlds, especially when framed within a queer Latinx aesthetic. Thinking stone and the human together "might help open passages for a praxis of care and response—response-ability—in ongoing multispecies worlding on a wounded terra."[31] Aguilar's stony becomings seek to know what it might be like to be a boulder: to sense, feel, know, and exist otherwise. This is a different kind of humanism, one akin to Eunjung Kim's elaboration that "beyond simply being deployed as a condemnatory last word, can 'objectification' as a mode of 'dehumanization' offer a new way to challenge the exclusionary configurations of humanity that create otherness?" Kim's article looks to see how "unbecoming human" might be a means through which to activate an "anti-ableism, antiviolence queer ethics of proximity that reveals the workings of the boundary of the human."[32] For Kim, dehumanization, as an analytic and practice, can be the means through which to interrogate the differences between objects and people, and how becoming object-like can orient us against the grain of Western conceptions of Man. Samera Esmeir further elucidates the point, in relation to processes of humanization undertaken by nation-states: "The task is not to recognize the other's humanity, for, like dehumanization, that task risks repeating colonial juridical logics."[33] These modes of humanizing, as she notes, are tied to colonial rationalities, which gave themselves the power to create humans who are dehumanized and in need of humanizing by colonial law. In this way, colonial power and violence prove to be tautological, able to adapt and reconfigure themselves according to new social, historical, and political contexts. If conceptualized in this antihumanist manner, Aguilar's fleshy-stone portrait-landscapes call into question our commonsense binaries like animate/inanimate, subject/object, and human/nonhuman, all the while evidencing modes of cohabiting that do not depend upon Western, Enlightenment fantasies of mastery, subjugation, exploitation, borders, or hierarchy. Her work offers an alternative framework for queer of color worlding, by placing at the analytical core an other-than-human episteme. The centering of the nonhuman does not require, or even necessitate, an evacuation of human social differences or sociopolitical analytics deriving from social justice movements, but, as her fleshy-stone portraits attest, the nonhuman and the minoritized human enter into a feedback loop. Their mutual imbrication allows for the posing of questions and formulating of solutions that honor their coextensiveness, a subaltern mutuality toward common liberatory goals and agendas. How can one be human otherwise? Aguilar's photos query, and the matter is a distinctly nonwhite and queer polemic.

Although Aguilar's artistic approach to human-stone assemblages is realist and photographic, the sensual transmogrifications of human-boulder corporealities and the immersive intimacies of fleshy-rock spatiotemporalities prove to be an instructive conceptual framework for critically apprehending Zapata's installation. How do we foster fantastical becomings with plushy-rock sculptures? What sensorial, affective, and imaginative liberties must we make to enmesh ourselves into the worlds of Zapata's texture-rich, color-saturated installation? How do we forge plushy, shaggy, polyvalent worlds like the installation? The installations propose a world-making practice premised on indolent haptics. Their plushy rock entices us to fall into their shaggy cushions, to lay back and sink into their clashing, psychedelic colors, to indulge excessively, languorously, extensively, in a daydreaming fantasia inspired by the variety of plushy-rock piles. Each cluster in the installation offers differing textures, colors, arrangements, and haptic experiences. In order to garner the widest range of experiential possibilities, we need to move a bit more slowly across each pile of plush, caress a bit more carefully and considerately each plushy rock, rove more thoroughly and capaciously across each and every fabric, each and every decorative face, each and every stitching. The indolent haptics becomes a matter of attuning oneself to the differences in scale, and what such a scaling attention does to how we pay attention, how we perceive, how we nuzzle the what is and what can be. These piles of plush impress upon skin and tissue the urgency of slowing down, attuning differently, an ethico-political haptic that prioritizes carefulness, care taken in every micromovement our mind-bodies make. Such a lounging practice resonates with Jeanne Vaccaro's theorizations on handicraft, felt matter, and embodiment in trans studies: "Connecting transgender corporealities to the politics and labor of the handmade is a way to explore alternate modes of identity production, and to resist institutional and institutionally sanctioned gender formation."[34] For Vaccaro, the handmade allows us to think process, the how of perpetually becoming oneself and becoming in relation, rather than reinscribing fixed, determinate, teleological end goals for trans identity formation. "A different epistemology is at work in the figuration of transgender as crafted," Vaccaro posits, "one that puts to the side the textual to animate textured modes of labor, process, collectivity, duration, and pattern."[35]

According to Zapata, she sees installations as a means of inviting in fantasy:[36] "I want to create these otherworldly experiences in order for the viewer to access ideas of potential and futurity."[37] Installations allow for fantasies to emerge in the here and now, right there on the gallery floor, tangibly present. "Zapata's objects can hold our fantasies," explains the installation description for *A Famine of Hearing*. "They form a landscape in which we can spend time and experience ourselves with other bodies."[38] In the festively fuzzy realms of Zapata's installation one can bring their fantasies, and share them with others, through the sensorial-sensual proximity of being near another, skin to skin, follicle to follicle, breath to breath. Maybe even new collective fantasies may emerge mediated by the installation. The fantasies of *In vastness of borrowed time (The taxing of a fruitful procession)* are ones that traffic in topsy-turvy imaginaries, playfully unserious spatiotemporalities, and fuzzily sensuous and indolent haptic worlds through horizontal lowness. We must plunge down, roll, and frolic near to the ground, lying and lounging and daydreaming in plushy-rock fluffiness. Zapata's low, horizontal installation shares much in common with the trench scene in *We the Animals*. There is a seduction in the sinking and plummeting into lowness. Lowering ourselves down into depths unfamiliar, down into depths unthinkable, lower and lower our minds and bodies go, which, all the while, arouses in us that most keen, and tantalizing, desire for emancipatory being and knowing, liberating sensations and feelings in worlds organized according to our mutual flourishing, our mutual becoming.

Installation is not the only medium through which Zapata's indolent haptics takes shape. Included in a New York City solo show, *Of This World Rather, I want you to know how hard I am* (2019) is a series of three ceramic pots enrobed in woven synthetic fibers, with two mannequin feet wearing crocheted socks jutting out the sides (see fig. 5.5). The ceramic sculptures speak to Zapata's principal aesthetic interest in weaving, and the socks her fascination with soft, shaggy textures, but these three sculptures add in a new element with the introduction of the ceramic. "When I was in Lambayeque," notes Zapata of her time in Peru, "I visited the museum for the tomb of Sipán with its examples of Moche ceramics and metallurgy. The ceramics were very inspiring to me, and a lot of the imagery on the rugs are from that excavation. It made a lot of sense to expand into ceramics for this show, and I loved how it also spoke to earth, and a grounded sensibility."[39] Here Zapata combines her sustained interest in pre-Columbian and Andean iconography and

Figure 5.5 Sarah Zapata, *I want you to know how hard I am*, 2019. Courtesy of the artist.

artistic practices with postmodern absurdity and sexual humor. The feet seem to suggest that a person is stuck in the ceramic pot, a tableau akin to Alice in Wonderland when she grows too big from the potion and her limbs explode out through the White Rabbit's house. Moreover, the feet wear those soft, thick socks, typically worn to go to bed or lounge about on a cold winter's day. The three iterations of *I want you to know how hard I am* present a kind of kitschy, snuggly absurdity. Whatever wonky world is in the pot, the entity whose feet protrude out desperately wants to be there. There is something about that enrobed vessel compelling this fuzzy sock wearer to crash through into it. There is something about the sculpture's nonwhite queer specificity that entrances this bootied being, who flies in the face of decorum by staying stuck there, indefinitely. Those stuck feet are in on a secret the viewer can only speculate upon.

The stuckness *I want you to know how hard I am* raises brings us full circle, to Torres's child in the mud. What worlds may lazing about in stuckness conjure? What might it mean to get stuck in a queer Latinx aesthetic fantasy, to want to stay stuck in such a realm? How might a critical aesthetic and political practice emerge from the pleasures of being stuck? Torres and Zapata demonstrate to us how getting stuck in a common fantasy, a fantasy comprised of a plurality of desires, pleasures, joys, and other life-affirming modes of queer Latinx imagining, yearns to unmake reality as we know it. Getting stuck in the plushy-rock installations or the snuggly ceramic pots of Zapata's imagination, or Torres's mud-lounge, doesn't seem all that bad. Yet their indolent worlds, materialities, and fantasies remind us that any alternative sensorial, affective, imaginative, and aesthetic practice requires work. The ethical and political possibilities of indolence will be labor-intensive, a commitment of resources and time, successes and failures. Social and political transformation always is. But the pleasures, and rewards, of indolent living, of thriving and flourishing against the grain of exploitative and destructive colonial-capitalist regimes, are worth it.

Coda

NOBODY WANTS TO WORK ANYMORE

Indolence is in vogue. When solicited to give advice to working women in a 2022 interview with *Variety* magazine, Kim Kardashian, billionaire mogul, responded: "I have the best advice for women in business: Get your fucking ass up and work. It seems like nobody wants to work these days."[1] The advice against indolence—or complaint, depending on how you look at it, perhaps even a rallying cry to her fellow capitalists— became the target of widespread criticism on social media pointing out how Kardashian, a child of nepotism, came from money and has not had to work very hard at all to secure her billions. In 2023, the *Washington Post* ran a series of columns about the problem of "lazy girl jobs," or why young professional women should opt out of working from home.[2] The column's thesis: women working from home may jeopardize their ability to make in-person connections with their superiors and, if push comes to shove, they may be the first on the chopping block when firings happen during recessions. Since the onset of the COVID-19 pandemic, employers have been urging, and coercing, employees back into the office, finger-wagging at the supposed insolent laziness plaguing contemporary workers who want to work from home. The bosses and the billionaires condemn indolence because they know it is a threat to the existing order. CEOs need workers to get up off their asses and work to make them their wealth. Management needs workers in offices, loyal to the company and therefore loyal to capital, in order to properly surveil and extract as much labor power from them as they can. Landlords, electric companies, car manufacturers, and a host of other capitalist industries profit off workers commuting to work and laboring in office buildings. The production of profit and the accumulation of wealth runs off a nebulous yet wholly interconnected web of nodes and relays, all of which, as the bourgeoisie unshamefacedly express, is endangered by workers refusing to work according to capitalism's destructive tenets. Workers are making demands for better wages, requesting a shorter workweek, forming unions, and striking if necessary, and the ruling class responds accordingly.

But the jig is up. We have seen how in the COVID-19 era indolence has become a straw man for capitalism's growing inability to manipulate workers and the working class into believing the ruse of capitalist exploitation. Working hard, working a lot, and work as moral good are no guarantee of stable housing, food security, and a good life, which becomes more and more evident in this advanced stage of twenty-first-century capitalism. Indolence, again, as in prior epochs, serves as the necessary boogeyman by the bourgeoisie to attempt to discipline the deluge of workers across the globe who are questioning their relation to work, and how they want to spend their time on this planet. As Judy Wajcman notes, "temporal sovereignty and sufficient leisure time are important indicators of a good life,"[3] and workers are demanding to live better lives distinct from the dictates of capitalist profit and edicts. Workers are refusing the terms and conditions of work set up by capitalism. Humans are refusing capitalism. It is as if the workers of the world are heeding the words of theoretician of *operaismo* Mario Tronti: "Work equals exploitation: this is the logical prerequisite and historical result of capitalist civilization."[4] "Operistas understand that capitalism is not simply the problem because workers are exploited, but because work has become the dominating condition of human life," summarizes Muñoz of the *operaismo* movement, where he also poses a series of pertinent questions: "What would it mean, on an emotional level, to make work not the defining features of our lives? How could such a procedure be carried out?"[5] I hope my discussion in this book has helped to address Muñoz's invigorating queries that center the affective dimensions of what a life not defined by work can be. What such a life can feel like. My aim has been to mobilize a critique of capitalist logics and rhetorics that have been made commonsense for far too long.

Figure 6.1 David Antonio Cruz, *Puerto Rican Pieta en la calle de la Fortaleza*, 2006. Oil on canvas with wood frame, 80 1/2 x 78 3/4 x 4 1/2 inches. Collection of El Museo del Barrio, New York. Museum purchase through a gift from the Jacques and Natasha Gelman Foundation, 2015. Installation view, 2023. Institute of Contemporary Art, University of Pennsylvania. Photo by Constance Mensh. Courtesy of the artist and Monique Meloche Gallery.

My larger aim beyond critique has been to articulate various indolent strategies and blueprints for imagining alternative pasts, presents, and futures distinct from the interlocking oppressive structures that are white supremacy, homophobia, transphobia, patriarchy, and capitalism.

By way of conclusion, I turn to one final indolent interlocutor, David Antonio Cruz, in particular, his painting *Puerto Rican Pieta en la calle de la Fortaleza* (see fig. 6.1). Riffing off the Pietà sculpture in Saint Peter's Basilica in Vatican City, the painting is a self-portrait of Cruz and his mother. Cruz, with puckered lips and cocky demeanor, lies lavishly on his mother's lap, her hands resting on his chest and shoulders, his hands brushing tenderly against her skin. The Puerto Rican mother holds the queer Puerto Rican child, lovingly protective. Both stare at the viewer while seated on a yellow couch, all rest and relaxation.

Couches and chaises figure prominently in Cruz's portraits. Queer subjects indulgently lounge on them, typically cozying up to one another, with "bodies in postures at once surprising yet also undeniably comfortable," as one reviewer summarizes.[6] Cruz's portraits remind us how couches are a furniture made to relax in, to lounge and laze, taking time to be with oneself or in the company of beloveds. Couches signify the temporality of rest and time off from waged labor, the symbolic antithesis of furniture like the office chair, which denotes work and exhaustion. Cruz's couches visually materialize as queer, nonwhite, and antiwork fixtures, signaling a distinctly lush and cushiony space-time created by the portraits.

Work has no dominion in portraits like *Puerto Rican Pieta en la calle de la Fortaleza*. The organizing logic of Cruz's lazing, languorous paintings is not that of waged labor, productivism, or capitalist profit above all else. The viewer gets a taste of an indolent something else. The pleasantness of a mother embracing her queer child, as he basks in all his sassy, sensual fullness. The pleasure of lounging on a couch or chaise, limbs and muscles and tissue in total repose, a lax levity. An indolent sensibility, where people can roam about more slowly, more appreciatively, more pleasurably, fostering relations between one another and the world they inhabit, without capitalist mandate, capitalism's drive to facilitate every facet of human experience and life.

Nobody wants to work anymore, so goes the billionaire's proverb. Let us take them at their word. If nobody wants to work anymore, then what comes next? The billion-dollar question we need to keep on asking.

Acknowledgments

This book was completed with the generous support from a Career Enhancement Fellowship for Junior Faculty from the Institute for Citizens and Scholars. I am infinitely grateful to the Mellon Foundation and Adelphi University for sponsoring the sabbatical required to focus on this project. I am also thankful to the Ford Foundation for supporting my early research into what would become this book. These multiple institutions have been integral to the completion of this research.

There are many who have guided my thinking on this project throughout the years. Lawrence La Fountain–Stokes, Francisco Galarte, and Ramón H. Rivera-Servera provided generously thorough and challenging feedback that has made this book all the better. I had the opportunity to present versions of this research at annual meetings of the Latinx Studies Association and the Modern Language Association and American Comparative Literature Association and at the US Latinx Literary Theory and Criticism Conference. My co-panelists and those colleagues in attendance helped improve and clarify my thinking. Various mentors and friends at CUNY who nurtured the first seeds: Kandice Chuh, Wayne Koestenbaum, Eric Lott, and Karl Steel. My colleagues at Adelphi University have been amazingly encouraging and supportive of this project. Kerry Webb has been a tremendously encouraging and supportive editor since day one. All my thanks to the staff at the University of Texas Press, whose work and dedication shepherded this book into existence, especially Christina Vargas, who fielded many of my queries related to the process. Lauren Abramo, my fabulous agent, whose unwavering support for all I do sustains me. And my gratitude to the many who nurtured my thinking and spirit along the way, a partial list of whom includes K'eguro Macharia, Joe Osmundson, Alex Polish, Christopher Gonzalez, Urayoán Noel, Jennifer Baker, Elan Abitbol, and Tatiana Milcent.

My father, Santiago, who taught me that work is not everything in life. Never everything.

Emmanuel, whose wisdom sharpened my ideas, whose kindness lifted me when I felt down and out, whose care kept me grounded. Con tanto amor.

Notes

Introduction

1. CS/CS/SB 1718: Immigration, Florida Senate (2023), https://www.flsenate.gov/Session/Bill/2023/1718.

2. Prem Thakker, "Florida Republicans Admit They Made a Big Mistake with Anti-immigrant Law," *New Republic*, June 5, 2023, https://newrepublic.com/post/173247/florida-republicans-admit-made-big-mistake-anti-immigrant-law.

3. elmannyviejero, "Before and After Inmigrants [sic] Workers Leave Florida Fields," TikTok, May 9, 2023, https://www.tiktok.com/@elmannyviajero/video/7231285360335113518.

4. Michael Dango, *Crisis Style: The Aesthetics of Repair* (Stanford, CA: Stanford University Press, 2022), 33.

5. Herman Melville, "Bartleby, the Scrivener," in *Billy Budd, Bartleby, and Other Stories* (New York: Penguin, 2016), 34.

6. Melville, "Bartleby," 35.

7. Melville, "Bartleby," 45.

8. Kathi Weeks, *The Problem with Work: Feminism, Marxism, Antiwork Politics, and Postwork Imaginaries* (Durham, NC: Duke University Press, 2011), 11.

9. Weeks, *Problem with Work*, 124.

10. Gigi Roggero, *Italian Operaismo: Genealogy, History, Method*, trans. Clara Pope (Cambridge, MA: MIT Press, 2023), 159–160.

11. Steve Wright, *Storming Heaven: Class Composition and Struggle in Italian Autonomist Marxism* (London: Pluto Press, 2017), 210.

12. Mario Tronti, *Workers and Capital*, trans. David Broder (New York: Verso, 2019), 221.

13. Tronti, *Workers and Capital*, 231.

14. Melville, "Bartleby," 29.

15. Melville, "Bartleby," 32.

16. Melville, "Bartleby," 32.

17. Melville, "Bartleby," 48.

18. Jacopo Galimberti, *Images of Class: Operaismo, Autonomia and the Visual Arts (1962–1988)* (New York: Verso, 2022), 13.

19. Sarah Jaffe, *Work Won't Love You Back: How Devotion to Our Jobs Keeps Us Exploited, Exhausted, and Alone* (New York: Bold Type Books, 2021).

20. Amelia Horgan, *Lost in Work: Escaping Capitalism* (London: Pluto Press, 2021), 54.

21. Jaffe, *Work Won't Love You Back*, 9.

22. Jennifer Ponce de León, *Another Aesthetics Is Possible: Arts of Rebellion in the Fourth World War* (Durham, NC: Duke University Press, 2021), 29.

23. Jaffe, *Work Won't Love You Back*, 18.

24. Paul Lafargue, *The Right to Be Lazy: And Other Writings* (New York: New York Review of Books, 2023), 5.

25. Lafargue, *Right to Be Lazy*, 35.

26. Bertrand Russell, *In Praise of Idleness, and Other Essays* (New York: Routledge, 2004), 3.

27. Devon Price, *Laziness Does Not Exist* (New York: Atria, 2021), 9.

28. Price, *Laziness*, 206.

29. Jenny Odell, *How to Do Nothing: Resisting the Attention Economy* (Brooklyn: Melville House, 2019), xviii.

30. Odell, *How to Do Nothing*, 12, 198.

31. Karl Marx, *Capital Volume 1* (New York: Penguin, 1992), 381.

32. L. H. Stallings, *Funk the Erotic: Transaesthetics and Black Sexual Cultures* (Urbana: University of Illinois Press, 2015), 14.

33. Brian O'Connor, *Idleness: A Philosophical Essay* (Princeton, NJ: Princeton University Press, 2018), 5.

34. Tung-Hui Hu, *Digital Lethargy: Dispatches from an Age of Disconnection* (Cambridge, MA: MIT Press, 2022), xxvii.

35. Pierre Saint-Amand, *The Pursuit of Laziness: An Idle Interpretation of the Enlightenment*, trans. Jennifer Curtiss Gage (Princeton, NJ: Princeton University Press, 2011), 123.

36. Nick Salvato, *Obstruction* (Durham, NC: Duke University Press, 2016), 19.

37. Salvato, *Obstruction*, 69.

38. Immanuel Kant, *An Answer to the Question: "What Is Enlightenment?,"* trans. H. B. Nisbet (London: Penguin Books, 2009), 1.

39. Kant, *Answer to the Question*, 1.

40. Kant, *Answer to the Question*, 2.

41. Kant, *Answer to the Question*, 4.

42. Michel Foucault, "What Is Enlightenment?," in *The Foucault Reader*, ed. Paul Rabinow (New York: Vintage, 2010), 34.

43. Foucault, "What Is Enlightenment?," 35.

44. Roger Scruton, *Kant: A Very Short Introduction* (London: Oxford University Press, 2001), 97.

45. Kant, *Critique of Judgement*, (London: Oxford University Press, 2007) 109.

46. Kant, *Critique of Judgement*, 88.

47. Kant, *Critique of Judgement*, 102–103.

48. Kant, *Critique of Judgement*, 106.

49. Kant, *Critique of Judgement*, 103.

50. Kant, *Critique of Judgement*, 123.

51. Kant, *Critique of Judgement*, 180.

52. Kant, *Critique of Judgement*, 132.

53. Georg Wilhelm Friedrich Hegel, *Introductory Lectures on Aesthetics* (New York: Penguin, 1993), 43.

54. When it comes to parsing the question of *what is man*, the *Anthropology* "is of great interest, but disappointing," as one scholar of Kant notes, though no explanation is provided for the harsh assessment. One wonders if such dismissal is due to the fact the *Anthropology* skews too heavily into human matters, is too exposing of the subjective, particular, and embodied philosopher behind the curtain. See Karl Jaspers, *Kant* (New York: Harcourt Brace 1957), 93.

55. Immanuel Kant, *Anthropology from a Pragmatic Point of View* (Cambridge: Cambridge University Press, 2006), 176.

56. Kant, *Anthropology*, 176–177.

57. Michel Foucault, *Introduction to Kant's Anthropology* (South Pasadena, CA: Semiotext(e), 2008), 97.

58. Sarah Jane Cervenak, *Wandering: Philosophical Performances of Racial and Sexual Freedom* (Durham, NC: Duke University Press, 2014), 58.

59. Robert Bernasconi, quoted in Cervenak, *Wandering*, 28.

60. Cervenak, *Wandering*, 28.

61. Cervenak, *Wandering*, 44.

62. Kant, *Anthropology*, 128.

63. Kant only makes this one mention of "South Americans," and it is in the annotated remarks Kant made postpublication to *Observations on the Feeling of the Beautiful and Sublime*. See Immanuel Kant, *Observations on the Feeling of the Beautiful and Sublime and Other Writings* (Cambridge: Cambridge University Press, 2011), 181.

64. Kant, *Observations*, 59.

65. Kant, *Observations*, 58.

66. Tom Lutz, *Doing Nothing: A History of Loafers, Loungers, Slackers, and Bums in America* (New York: Farrar, Straus and Giroux, 2006), 53.

67. José Esteban Muñoz, *Cruising Utopia: The Then and There of Queer Futurity* (New York: New York University Press, 2009), 1.

68. John Sharp and David Thomas distinguish between hedonic and eudaemonic experiences in the playing of video games. Hedonic experience is nonutilitarian, undertaken for the sake of their own enjoyment, with no larger purpose in mind. In contrast, eudaimonic experiences "have an outcome in addition to the experience itself," are "tangibly unproductive," and are "pleasurable but only so long as they fit within a larger purview of personal excellence or ethical living or both." See John Sharp and David Thomas, *Fun, Taste, and Games: An Aesthetics of the Idle, Unproductive, and Otherwise Playful* (Cambridge, MA: MIT Press, 2019), 49.

69. Thorstein Veblen, *Theory of the Leisure Class* (London: Oxford World's Classics, 2007), 27.

70. O'Connor, *Idleness*, 7–8.

71. Ross Chambers, *Loiterature* (Lincoln: University of Nebraska Press, 1999), 9.

72. Chambers, *Loiterature*, 9.

73. Chambers, *Loiterature*, 10.

74. Chambers, *Loiterature*, 11.

75. La Marr Jurelle Bruce, "Shore, Unsure: Loitering as a Way of Life," *GLQ: A Journal of Gay and Lesbian Studies* 25, no. 2 (2019): 353.

76. Antonio Viego, *Dead Subjects: Toward a Politics of Loss in Latino Studies* (Durham, NC: Duke University Press, 2007), 6.

77. José Esteban Muñoz, *The Sense of Brown* (Durham, NC: Duke University Press, 2020), 11.
78. Muñoz, *Sense of Brown*, 39.
79. Marcos Gonsalez, "José Muñoz's *The Sense of Brown*," *ASAP/Journal*, 2020, https://asapjournal.com/review/jose-munozs-the-sense-of-brown-marcos-gonsalez.
80. Joshua Javier Guzmán, "Brown," in *Keywords for Latina/o Studies*, ed. Deborah R. Vargas, Nancy Raquel Mirabal, and Lawrence La Fountain–Stokes (New York: New York University Press, 2017), 25.
81. Ellis Neyra, "The Question of Ethics in the Semiotics of Brownness," *SX Salon*, October 2020, http://smallaxe.net/sxsalon/discussions/question-ethics-semiotics-brownness.
82. Alan Pelaez Lopez, "The X in Latinx Is a Wound, Not a Trend," *Color Bloq*, September 2018, https://www.colorbloq.org/article/the-x-in-latinx-is-a-wound-not-a-trend.
83. Lorgia García-Peña, "Dismantling Anti-Blackness Together," NACLA, June 8, 2020, https://nacla.org/news/2020/06/09/dismantling-anti-blackness-together.
84. Yomaira Figueroa-Vásquez, *Decolonizing Diasporas: Radical Mappings of Afro-Atlantic Literature* (Evanston, IL: Northwestern University Press, 2020), 4.
85. Miriam Jiménez Román and Juan Flores, introduction to *The Afro-Latin@ Reader: History and Culture in the United States* (Durham, NC: Duke University Press, 2010), 15.
86. Dora Silva Santana, "*Mais Viva!* Reassembling Transness, Blackness, and Feminism," *TSQ: Transgender Studies Quarterly* 6, no. 2 (2019): 218.
87. Leticia Alvarado, *Abject Performances: Aesthetic Strategies in Latino Cultural Production* (Durham, NC: Duke University Press, 2018), 11.
88. Marissa K. López, *Racial Immanence: Chicanx Bodies beyond Representation* (New York: New York University Press, 2019), 15.
89. Frances R. Aparicio, "(Re)constructing Latinidad: The Challenge of Latina/o Studies," in *The New Latino Studies Reader: A Twenty-First-Century Perspective*, ed. Ramón A. Gutiérrez and Tomás Almaguer (Oakland: University of California Press, 2016), 62.
90. Carlos Ulises Decena, *Tacit Subjects: Belonging and Same-Sex Desire among Dominican Immigrant Men* (Durham, NC: Duke University Press, 2011), 70.
91. Joshua Chambers-Letson, *After the Party: A Manifesto for Queer of Color Life* (New York: New York University Press, 2018), 19.
92. Dixa Ramírez, *Colonial Phantoms: Belonging and Refusal in the Dominican Americas, from the 19th Century to the Present* (New York: New York University Press, 2018), 164.
93. Kadji Amin, *Disturbing Attachments: Genet, Modern Pederasty, and Queer History* (Durham, NC: Duke University Press, 2017), 10.
94. Juana María Rodríguez, *Sexual Futures, Queer Gestures, and Other Latina Longings* (New York: New York University Press, 2014), 4.

Chapter 1: Glimpsing Angie Xtravaganza

1. *Paris Is Burning*, directed by Jennie Livingston (1990; New York: Criterion Collection, 2020), Blu-ray.
2. Lucas Hilderbrand, *Paris Is Burning* (Vancouver, BC: Arsenal Pulp Press, 2021), 122.
3. bell hooks, *Black Looks: Race and Representation* (New York: Routledge, 1992), 152.

4. See Jesse Green, "Paris Has Burned," *New York Times*, April 18, 1993, https://www.nytimes.com/1993/04/18/style/paris-has-burned.html.

5. José Esteban Muñoz, *Disidentifications: Queers of Color and the Performance of Politics* (Minneapolis: University of Minnesota Press, 1999), 162.

6. Muñoz, *Sense of Brown*, 139.

7. Judith Butler, *Bodies That Matter* (New York: Routledge, 1993), 88.

8. See Jules Gill-Peterson, "General Editor's Introduction," *Transgender Studies Quarterly* 8, no. 4 (2021): 413.

9. Jay Prosser, "Judith Butler: Queer Feminism, Transgender, and the Transubstantiation of Sex," in *The Transgender Studies Reader*, ed. Susan Stryker and Stephen Whittle (New York: Routledge, 2006), 277.

10. Jian Neo Chen, *Trans Exploits: Trans of Color Cultures and Technologies in Movement* (Durham, NC: Duke University Press, 2019), 36.

11. *Oxford English Dictionary Online*, s.v. "otiose, adj.," accessed September 2023, https://doi.org/10.1093/OED/1820282217.

12. D. A. Miller, *Second Time Around: From Art House to DVD* (New York: Columbia University Press, 2021), 15.

13. Boyd McDonald, *Cruising the Movies: A Sexual Guide to Oldies on TV* (South Pasadena, CA: Semiotext(e), 2015), 293.

14. Jeffrey Geiger, "Intimate Media: New Queer Documentary and the Sensory Turn," *Studies in Documentary Film* 14, no. 3 (2020): 196.

15. Geiger, "Intimate Media," 198.

16. Gill-Peterson, "General Editor's Introduction," 414.

17. Cole Rizki, "Latin/x American Trans Studies: Toward a Travesti-Trans Analytic," *TSQ: Transgender Studies Quarterly* 6, no. 2 (2019): 149.

18. Silva Santana, *"Mais Viva!,"* 211.

19. Giancarlo Cornejo, *"Travesti* Dreams Outside in the Ethnographic Machine," *GLQ: A Journal of Lesbian and Gay Studies* 25, no. 3 (2019): 458.

20. Franciso J. Galarte, *Brown Trans Figurations: Rethinking Race, Gender, and Sexuality in Chicanx/Latinx Studies* (Austin: University of Texas Press, 2021), 131.

21. L. Heidenreich, *Nepantla Squared: Transgender Mestiz@ Histories in Times of Global Shift* (Lincoln: University of Nebraska Press, 2020), 45.

22. Erika Balsam and Hila Peleg, "Introduction: The Documentary Attitude," in *Documentary across Disciplines*, ed. Balsom and Peleg (Cambridge, MA: MIT Press, 2016), 13.

23. C. Riley Snorton, *Black on Both Sides: A Racial History of Trans Identity* (Minneapolis: University of Minnesota Press, 2017), 183.

24. Saidiya Hartman, *Wayward Lives, Beautiful Experiments: Intimate Histories of Social Upheaval* (New York: W. W. Norton 2019), 33.

25. Saidiya Hartman, "Venus in Two Acts," *Small Axe* 12, no. 26 (2008): 12.

26. LaVelle Ridley, "Imagining Otherly: Performing Possible Black Trans Futures in Tangerine," *TSQ: Transgender Studies Quarterly* 6, no. 4 (2019): 482–483.

27. Marquis Bey, *Black Trans Feminism* (Durham, NC: Duke University Press, 2022), 23.

28. Bey, *Black Trans Feminism*, 60.

29. micha cárdenas, *Poetic Operations: Trans of Color Art in Digital Media* (Durham, NC: Duke University Press, 2022), 25.

30. Lawrence La Fountain-Stokes, *Translocas: The Politics of Puerto Rican Drag and Trans Performance* (Ann Arbor: University of Michigan Press, 2021), 47.

31. Leah Devun and Zeb Tortorici, "Trans, Time, and History," *TSQ: Transgender Studies Quarterly* 5, no. 4 (2018): 535.

32. See Marta V. Vicente for more on how transgender as a category can work to suppress other identificatory terminology and applications of gendered variance across social, historical, and geographical locations: Marta V. Vicente, "Transgender: A Useful Category? Or, How the Historical Study of 'Transsexual' and 'Transvestite' Can Help Us Rethink 'Transgender' as Category," *TSQ: Transgender Studies Quarterly* 8, no. 4 (2021): 426–442.

33. Giancarlo Cornejo, "Thinking *Travesti* Tears: Reading *Loxoro*," *Camera Obscura* 36, no. 3 (2021): 54.

34. Joseph Cassara, *The House of Impossible Beauties* (New York: Ecco Press, 2018), 140.

35. Michael Cunningham, "The Slap of Love," *Open City*, accessed January 12, 2024, https://opencity.org/archive/issue-6/the-slap-of-love.

36. Cassara, *House of Impossible Beauties*, 275.

37. Cassara, *House of Impossible Beauties*, 245.

38. The author's note reminds the reader: "The portraits of the characters who appear in this story, along with the events and journeys covered, should not be taken as a historical record."

39. The page location: https://www.facebook.com/AngieXtravaganza.

40. Emmett Harsin Drager and Lucas Platero, "At the Margins of Time and Place: Transsexuals and Transvestites in Trans Studies," *TSQ: Transgender Studies Quarterly* 8, no. 4 (2021): 420.

41. Robb Hernández, "Chasing Papi: A Study in Virulence and Virtuality," *TSQ: Transgender Studies Quarterly* 8, no. 1 (2021): 20–21.

Chapter 2: Lounge Lizard Aesthetics

1. Muñoz, *Cruising Utopia*, 97.

2. Muñoz, *Cruising Utopia*, 1.

3. Muñoz, *Cruising Utopia*, 113.

4. Reynaldo Rivera, *Reynaldo Rivera: Provisional Notes for a Disappeared City* (South Pasadena, CA: Semiotext(e), 2020), 22.

5. Tina M. Campt, *Listening to Images* (Durham, NC: Duke University Press, 2017), 9.

6. Celeste Fraser Delgado and José Esteban Muñoz, "Rebellions of Everynight Life," in *Everynight Life: Culture and Dance in Latin/o America*, ed. Delgado and Muñoz (Durham, NC: Duke University Press, 1997), 10.

7. Kemi Adeyemi, Kareem Khubchandani, and Ramón H. Rivera-Servera, introduction to *Queer Nightlife*, ed. Adeyemi, Khubchandani, and Rivera-Servera (Ann Arbor: University of Michigan Press, 2021), 7.

8. Ramón Rivera-Servera, "History in Drag: Latina/o Queer Affective Circuits in Chicago," in *The Latina/o Midwest Reader*, ed. Omar Valerio-Jiménez, Santiago R. Vaquera Vásquez, and Claire F. Fox (Urbana: University of Illinois Press, 2017), 191.

9. Rivera-Servera, "History in Drag," 193.

10. Richard T. Rodríguez, "Beyond Boystown: Latinidad on the Outskirts of Queer Chicago Nightlife," *Latino Studies* 18, no. 2 (2020): 279.

11. Kemi Adeyemi, "The Practice of Slowness: Black Queer Women and the Right to the City," *GLQ: A Journal of Lesbian and Gay Studies* 25, no. 4 (2019): 552.

12. Elizabeth Ferrer, *Latinx Photography in the United States: A Visual History* (Seattle: University of Washington Press, 2020), 67.

13. Though Rivera's photography was not the subject of study in David William Foster's monograph *Picturing the Barrio*, Foster examines the eminent role played by the urban barrio in the photographic oeuvres of various Chicanx photographers. Moreover, the urban scene has also been of considerable importance for queer artistic production and dissemination. In the case of Rivera, the urban scene provides a bountiful repository for photographic practice spotlighting nightlife, especially the nightlife cultures of those who are simultaneously raced, trans, and queer.

14. Rivera, *Provisional Notes*, 239.

15. Rivera, *Provisional Notes*, 26.

16. Rivera, *Provisional Notes*, 26.

17. Rivera, *Provisional Notes*, 26.

18. Rivera, *Provisional Notes*, 239.

19. Pierre Bourdieu, *Photography: A Middle-Brow Art* (Stanford, CA: Stanford University Press, 1990), 76.

20. John Berger, *Understanding a Photograph* (New York: Aperture, 2013), 57.

21. Eduardo Cadava, *Paper Graveyards* (Cambridge, MA: MIT Press, 2021), 113.

22. Elspeth H. Brown and Thy Phu, in their introduction to the anthology *Feeling Photography*, mount a defense of the role of feeling and affect in photography studies. Their intervention stresses how introducing feeling and affect into the study of photos does not, as more discourse-oriented analyses purport, diminish scholarly rigor or political saliency. Rather, as they contend, "feeling allows photo scholars a rich theoretical terrain to reimagine the complex relationship between images, power, and subjects." Elspeth H. Brown and Thy Phu, introduction to *Feeling Photography*, ed. Brown and Phu (Durham, NC: Duke University Press, 2014), 21.

23. Susan Sontag, *On Photography* (New York: Library of America, 2013), 554.

24. Sontag, *On Photography*, 554.

25. Christina Catherine Martínez, "Glitter for the Fire: How Reynaldo Rivera Chronicled the Chaotic Glamour of LA Nightlife," *Aperture*, no. 245, n.p.

26. Kareem Khubchandani, *Ishtyle: Accenting Gay Indian Nightlife* (Ann Arbor: University of Michigan Press, 2020), 23.

27. Rivera, *Provisional Notes*, 239.

28. Hagi Kenaan, *Photography and Its Shadow* (Stanford, CA: Stanford University Press, 2020), 30.

29. Discussing the portraits of Catherine Opie, Dana Seitler persuasively argues for how queer photographic practice conjures queerness in and as form, especially those formal properties frequently considered ornamental or superfluous. Though not applying a stringent or strong anti-identitarian and nonrepresentational analytic, Seitler posits how "the luxuriant folds, intricate patterns, and intense colors of [Opie's] backdrops become a measure of the figure's depth," where "they make identity manifest as something sensually perceptible." See Dana Seitler, "Making Sexuality Sensible: Tammy Rae Carland's and Catherine Opie's Queer Aesthetic Forms," in Brown and Phu, *Feeling Photography*, 58.

30. John Tagg, *The Burden of Representation: Essays on Photographies and Histories* (Minneapolis: University of Minnesota Press, 2021), 36.

31. Tagg, *Burden of Representation*, 37.

32. Eduardo Cadava and Cortés Rocca, "Notes on Love and Photography," in Cadava, *Paper Graveyards*, 161.

33. Rivera, *Provisional Notes*, 22.

34. C. Ondine Chavoya, introduction to *Chicano and Chicana Art: A Critical Anthology*, ed. Jennifer A. González, C. Ondine Chavoya, Chon A. Noriega, and Terecita Romo (Durham, NC: Duke University Press, 2019), 267.

35. For a compelling reading of how Chicano youth gang artists implemented graffiti art like placas, Chicano insignias that communicate messages via a stylized writing, across barrios, see Marcos Sánchez-Tranquilino, "Space, Power, and Youth Culture," in González et al., *Chicano and Chicana Art*.

36. Sandra de la Loza, "La Raza Cósmica: An Investigation into the Space of Chicana/o Muralism," in *L.A. Xicano*, ed. Chon A. Noriega, Terezita Romo, and Pilar Tompkins Rivas (Los Angeles: UCLA Chicano Studies Research Center Press, 2011), 61.

37. For a thorough analysis of the anti-queer and anti-trans attacks on *Por Vida* and the representational complexities the transmasculine figure draws up, see Galarte, "Introduction: Thinking Brown and Trans Together," in *Brown Transfigurations*, 1–22.

38. Robb Hernández, *Archiving an Epidemic: Art, AIDS, and the Queer Chicanx Avant Garde* (New York: New York University Press, 2019), 44.

39. During the initial onset of the COVID-19 pandemic in 2020, the New Jalisco Bar undertook a fundraising campaign to pay for rent and other expenses accrued due to the lockdown. Like many other queer bars across the United States during the COVID-19 pandemic, and even before, they were struggling to make ends meet and were at risk of shuttering their doors. Thankfully, they met the goal; however, the ongoing threat of rising rents and displacement, which have historically disproportionately threatened queer bars, looms.

Chapter 3: The Poetics of Latin Night

1. Roque Raquel Salas Rivera, *the tertiary / lo terciario* (Blacksburg, VA: Noemi Press, 2019), 50.

2. Salas Rivera, *the tertiary / lo terciario*, 52.

3. Salas Rivera, *the tertiary / lo terciario*, 53.

4. As the editors importantly point out in the introduction of the anthology *Queer Nightlife*, queer and trans nightlife scenes happen in bars, chat rooms, cafés, living rooms, social media, and a myriad of other sites. Nightlife spaces unfold in situated ways in response to geographical location, age, costs, and other parameters that queer and trans people must navigate in order to "go out."

5. Lawrence La Fountain–Stokes, "Queer Puerto Ricans and the Burdens of Violence," *QED: A Journal in GLBTQ Worldmaking* 3, no. 3 (2016): 99.

6. See Randell-Moon for more on how framing mass shootings in the twenty-first century with phrasal superlatives like "the worst mass shooting" occludes and disavows the long history of settler colonial mass killings of Indigenous, Black, and other nonwhite racialized peoples. Holly Randell-Moon, "Mediations of Security, Race, and Violence in the Pulse Nightclub Shooting: Homonationalism in Anti-immigration Times," *GLQ: A Journal of Lesbian and Gay Studies* 28, no. 1 (2022): 1–28.

7. See Doug Meyer, "Omar Mateen as US Citizen, Not Foreign Threat: Homonationalism and LGBTQ Online Representations of the Pulse Nightclub Shooting," *Sexualities* 23, no. 3 (2019): 249–268. The work of Hiram Pérez also bears mentioning for

how hate-based LGBTQ+ rights discourses were immediately invoked on behalf of a "gay modernity" threatened by Mateen's symbolic homophobic nonwhite backwardness, reifying, in the process, "complicities with U.S. empire." Hiram Pérez, *A Taste for Brown Bodies* (New York: New York University Press, 2015), 9.

8. For more on how the media reported on and represented the victims of the shooting, see Doug Meyer, "An Intersectional Analysis of LGBTQ Online Media Coverage of the Pulse Nightclub Shooting Victims," *Journal of Homosexuality* 67, no. 10 (2019): 1343–1366.

9. Jack Halberstam instructively analyzes the rhetorical strategies deployed in magazines like *The Atlantic*, which sought to create false dichotomies between the violences faced by queer communities and communities of color. Jack Halberstam, "Who Are 'We' After Orlando?," *Bully Bloggers*, June 22, 2016, https://bullybloggers.wordpress.com/2016/06/22/who-are-we-after-orlando-by-jack-halberstam.

10. Justin Torres, "In Praise of Latin Night at the Queer Club," *Washington Post*, June 13, 2016, https://www.washingtonpost.com/opinions/in-praise-of-latin-night-at-the-queer club/2016/06/13/e841867e-317b-11e6-95c0-2a6873031302_story.html.

11. Amanda Torres and William Orchard, "Poetry, Pulse, and the Anthology," *Post45*, January 21, 2020, https://post45.org/2020/01/poetry-pulse-and-the-anthology.

12. Belcourt, *A History of My Brief Body*, (Columbus, OH: Two Dollar Radio, 2020), 125; Edgar Gomez, *High-Risk Homosexual* (New York: Soft Skull, 2022).

13. Julia Leslie Guarch, "Shh. Shh. Be Quiet," in *Pulse/Pulso: In Remembrance of Orlando*, ed. Roy G. Guzmán and Miguel M. Morales (Richmond, VA: Damaged Goods Press, 2018), 22.

14. Baruch Porras-Hernandez, "Ceremonias De La Superviviencia," in Guzmán and Morales, *Pulse/Pulso*, 14.

15. Caridad Moro-Gronlier, "Pulse: A Memorial in Driftwood, Cannon Beach, OR," in Guzmán and Morales, *Pulse/Pulso*, 39.

16. Juana María Rodríguez, "Pulse," *GLQ: A Journal of Lesbian and Gay Studies* 24, no. 1 (2018): 51.

17. Rodríguez, "Pulse," 53.

18. Chris Soto, "All the Dead Boys Look Like Me," in *Bullets into Bells: Poets and Citizens Respond to Gun Violence*, ed. Brian Clements, Alexandra Teague, and Dean Rader (Boston: Beacon Press, 2017), 153.

19. This unthinkability is paramount given the widespread reporting of the shooting, which sought to exclusively frame the event as an attack against a racially unmarked LGBTQ+ community, rather than a specifically racialized and Latinx population. Michael Hames-García's critique of queer theory's elisions of race in efforts to maintain an epistemologically pure sense of queerness proves instructive for why Pulse needs to be considered along multiple vectors of social difference. Michael Hames-García, "Queer Theory Revisited," in *Gay Latino Studies: A Critical Reader*, ed. Michael Hames-García and Ernesto Javier Martínez (Durham, NC: Duke University Press, 2011), 19–45.

20. Nolan Kline and Christopher Cuevas assess how the erasure of queer and trans Latinx Orlando populations from popular invocations of Pulse required local queer- and trans of color–focused organizations to bear the bulk of the responsibility to address and serve the needs of queer and trans Latinx Orlandoans in absence of state-based support and care. See Nolan Kline and Christohper Cuevas, "Resisting Identity

Erasure after Pulse: Intersectional LGBTQ+ Latinx Activism in Orlando, FL," *Chiricú Journal: Latina/o Literatures, Arts, and Cultures* 2, no. 2 (2018): 68–71.

21. Lawrence La Fountain-Stokes, "Queering Latina/o Literature," in *The Cambridge Companion to Latina/o American Literature*, ed. John Morán González (Cambridge: Cambridge University Press, 2016), 178–194.

22. See Alicia Gaspar de Alba, "Thirty Years of Chicana/Latina Lesbian Literary Production," in *The Routledge Companion to Latina/o Literature*, ed. Suzanne Bost and Frances R. Aparicio (New York: Routledge, 2013), 462–475.

23. Kristen Silva Gruesz, "What Was Latino Literature?," *PMLA* 127, no. 2 (2012): 336.

24. See Doug P. Bush's *Capturing Mariposas: Reading Cultural Schema in Gay Chicano Literature* (Columbus: Ohio State University Press, 2019) for a thorough examination into how identity-based literature designations prove useful for marketing, studying, and building readerships for minoritized writers.

25. María Josefina Saldaña-Portillo, "Latina/o Literature: The Borders Are Burning," in *The Cambridge History of Latina/o American Literature*, ed. John Morán González and Laura Lomas (Cambridge: Cambridge University Press, 2018), 741.

26. I am thinking here of scholarly studies on how literature depicts 9/11 or how the aftermaths of 9/11 take shape as a literary phenomenon. For example, Martin Randall's *9/11 and the Literature of Terror* (2011) and Georgiana Banita's *Plotting Justice: Narrative Ethics and Literary Culture after 9/11* (2012) demonstrate how 9/11 is aesthetically rendered and mediated, with novels and fiction being the primary genre in which scholars reckon with representing and accounting for 9/11.

27. The literatures of 9/11 are predominately concentrated around the novel genre, while the literatures of Pulse find their rendering as poetry.

28. The literatures of Pulse also notably participate in "pinpointing a series of issues that articulate beyond identitarian politics," as Elijah Adiv Edelman calls for in how we can mobilize queer and trans activism in the post-Pulse moment, being that identitarian calls for social justice overwhelmingly rely on homonormative and homonationalist logics that only "maintain systems of inequality." Elijah Adiv Edelman, "Why We Forget the Pulse Nightclub Murders: Bodies That (Never) Matter and a Call for Coalitional Models of Queer and Trans Social Justice," *GLQ: A Journal of Lesbian and Gay Studies* 24, no. 1 (2018): 34.

29. Ralph E. Rodriguez, *Latinx Literature Unbound: Undoing Ethnic Expectation* (New York: Fordham University Press, 2018), 12.

30. Sandra K. Soto, *Reading Chican@ Like a Queer: The De-mastery of Desire* (Austin: University of Texas Press, 2010), 18.

31. Ricardo L. Ortiz, *Latinx Literature Now: Between Evanescent and Event* (Palgrave Macmillan, 2019), 80.

32. Christopher González, *Permissible Narratives: The Promise of Latino/a Literature* (Columbus: Ohio State University Press, 2017), 8.

33. See Ernesto Javier Martínez for more on how queer of color realist knowledge production creates alternative schemas of intelligibility. Ernesto Javier Martínez, *On Making Sense: Queer Race Narratives of Intelligibility* (Stanford, CA: Stanford University Press, 2012).

34. Gloria Anzaldúa and Cherríe Moraga, "Entering the Lives of Others: Theory in the Flesh," in *This Bridge Called My Back: Writings by Radical Women of Color*, 4th ed. (Albany: State University of New York Press, 2015), 19.

35. Maya Chinchilla, "Church at Night," in Guzmán and Morales, *Pulse/Pulso*, 12.

36. Chinchilla, "Church at Night," 11.

37. "[Queer nightlife spaces] can also be sites of alienation that are circumscribed by normative modes of exclusion," note Adeyemi, Khubchandani, and Rivera-Servera in the introduction to *Queer Nightlife* (2–3). The all-too-familiar isms and phobias constituting the world writ large also shape queer and trans nightlife: "Who then comes out at night, capitalizes on its flexibility and ambiguity, and risks the surveillance that penetrates the darkness?"

38. Chinchilla, "Church at Night," 10–11.

39. Richard Blanco, "One Pulse—One Poem," in Clements, Teague, and Rader, *Bullets into Bells*, 18.

40. Chinchilla, "Church at Night," 10.

41. T. Jackie Cuevas, *Post-borderlandia: Chicana Literature and Gender Variant Critique* (New Brunswick, NJ: Rutgers University Press, 2018), 26.

42. Chinchilla, "Church at Night," 10.

43. Chinchilla, "Church at Night," 13.

44. Chinchilla, "Church at Night," 11.

45. Gomez, *High-Risk Homosexual*, 184.

46. Gomez, *High-Risk Homosexual*, 183.

47. Gomez, *High-Risk Homosexual*, 184.

48. María DeGuzmán, *Buenas Noches, American Culture: Latina/o Aesthetics of Night* (Bloomington: Indiana University Press, 2012), 30.

49. Che Gossett, "Silhouettes of Defiance: Memorializing Historical Sites of Queer and Transgender Resistance in an Age of Neoliberal Inclusivity," in *The Transgender Studies Reader 2*, ed. Susan Stryker and Aren Z. Aizura (New York: Routledge, 2013), 581.

50. Gossett, "Silhouettes of Defiance," 588.

51. The poem itself was originally published in the immediate aftermath of the Pulse shooting, which probably explains the narrative tone.

52. Roy G. Guzmán, "Restored Mural for Orlando," in *Catrachos* (Minneapolis, MN: Graywolf Press, 2020), 49.

53. Guzmán, "Restored Mural," 49.

54. Guzmán, "Restored Mural," 50.

55. Guzmán, "Restored Mural," 51.

56. Guzmán, "Restored Mural," 51.

57. Torres, "In Praise of Latin Night."

58. Ricardo L. Ortiz instructively notes how the use of the "you" throughout the essay enacts "an expressive performance of address that implicates the reader in a different kind of discursive exchange." The reader experiences what the poem recounts. Ricardo L. Ortiz, "Queer Latinx Studies and Queer Latinx Literature 'after' Queer Theory, or Thought and Art and Sex after Pulse," in *After Queer Studies: Literature, Theory and Sexuality in the 21st Century*, ed. Tyler Bradway and E. L. McCallum (Cambridge: Cambridge University Press, 2019), 53.

59. Torres, "In Praise of Latin Night."

60. Chandan Reddy, *Freedom with Violence: Race, Sexuality, and the US State* (Durham, NC: Duke University Press, 2011), 8.

61. Torres, "In Praise of Latin Night."

62. Torres, "In Praise of Latin Night."

63. Torres, "In Praise of Latin Night."
64. Torres, "In Praise of Latin Night."

Chapter 4: Slacking Off on the Main Stage

1. *Vogue México y Latinoamérica*, "Ella es Valentina, conocida drag queen de *RuPaul's Drag Race*: 'Es bello ser diferente,'" YouTube, April 1, 2019, https://www.youtube.com/watch?v=ALa7l7koINs.

2. For an incisive assessment of the neoliberal positivism displayed by RuPaul and the management of racialized difference the show undertakes in season 1, see Matthew Goldmark, "National Drag: The Language of Inclusion in *RuPaul's Drag Race*," *GLQ: A Journal of Lesbian and Gay Studies* 21, no. 4 (2015): 501–520.

3. I play up the multivalent meanings of words like *spectacle* and *spectacular* throughout. Valentina is a spectacle and is spectacular both at once: hypervisible, hypertheatrical, and a fantastic drag star who knows how to wow an audience. However, spectacle and spectacularity—often barely perceptible—also do subversive work, as seen in the ways Valentina presents her trans and queer Latinxness, which effectively scrambles the televisual logics of *Drag Race* and US popular-cultural consumption. I toggle between these various spectra that Valentina's spectacularity invites.

4. Édouard Glissant, *Poetics of Relation*, trans. Betsy Wing (Ann Arbor: University of Michigan Press, 2010).

5. *Oxford English Dictionary Online*, s.v. "obfuscate," accessed September 2022, https://www.oed.com/view/Entry/129592.

6. Amy Villarejo, "Adorno by the Pool; or, Television Then and Now," *Social Text* 34, no. 3 (2016): 80.

7. Nick Salvato, *Television Scales* (Goleta, CA: Punctum Books, 2019).

8. For more on how reality television negotiates authenticity and truth, see Leigh H. Edwards, *Triumph of Reality TV: The Revolution in American Television* (Santa Barbara, CA: Praeger, 2013); and Jon Kraszewski, *Reality TV* (New York: Routledge, 2017).

9. See Susan Stryker's important essay "Institutionalizing Trans* Studies at the University of Arizona" on the labor involved in establishing one of the first transgender studies programs at a university, and why that is crucially important for the continuing work to develop trans studies and curricula. Susan Stryker, "Institutionalizing Trans* Studies at the University of Arizona," *TSQ: Transgender Studies Quarterly* 7, no. 3 (2020): 354–366.

10. For example, Grace Lavery incisively formulates how early queer theory published by those like Eve Sedgwick helped propagate a "construction of queer universalism" that was "predicated on the impossibilization of transition." Grace Lavery, "Egg Theory's Early Style," *TSQ: Transgender Studies Quarterly* 7, no. 3 (2020): 395.

11. Snorton, *Black on Both Sides*.

12. Jules Gill-Peterson, "Trans of Color Critique before Transsexuality," *Transgender Studies Quarterly* 5, no. 4 (2018): 615.

13. Chen, *Trans Exploits*, 7.

14. Galarte, *Brown Trans Figurations*, 15.

15. Joseph M. Pierce, "I Monster: Embodying Trans and Travesti Resistance in Latin America," *Latin American Review* 55, no. 2 (2020): 318.

16. Malú Machuca Rose, "Giuseppe Campuzano's Afterlife: Toward a Travesti Methodology for Critique, Care, and Radical Resistance," *TSQ: Transgender Studies Quarterly* 6, no. 2 (2019): 242.

17. Machuca Rose, "Giuseppe Campuzano's Afterlife," 242.

18. *RuPaul's Drag Race*, season 9, episode 9, "Your Pilot's on Fire."

19. These confessional, direct-to-camera commentaries, and their subsequent sampling on social media, produce what Grobe describes as a "self [that] is not only 'performative,' but something literally to be performed; that it can never be captured, only conjured in live performance with the help of dead media; and that roleplay—especially the 'inverted Method acting' of people playing themselves—can reveal as much as it obscures" (187). Through the confessional format, the queens perform themselves, exaggeratedly so, and then become humorous fodder for digital media for a mass online audience. Christopher Grobe, *The Art of Confession: The Performance of Self from Robert Lowell to Reality TV* (New York: New York University Press, 2017).

20. June Deery defines reality television as "relations between the camera, the participants, and the viewers." June Deery, *Reality TV* (Cambridge: Polity, 2015), 3. *RuPaul's Drag Race* fits perfectly into this definition and, as I would argue, even exceeds such parameters because of its international branding and crossover status appealing to both LGBTQ+ and cishet audiences. *Drag Race* has produced its own fandom universe, highly intricate and networked, which is enthusiastically supported and engaged with by a global audience.

21. See this post by u/OvernightSiren on Reddit, which contains a screenshot of Valentina's Instagram address to fans about the mask incident. u/OvernightSiren, "Valentina Opens Up about Maskgate," Reddit, July 26, 2020, 3:32 p.m., https://www.reddit.com/r/RPDRDRAMA/comments/hyd51z/valentina_opens_up_about_maskgate.

22. In a 2019 profile conducted in *Vogue México y Latinoamérica*, it is noted that Valentina studied fashion design in college. Many of her outfits and accessories are handmade. Roberto Sierra Román, "James y Valentina, una fuerza dual," *Vogue México y Latinoamérica*, April 19, 2019, https://www.vogue.mx/moda/articulo/valentina-drag-queen-en-vogue-mexico.

23. Edwards, *Triumph of Reality TV*, 54.

24. Eliza Steinbock, *Shimmering Images: Trans Cinema, Embodiment, and the Aesthetics of Change* (Durham, NC: Duke University Press, 2019), 17.

25. Katherine Sender, *The Makeover: Reality TV and Reflexive Audiences* (New York: New York University Press, 2012), 6.

26. Laurie Ouellette, *Lifestyle TV* (New York: Routledge, 2016), 5.

27. Cory G. Collins summarizes the economic and aesthetic biases of the show that *RuPaul's Drag Race* downplays or omits from view. Cory G. Collins, "Drag Race to the Bottom? Updated Notes on the Aesthetic and Political Economy of *RuPaul's Drag Race*," *TSQ: Transgender Studies Quarterly* 4, no. 1 (2017): 128–134.

28. *RuPaul's Drag Race: Untucked!*, season 8, episode 9, "Your Pilot's on Fire."

29. *RuPaul's Drag Race: Untucked!*, season 8, episode 9, "Your Pilot's on Fire."

30. For more on the technical aspects of producing the *Drag Race* show, see Bean Urquhart, "These Nineteen Crazy Production Secrets Reveal Exactly How RuPaul's Drag Race Is Filmed," *The Tab*, April 10, 2020, https://thetab.com/uk/2020/04/10/rupauls-drag-race-production-secrets-151703.

31. Vanessa Angélica Villarreal, "Valentina's Downfall on 'Rupaul's Drag Race' Revealed Some Ugly Truths about the Show," *Buzzfeed*, September 25, 2017, https://www.buzzfeednews.com/article/olliphant/valentina-rupauls-drag-race.

32. Many strains of queer theory glorify failure as a means of critiquing

aspirational forms of normalcy tied to neoliberal capitalism. Though I find these studies intellectually interesting and provocative, I don't subscribe to failure writ large as a means of countering such restrictive logics, especially for queer and trans people of color.

33. For a foundational and thorough engagement with Latinx stereotype and stereotyping in US film and TV across the twentieth century, see Charles Ramírez Berg, *Latino Images in Film: Stereotypes, Subversion, Resistance* (Austin: University of Texas Press, 2002).

34. Mary C. Beltrán, *Latina/o Stars in U.S. Eyes: The Making and Meanings of Film and TV Stardom* (Urbana: University of Illinois Press, 2009), 12.

35. Isabel Molina-Guzmán, *Latinas and Latinos on TV: Colorblind Comedy in the Post Racial Network Era* (Tucson: University of Arizona Press, 2018), 10.

36. La Fountain-Stokes, *Translocas*, 47.

37. My analytic attention on Valentina follows Amy Villarejo's provocative proposition of "understanding more boldly what television can think, what it is possible to think on television, not just about television, for we are 'live' as television is, we live life as and through television." Amy Villarejo, *Ethereal Queer: Television, Historicity, Desire* (Durham, NC: Duke University Press, 2014), 11. Valentina activates a host of associations, memories, longings, politics, and other affect relations, which is precisely why I, and her fans, take an interest in her.

38. Mary C. Beltrán, "Television," in Vargas, Mirabal, and La Fountain-Stokes, *Keywords for Latina/o Studies*, 221.

39. *RuPaul's Drag Race*, season 9, episode 1, "Oh. My. Gaga!"

40. *RuPaul's Drag Race All Stars*, season 4, episode 2, "Super Girl Groups, Henny!"

41. *RuPaul's Drag Race*, season 9, episode 2, "She Done Already Done Brought It."

42. *RuPaul's Drag Race All Stars*, season 4, episode 1, "All Star Super Queen Variety Show."

43. *RuPaul's Drag Race*, "Meet Valentina: All About the Fantasy," YouTube, November 9, 2018, https://www.youtube.com/watch?v=m0pRkTFX66g.

44. *RuPaul's Drag Race All Stars*, season 4, episode 2, "Super Girl Groups, Henny!"

45. For a survey of the impact of popular telenovelas, and their attendant televisual styles, see June Carolyn Erlick, *Telenovelas in Pan-Latino Context* (New York: Routledge, 2018).

46. For the telenovela villain referencing, see "Meet Valentina."

47. Elaborating on ways of reading gendered variance and trans embodiment in mid-century sitcoms, Quinlan Miller explains that camp was not initiated by individuals sneakily trafficking in trans- and queer-related content; rather, it was integral to the production methods themselves: "Camp modes of production hinged on standardized industry practices rather than on specific auteurs. Patterns at play in characterization, casting, performance, and the construction of intertextual story worlds created an infrastructure for camp. . . . Methods of censoring nonconformity from TV screens can actually produce trans gender queer representation." Quinlan Miller, *Camp TV: Trans Gender Queer Sitcom History* (Durham, NC: Duke University Press, 2019), 125.

48. *RuPaul's Drag Race All Stars*, season 4, episode 3, "Snatch Game of Love."

49. *RuPaul's Drag Race All Stars*, season 4, episode 3, "Snatch Game of Love."

50. *RuPaul's Drag Race*, season 9, episode 6, "Snatch Game."

51. Marcia Ochoa, *Queen for a Day: Transformistas, Beauty Queens, and the Performance of Femininity in Venezuela* (Durham, NC: Duke University Press, 2014), 89.

52. *RuPaul's Drag Race All Stars*, season 4, episode 4, "Jersey Justice."
53. *RuPaul's Drag Race All Stars*, season 4, episode 6, "LaLaPaRUza."
54. For the original post and the subsequent replies that I discuss, see u/avp_1309, "Valentina in Season 9," Reddit, May 24, 2020, 3:52 p.m., https://www.reddit.com/r/rupaulsdragrace/comments/gpw4rf/valentina_in_season _9/?context=3.
55. *RuPaul's Drag Race*, "Valentina's Signature Look," YouTube, January 28, 2019, https://www.youtube.com/watch?v=S-xcjHS3wec.

Chapter 5: The Textures of Our Daydreaming

1. Justin Torres, *We the Animals* (New York: Mariner Books, 2011), 76.
2. Zorimar Rivera Montes, "'For Opacity'": Queerness and Latinidad in Justin Torres' *We the Animals*," *Latino Studies* 18, no. 2 (2020): 226.
3. Torres, *We the Animals*, 79.
4. Torres, *We the Animals*, 80–81.
5. Torres, *We the Animals*, 81.
6. Marion Christina Rohrleitner, "Refusing the Referendum: Queer Latino Masculinities and Utopian Citizenship in Justin Torres' *We the Animals*," *European Journal of American Studies* 11, no. 3 (2017): 7.
7. Alvarado, *Abject Performances*, 11.
8. T. Jackie Cuevas, "Fighting the Good Fight: Grappling with Queerness, Masculinities, and Violence in Contemporary Latinx Literature and Film," in *Decolonizing Latinx Masculinities*, ed. Arturo J. Aldama and Frederick Luis Aldama (Tucson: University of Arizona Press, 2020), 141.
9. Muñoz, *Sense of Brown*, 126–127.
10. Muñoz, *Sense of Brown*, 127.
11. Marcos Gonsalez, "Transmogrifying Guadalupes, Transmogrifying Selves: The Queer Inhumanist Aesthetics of Gloria Anzaldúa's *Light in the Dark / Luz en lo oscuro*," *ASAP/Journal* 6, no. 3 (2021): 631–651.
12. Mel Y. Chen, *Animacies: Biopolitics, Racial Mattering, and Queer Affect* (Durham, NC: Duke University Press, 2012), 2.
13. Chen, *Animacies*, 2.
14. Mel Y. Chen and Dana Luciano, "Introduction: Has the Queer Ever Been Human?," *GLQ: A Journal of Lesbian and Gay Studies* 21, nos. 2–3 (2015): 195.
15. Nathan Snaza, *Animate Literacies: Literature, Affect, and the Politics of Humanism* (Durham, NC: Duke University Press, 2019), 77.
16. Steve Mentz, "Brown," in *Prismatic Ecology: Ecotheory beyond Green*, ed. Jeffrey Jerome Cohen (Minneapolis: University of Minnesota Press, 2013), 193.
17. Julie Livingston and Jasbir Puar, "Interspecies," *Social Text* 29, no. 1 (2011): 7.
18. Karl Steel, *How Not to Make a Human: Pets, Feral Children, Worms, Sky Burial, Oysters* (Minneapolis: University of Minnesota Press, 2019), 109.
19. Rosamond S. King, *Island Bodies: Transgressive Sexualities in the Caribbean Imagination* (Gainesville: University Press of Florida, 2014), 19.
20. Eben Kirksey, Brandon Costelloe-Kuehn, and Dorion Sagan, "Life in the Age of Biotechnology," in *The Multispecies Salon*, ed. Eben Kirksey (Durham, NC: Duke University Press, 2014), 213.
21. Eva Hayward, "More Lessons from a Starfish: Prefixial Flesh and Transspeciated Selves," *Women's Studies Quarterly* 36, nos. 3–4 (2008): 76.
22. Hayward, "More Lessons," 77.

23. Mimi Sheller, *Citizenship from Below: Erotic Agency and Caribbean Freedom* (Durham, NC: Duke University Press, 2012), 17–18.

24. Ren Ellis Neyra, *The Cry of the Senses: Listening to Latinx and Caribbean Poetics* (Durham, NC: Duke University Press, 2020), 115.

25. Joseph R. Wolin, "Context, Collapsed and Expanded," in *Latinx Abstract*, ed. Elizabeth Ferrer, Joseph R. Wolin, and Analucia Zepeda (Brooklyn: BRIC Arts Media, 2021), 73.

26. Aileen Kwun, "The Textile Artist Employing Centuries-Old Practices and Pop Culture Imagery," *New York Times*, October 4, 2021, https://www.nytimes.com/2021/10/04/t-magazine/sarah-zapata-weaving-art.html.

27. Johanna Fateman, "Sarah Zapata," *New Yorker*, https://www.newyorker.com/goings-on-about-town/art/sarah-zapata.

28. Macarena Gómez-Barris, "Mestiza Cultural Memory: The Self-Ecologies of Laura Aguilar," in *Laura Aguilar: Show and Tell*, ed. Rebecca Epstein (Los Angeles: UCLA Chicano Studies Research Center Press, 2017), 82.

29. See Macarena Gómez-Barris, *The Extractive Zone: Social Ecologies and Decolonial Perspectives* (Durham, NC: Duke University Press, 2017).

30. Jeffrey Jerome Cohen, *Stone: An Ecology of the Inhuman* (Minneapolis: University of Minnesota Press, 2015), 65.

31. Donna J. Haraway, *Staying with the Trouble: Making Kin in the Chthulucene* (Durham, NC: Duke University Press, 2016), 105.

32. Eunjung Kim, "Unbecoming Human: An Ethics of Objects," *GLQ: A Journal of Lesbian and Gay Studies* 21, no. 2 (2015): 295–320.

33. Samera Esmeir, "On Making Dehumanization Possible," *PMLA* 121, no. 5 (2006): 1545.

34. Jeanne Vaccaro, "Felt Matters," in Stryker and Aizura, *Transgender Studies Reader 2*, 92.

35. Jeanne Vaccaro, "Feelings and Fractals: Wooly Ecologies of Transgender Matter," *GLQ: A Journal of Lesbian and Gay Studies* 21, nos. 2–3 (2015): 288.

36. See Zapata's interview with Jeanne Vaccaro, "Sarah Zapata Interviewed by Jeanne Vaccaro," *Bomb*, April 10, 2019, https://bombmagazine.org/articles/2019/04/10/ritualization-and-embodiment-sarah-zapata-interviewed.

37. Zapata's conceptualizing of installation as fantasy and otherworldliness derives from her reading of José Muñoz's *Cruising Utopia: The Then and There of Queer Futurity*. See her interview with Jeanne Vaccaro.

38. "A Famine of Hearing," Performance Space, accessed January 16, 2024, https://performancespacenewyork.org/shows/famine-of-hearing.

39. Vaccaro, "Sarah Zapata Interviewed by Jeanne Vaccaro."

Coda

1. *Variety*, "Kim Kardashian's Business Advice: 'Get Your F**king Ass Up and Work,'" YouTube, March 9, 2022, https://m.youtube.com/watch?v=XX2izzshRmI.

2. See Megan McArdle, "Want a 'Lazy Girl Job'? Think Again," *Washington Post*, July 27, 2027, https://www.washingtonpost.com/opinions/2023/07/27/lazy-girl-job-employment-women; Megan McArdle, "Want Employees to Return to the Office? Then Give Each One an Office," *Washington Post*, August 8, 2023, https://www.washingtonpost.com/opinions/2023/08/09/remote-work-offices-floorplan-privacy.

3. Judy Wajcman, *Pressed for Time: The Acceleration of Life in Digital Capitalism* (Chicago: University of Chicago Press, 2015), 11.

4. Tronti, *Workers and Capital*, 273.

5. Lisa Duggan and José Esteban Muñoz, "Hope and Hopelessness: A Dialogue," *Women and Performance: A Journal of Feminist Theory* 19, no. 2 (2009): 277.

6. Betsy Reed, "'They Don't Come with Rules': David Antonio Cruz Celebrates Queer Chosen Families," *The Guardian*, August 15, 2023, https://www.theguardian.com/artanddesign/2023/aug/15/artist-david-antonio-cruz-lgbtq-chosen-families-exhibition-philadelphia.

Index

abjection, 14, 27, 29, 135
Abject Performances (Alvarado), 29
Abya Yala, 2
Adeyemi, Kemi, 66–68
aesthetic judgement, 17–18
aesthetic strategies, 4, 5, 24, 79
affect, 169n22; beauty and, 17; Latinx, 27; negative, 5, 27
Afghanistan, 106
Agamben, Giorgio, 45
Age of Enlightenment, 15
Aguilar, Laura, 150–153
AIDS, 41, 58, 61, 69, 70
"All the Dead Boys Look Like Me" (Soto, C.), 92
Alquati, Romano, 7
Alvarado, Leticia, 29, 135
America's Next Top Model (TV series), 114
Amin, Kadji, 31
Angie Xtravaganza, 32, 39, 41, 43, 45, 60; dancing of, 46–50; glimpse of, 51–56, *52*, *53*; literary and digital afterlives of, 56–61
"Angi Xtravaganza and Friends at The World, 1988" (Simone), 59
animacy, 138
"Answer to the Question, An: 'What Is Enlightenment?'" (Kant), 15
Anthropology from a Pragmatic Point of View (Kant), 19, 22
anti-Blackness, 12, 28–29, 65, 126
anti-capitalism, 8

antiportrait, *Silverlake Lounge* as, 77
antiwork: politics, 7, 12, ; modes and practices, 25–26
Anzaldúa, Gloria, 47, 97–98, 138
Aparicio, Frances, 29–30
Arbus, Diane, 72, 74
Armendariz, Alicia, 68
artistic laziness, 13
Atlantic, (magazine), 171n9
attention economy, 10–11, 117

ball culture. *See Paris Is Burning*
"Bartleby, the Scrivener" (Melville), 5–6, 8–9
Bauz, Luis, 64
beauty, 49; affect and, 17; pageants, 123, 126–127; regimes of, 14
Belcourt, Billy-Ray, 91
Beltrán, Mary C., 120
Berger, John, 70, 71
Berwyn, Illinois, 67
bewilderment, 140
Bey, Marquis, 48–50
Black feminist method, 65
Black Lives Matter, 83
Blackness, 28, 65. *See also* Latinx Blackness
Black queer: life in the US, 41; women, 67–68, 112; world-making, 26
Black trans feminism, 48, 49–50
Black trans latinidades, 29
Blanco, Richard, 99

Bodies That Matter (Butler), 42
boredom, 20–22
bourgeois capitalists, 6, 8, 87, 158
BRIC Brooklyn, 144, 146
Brown, Elspeth H., 169n22
Brown, Nina Bo'nina, 116, 120
brownness, 27–28, 45–46, 136–137
Brown Trans Figurations (Galarte), 46, 113
Bruce, La Marr Jurelle, 26
burnout, 10–11
Butler, Judith, 42

Cadava, Eduardo, 71, 78
Campt, Tina M., 65
Campuzano, Giuseppe, 113
Capital (Marx), 89
capitalism, 1, 2, 5, 16, 26, 108; anti-capitalism, 8; bourgeois capitalists, 6, 8, 87, 158; burnout and, 11; COVID-19 and, 158; exploitation and, 7, 9, 10, 54, 158; "labor of love" myth and, 9; leisure and, 25; modernity and, 74; neoliberal, 4, 23–24, 81, 127, 176n32; *operaismo* and, 8; productivist work under, 9–10; white supremacist, 12
capitalist productivism, 5, 127
Caribbean Native ("the Carib"), 20–22
Cassara, Joseph, 57
Catch One (nightclub), 63
Catrachos (Guzmán, R.), 103
"Ceremonias De La Supervivencia" (Porras-Hernandez), 92
Cervenak, Sarah Jane, 20
Chambers, Ross, 25–26
Chambers-Letson, Joshua, 30
chattel slavery, 3, 112
Chen, Jian Neo, 42, 112
Chen, Mel Y., 138
Chicanx movement, 83
Chicanx photography, 68
Chinchilla, Maya, 33, 97–108
Christian, Marcel, 40
"Church at Night" (Chinchilla), 97–101, 104, 107
cisheterosexist white supremacy, 34, 35
Cisneros, Sandra, 131
class, 7, 14, 65, 158; middle, 132–133;

multi-ethnic, 69, 85; upper-class culture, 118; working, 8–9, 10, 19, 83, 103
claws of Valentina, 114–122
close narration, 48
close-up shots, 47
Cohen, Jeffrey Jerome, 151
colonialism, 110, 152
coloniality, 65
Communist Manifesto, The (Engels), 10
Compton's Cafeteria, 102
Corey, Dorian, 39, 57
Cornejo, Giancarlo, 45, 55
Cortés Rocca, Paola, 3, 78
COVID-19 (coronavirus) pandemic, 114, 157–158, 170n39
cowardice, 15, 19
Crisis Galería, 146
critical fabulation, 48
critical otiosity, 40–41, 43–45, 48, 59, 117
Critique of Judgement (Kant), 16, 21
Critique of Practical Reason (Kant), 16
Critique of Pure Reason (Kant), 16, 21
Cruising Utopia (McCarty), 63
Cruz, Celia, 83, 86
Cruz, David Antonio, 36, *159*, 160
Cuevas, Christopher, 171n20
Cuevas, T. Jackie, 100, 136
Cunningham, Michael, 57

Dance of the Forty-One, 33, 85
dance practices, Latinx, 66
Dango, Michael, 5
Danny Xtravaganza, 59–60
Davis, Vaginal, 64, 69
daydreaming, 20, 137, 153
DC Comics, 91
Dead Subjects (Viego), 27
Decena, Carlos Ulises, 30
Decolonizing Diasporas (Figueroa-Vásquez), 28
Deery, June, 175n20
"Defund the Police" (slogan), 83
DeGuzmán, María, 102
dehumanization, 152
Delgado, Celeste Fraser, 66

DeVun, Leah, 54
discomfort, 31
Disidentifications (Muñoz, J.), 41
Disney World, 103
dominicanidad, 30
drag queens. *See specific queens*
Drag Race México (TV series), 129
dual-model identity, 97
duplicity, 19

Edelman, Elijah Adiv, 172n28
Ellis Neyra, Ren, 28, 143
Engels, Friedrich, 10
Enlightenment, 20–21, 140, 152; Age of, 15; humanism, 12; philosophy, 14, 21, 23; rationality, 22, 110; Western, 15, 23
Esmeir, Samera, 152
esparza, rafa, 33, 82–88
ethics of representation, 43
eudaemonic experiences, 165n68
Eurocentric bourgeois whiteness, 41
Everynight Life (Delgado and J. Muñoz), 66
exploitation: capitalist, 7, 9, 10, 54, 158; inequality and, 66, 68
"Extravas Host a Ball in DC, The" (*Paris Is Burning* outtake), 46

Facebook, 59
Famine of Hearing, A (Zapata), 146, 154
fantasy, 34, 113, 123, 125, 154
farmworkers, 1–2, 37
Feeling Philanthropy (Brown, E., and Phu), 169n22
Félix, María, 122
femininity, 126
feminism, Black trans, 49–50
Ferrer, Elizabeth, 68
Figueroa-Vásquez, Yomaira C., 28
Flowers, Nina, 121
form-content debate, 5
Fornés, María Irene, 136–137
Foster, David William, 169n13
Foucault, Michel, 15–16, 19–20
four-hour workday, 10
freedom, 4, 50, 142–143; moral, 20; with violence, 106

frivolity, 86–88
frontality, 74, 77–78
funk, 12–13
Funk the Erotic (Stalling), 12

Gabriel, Juan (singer), 86
Galarte, Francisco J., 46, 113
Galería de la Raza, 84
Galimberti, Jacopo, 9
García-Peña, Lorgia, 28
Garland, Jack, 47–48
Gaspar de Alba, Alicia, 93
Geiger, Jeffrey, 45
gender, 50; chattel slavery and, 112; Heidenreich on, 47; identity, 112; normative, 3, 23; as regeneration, 142; sexed variance of, 54; variant critique, 100
genocide against Native peoples, 2
gentrification, 70, 81
Gil de Montes, Roberto (painter), 68
Gills-Peterson, Jules, 45, 112
Glass: A Journal of Poetry, 91
Glissant, Édouard, 110, 133
Global North, 28, 36, 113
Global South, 36
GLQ: A Journal of Lesbian and Gay Studies, 91, 92, 97
Gomez, Edgar, 34, 91, 97–108
Gómez-Barris, Macarena, 150
González, Christopher, 96–97
Gossett, Che, 102–103
Grobe, Christopher, 175n19
Grounded #120 (Untitled) (Aguilar), 150
Gruesz, Kirsten Silva, 94
Guarch, Julia Leslie, 92
gun violence, 101, 106
Gutiérrez, Ariadna, 126
Guzmán, Joshua Javier, 28
Guzmán, Roy G., 34, 91, 97–108; *Catrachos*, 103; "Restored Mural for Orlando," 103

Halberstam, Jack, 171n9
Hames-García, Michael, 171n19
handicraft in trans studies, 153
Hartman, Saidiya, 48–49

Hayward, Eva, 142
Hector Xtravaganza, 57
hedonic experience, 165n68
Hegel, Georg Wilhelm Friedrich, 18
Heidenreich, L., 47–48
Hernández, Robb, 61, 85
high art, 74
high-femme glamour, 127
High-Risk Homosexual (Gomez), 91
Hilderbrand, Lucas, 41
History of My Brief Body, A (Belcourt), 91
HIV/AIDS, 41, 58, 61, 69, 70
hooks, bell, 41, 42
Horgan, Amelia, 9
horizontality, 140, 149
house culture. *See Paris Is Burning*
House of Impossible Beauties, The (Cassara), 57
House of Xtravaganza, 32, 39, 40, 46, 57, 60
House on Mango Street, The (Cisneros), 131
How to Do Nothing (Odell), 11
Hu, Tung-Hui, 12
human distinctiveness, 80
humanism, 152; Enlightenment, 12; liberal, 10
hyperproductive work, 1

identity, 100, 102, 106, 113; complexity of, 41; dual-model, 97; gender, 112; labor and, 4, 7, 8; Latinx, 28–29, 30, 121, 129; sensuality and, 169n29; social, 78; trans, 112, 153; of travesti people, 45; in Venezuela, 126
idle Native (trope), 3, 21
idleness, 12–13, 24
IDW Publishing, 91
If I Could (Zapata), 146, 149
immaturity, 15
imperialism, 28, 98, 106, 110
improper behavior, 31
in-betweenness, 47
Indigenous peoples, 90
individuality, 11, 80
indolent liberatory practices, 32
"In Praise of Idleness" (Russell), 10
"In Praise of Latin Night at the Queer Club" (Torres, J.), 91, 105–107

Instagram, 128, 129
installations, 146–150, 153–156, 159, 178n37
In the Heights (film), 128
In vastness of borrowed time (The taxing of a fruitful procession) (Zapata), 146, *147, 148*, 149, 154
"Is Paris Burning?" (bell hooks), 41
Italian Marxists, 7–8
I want you to know how hard I am (Zapata), 154, *155*, 156

Jaffe, Sarah, 9
Jefferson, Marshall, 46
Johnson, Samuel, 13
judgement, aesthetic, 17–18
Justice, Eddie Jamoldroy, 92

Kant, Immanuel, 14–23, 165n54, 165n63
Kardashian, Kim, 157
Khubchandani, Kareem, 66, 75, 173n37
Kim, Eunjung, 152
King, Rosamond S., 141
Kitt, Eartha, 125
Kline, Nolan, 171n20
Kraus, Chris, 64
Kressley, Carson, 115

LaBeija, Pepper, 39
"labor of love" myth (Jaffe), 9
Lafargue, Paul, 10
La Fountain–Stokes, Lawrence, 51, 90, 93, 121
languid affections, 17
La Plaza (bar), 68
Latinidad, 27, 29
Latin night, 33–34, 89–93, 95, 99–102, 105, 108
Latinx Abstract (exhibition), 144
Latinx affect, 27
Latinx Blackness, 28–29
Latinx identities, 28–29
Latinxness, 29, 113, 122
Latinx studies, 30
Laura Aguilar: Show and Tell (Aguilar), 150
Lavery, Grace, 174n10
laziness, 3, 14–15, 19, 22, 63; artistic, 13;

"the Laziness Lie," 11; literary, 13; typologies of, 23–36
Laziness Doesn't Exist (Price), 11
lazing, 13–14, 66, 96–97, 99–100, 132–134, 139, 156, 160
leisure, 24–26, 104
lesbianness, 93
lethargy, 12–13
"Let's Play Lawyer" (*Paris Is Burning* outtake), 40
Leyva, James Andrew, 111
liberal humanism, 10
"listening to images," 65
literary historicity, 94
literary laziness/lazing, 13, 96
Little Domestic Waste I, A (Zapata), 144, 145
Little Domestic Waste VII, A (Zapata), 144, 145
Livingston, Jennie, 41
loafer, 14, 31
loiterature, 25–26
loitering, 25–26
Lolita Banana (drag queen), 129
López, Marissa, 29
Love Is Love (anthology), 91
Luciano, Dana, 138
Lutz, Tom, 24

MacArthur Park, 82
Machuca Rose, Malú, 113
makeover television, 118, 123
Maricón Collective (DJ group), 85
Marx, Karl, 9–10, 11, 89
Marxists, Italian, 7–8
mask and claws of Valentina, 114–122
Mateen, Omar, 90, 91, 106
maxi challenge of *RuPaul's Drag Race*, 114–115
McCarty, Kevin, 63, 75
McDonald, Boyd, 44
"Meet Valentina: All About the Fantasy" (video), 123, 176n46
Melville, Herman, 5–6, 8–9
Mexico City raid (1901), 85
middle class, 132–133
Miller, D. A., 44
Miller, Quinlan, 176n47

mini challenge of *RuPaul's Drag Race*, 114
minoritarian critique, 138
minoritarian performance, 30
Miss Ketty (aka Ketty Teanga), 67
Miss Universe, 122, 126
Modern Family (TV series), 121
modernity, capitalist, 74
Molina-Guzmán, Isabel, 121
Monét X Change (drag queen), 124
Monique Heart (drag queen), 124
Moraga, Cherríe, 96, 98
Morales, Miguel M., 91
moral freedom, 20
Moro-Gronlier, Caridad, 92
motion-change, 47
"Move Your Body" (Jefferson), 46
mud, 132, 135–141, 143–144
Mud (Fornés), 136–137
Mugi's (bar), 68, 75
multispecies intimacy, 140
Muñoz, Beatriz Santiago, 143
Muñoz, José Esteban, 24, 29, 63, 121, 136, 158; *Disidentifications*, 41; *Everynight Life*, 66; *The Sense of Brown*, 27
mural, *Nostra Fiesta*, 82–88
muralism, 83, 84

Nacho Nava (DJ name of Ignacio Nava), 86
nationalism, Venezuelan, 126
nation-building, 3–4
Native peoples, 2
negative affect, 5, 27
Negri, Antonio, 7
neoliberal capitalism, 4, 23–24, 81, 127, 176n32
neoliberal positivism, 174n2
Nepantla Squared (Heidenreich), 47
New Jalisco Bar, 33, 82–88, *84*, 170n39
New World Native, 22
New York Times (newspaper), 11, 41
9/11 terrorist attacks, 94–95, 172nn26–27
normative gender, 3, 23
normativity, 118
North American Native, 21
Norton Anthology of Latino Literature (Gruesz), 94

Nostra Fiesta (mural by esparza and Ruiz), 82–88
"Not Our President" (slogan), 83

obfuscation, 111, 117; spectacular, 122–130
Observations on the Feeling of the Beautiful and Sublime (Kant), 20, 21
Obstruction (Salvato), 13
Ochoa, Marcia, 126
O'Connor, Brian, 12–13, 24–26
Odell, Jenny, 11
Of This World Rather (Zapata), 154
"One Pulse—One Poem" (Blanco), 99
"On the Highest Physical Good" (Kant), 19
opacity, 110
operaismo movement, 7–9, 158
Opie, Catherine, 169n29
Orchard, William, 91
Orlando, Florida. *See* Pulse nightclub shooting
Ortiz, Ricardo L., 96, 173n58
otiosity, critical, 40–41, 43–45, 48, 59, 117

Paris Is Burning (documentary), 32, 39–45, 64; Angie dancing in, 46–50; Angie glimpsed in, 51–56, *52*, *53*; "The Extravas Host a Ball in DC," 46; "Let's Play Lawyer," 40
passivity, 8
Paul, Manuel, 84–85
Pelaez Lopez, Alan, 28
people of color, 4. *See also* trans and queer people of color
Performer, Silverlake Lounge (Rivera), *73*
Philippine-American War, 47
Phu, Thy, 169n22
Picturing the Barrio (Foster), 169n13
Pierce, Joseph M., 113
Pier Kids (film), 43
plural historicities, 54
political transformation, 156
politics of representation, 120
Ponce de León, Jennifer, 9
Porras-Hernandez, Baruch, 92
Por Vida (mural), 84–85, 170n37

Posada, José Guadalupe, 33, 85
postwork imaginaries, 5, 7
Price, Devon, 11
Problem with Work, The (Weeks), 6
productivism, 3, 5, 12, 127, 160
productivist work, 9–10
Project Runway (TV series), 114
Prosser, Jay, 42
Protestant work ethic, 6, 21
Provisional Notes for a Disappeared City (Rivera), 33, 63–75, *71*
public resources, dismantling of, 4
Puerto Rican Pieta en la calle de la Fortaleza (Cruz, D.), *159*, 160
Puerto Rico, 3, 89–90, 106, 121
"Pulse" (Rodríguez, J.), 92
"Pulse: A Memorial in Driftwood, Cannon Beach, OR" (Moro-Gronlier), 92
Pulse nightclub shooting (Orlando, Florida, 2016), 33–34, 89–97, 171n20; literary lazing and, 96–108
Pulse/Pulso (anthology), 91, 92, 97

QED: A Journal in GLBTQ Worldmaking, 91
Queen for a Day (Ochoa), 126
"Queen of Clubs" (episode, *RuPaul's Drag Race All Stars*), 126
"Queering Latina/o Literature" (La Fountain-Stokes), 93
queer nightlife, 64, 66–67, 75, 81, 86
Queer Nightlife (anthology), 170n4
queer of color theory, 5, 66, 92, 112
queer studies, 31
queer theory, 171n19, 174n10, 176n32
queer utopia, 24, 63
quotidian digital sphere, 12

Racial Immanence (López), 29
Ramírez, Dixa, 31
rationality, Enlightenment, 22, 110
realism, representational, 78–79
reality television, 111, 115–118, 125, 175n20. *See also RuPaul's Drag Race*
Reddit, 127–128, 129
Reddy, Chandan, 106
refusals of work, 5, 7–8
refusenik, 14, 31
Rent: Live (TV musical event), 128

representation: ethics of, 43; politics of, 120
representational realism, 78–79
rest, power of, 11
"Restored Mural for Orlando" (Guzmán, R.), 103
Ridley, LaVelle, 48–49
Right to Be Lazy, The (Lafargue), 10
Rivera, Reynaldo (photographer), 33, 63–82, 169n13; *Performer, Silverlake Lounge*, *73*; *Silverlake Lounge*, 76–82, *77*; *Untitled, Downtown*, *71*
Rivera Montes, Zorimar, 133
Rivera-Servera, Ramón H., 66, 67
Rizki, Cole, 45
Rodríguez, Juana María, 32, 92
Rodriguez, Olivero, 61
Rodriguez, Ralph E., 96
Rohrleitner, Marion Christina, 135
Ruiz, Gabriela (artist), 33, 64, 68, 82–88
RuPaul, 60, 114, 118, 127, 174n2
RuPaul's Drag Race (TV series), 34, 109–113; maxi challenge, 114–115; mini challenge, 114; spectacular obfuscation and, 122–130; Valentina's mask and claws and, 114–122
RuPaul's Drag Race All Stars (TV series), 109, 111, 125; "Queen of Clubs," 126; "Super Girl Groups, Henny!," 124
RuPaul's Drag Race: Untucked! (TV series), 111, 115–116, 119
Russell, Bertrand, 10

Saint-Armand, Pierre, 13
Saint Peter's Basilica, 160
Salas Rivera, Roque Raquel, 89
Saldaña-Portillo, María Josefina, 94
Salvato, Nick, 13–14, 111
Santana, Dora Silva, 29, 45
Scaron, Pedro, 89
Sedgwick, Eve, 174n10
Seitler, Dana, 169n29
Selena, 122
self-help culture, 118
Senate Bill 1718 (Florida, 2023), 1–2
Sense of Brown, The (Muñoz, J.), 27
sensorial errancy, 143

"sensus communis," 17–18
Sharp, John, 165n68
Sheller, Mimi, 142
"Shh. Shh. Be Quiet" (Guarch), 92
"Siempre Unidos" (slogan), 83
Siempre X (Zapata), 149
Silverlake Lounge (bar), 68, 72, *73*, 77
Silverlake Lounge (Rivera photo), 76–82, *77*
Silver Platter (bar), 82
Simone, John, 59
singularity, 80, 87
Siqueiros, Francesco, 68
"skilled" labor, 1, 2
slackers, 24, 34
slavery, chattel, 3, 112
"Slap of Love, The" (Cunningham), 57
Slo 'Mo (party), 67
slowness, 67–68
Snaza, Nathan, 140
Snorton, C. Riley, 48, 112
social difference, 112
social distinction, 78
social identity, 78
social transformation, 156
social uplift, 6
social welfare services, dismantling of, 4
societal betterment, 6
Sontag, Susan, 72, 74
Soto, Christopher, 92
Soto, Sandra K., 96
South American Native, 21
Spaceland (nightclub), 63
space-time, surreal, 137
spatiality, 34, 98, 100
spectacle, tragedy as, 58
spectacular obfuscation, 122–130
Stalling, L. H., 12–13
Steel, Karl, 141
Steinbock, Eliza, 118
stereotyping, 122
Stevenson, Robert Louis, 13
stones, theorizing of, 151
Stonewall, 102
strenuous vigor, 16–17
strike, power of a, 8
Stroll, The (film), 43
sublimity, 16
suburban queer nightlife, 67

"Super Girl Groups, Henny!" (episode, *RuPaul's Drag Race All Stars*), 124
surreal space-time, 137

tactility, 36
Tagg, John, 78
Tangerine (film), 49
Teanga, Ketty, 67
television studies, 111
the tertiary / lo terciario (Salas Rivera), 89
Thalía, 122
"theory in the flesh," 98
This Bridge Called My Back (Moraga), 98
Thomas, David, 165n68
TikTok, 1
Torres, Amanda, 91
Torres, Justin, 34, 97–108, 156; "In Praise of Latin Night at the Queer Club," 91, 105–107; literary style of, 133; *We the Animals*, 35, 131–144, *138*, *139–140*
Tortorici, Zeb, 54
tragedy as spectacle, 58
trans and queer people of color, 41, 65, 92, 93, 107, 117, 120, 176n32; Latin night and, 99, 108; 9/11 terrorist attacks and, 95; Pulse shooting and, 90, 102–103; representational realism and, 78–79; representational schemas for depicting, 43
trans identity, 112, 153
transloca practices, 51
transness, 77, 79, 80, 113, 142; Black gender and, 50; Galarte on, 45–46; of Garland, 48; Latinx, 111–112
trans of color theory, 5, 48, 112–113
"Trans Rights" (slogan), 83
"transvestites," the word/category, 45, 69
travesti people, 29, 113; identity of, 45
"Trench," *We the Animals* (Torres, J.), 132
Trinity the Tuck (drag queen), 124–125
Tronti, Mario, 7, 8, 158
Tsang, Wu, 82
Turtle Island, 2

UCLA, 54
undocumented migrant, 1–2, 28, 36
United States, 41, 83; capitalism in, 2; as disciplining mechanism, 6; gun violence in, 101, 106; Latinx identity formation in, 28; Latinx literature in, 96–97; mask-wearing in, 114; mass shootings in, 90; migrant workforces in, 3; nation-building and, 3–4; neoliberal capitalism in, 24, 81, 127; Philippine-American War and, 47; pro-immigrant discourses in, 2; value system in, 3; whiteness in, 27
Universal Studios, 103
"unskilled" labor, 1
Untitled, Downtown (Rivera photo), *71*
upper-class culture, 118
urban scene, 169n13
utopia, queer, 24, 63

Vaccaro, Jeanne, 153
Valentina (drag queen), 34, 109–111, 113, *119*, 123–130, 174n3, 176n37; drag persona evolution of, 129; gloves of, 116–117, *117*; mask and claws of, 114–122; YouTube channel of, 130
"Valentina's Signature Look" (YouTube channel), 130
valorized wage labor, 7, 9–10
Variety (magazine), 157
Veblen, Thorstein, 24
Venezuelan nationalism, 126
Venus Xtravaganza, 39, 42, 45, 57–58, 61, 92
verticality, 140
video games, 165n68
Viego, Antonio, 27, 29
vigor, 16–17, 19
Villarejo, Amy, 111, 176n37
Villarreal, Vanessa Angélica, 120
Vincent Price Art Museum, 150
violence, 34, 42; freedom with, 106; gun, 101, 106; narratives of, 54; of 9/11 terrorist attacks, 94–95, 172nn26–28. *See also* Pulse nightclub shooting
Virgen de Guadalupe candle, 122
Visage, Michelle, 115
Vogue México y Latinoamérica (magazine), 109, 111
Volty, Tatiana, 64

wage labor, valorized, 7, 9–10
Wajcman, Judy, 158
Washington Post (newspaper), 105, 157
Weber, Max, 6
Weeks, Kathi, 6, 7
Western Enlightenment, 15, 23
We the Animals (Torres, J.), 35, 131–144; film version of, 136, *138*, 139–140
white Europeans, 22
white laborers, 1
whiteness, 136; Eurocentric bourgeois, 41; in United States, 27
white supremacy, 27, 88, 101; capitalism and, 12; cisheterosexist, 34, 35
Wilde, Oscar, 13
Wildness (film), 43, 82
work documentation, 1
workerism. *See operaismo* movement
working class, 8–9, 10, 19, 83, 103; multi-ethnic, 69, 85

The World (nightclub), 60
worms, 141–142, 144
Wright, Steve, 8
Wynter, Sylvia, 140

YouTube, 109, 130

Zagar, Jeremiah, 131
Zapata, Sarah (artist), 35–36, 144–156; *A Famine of Hearing*, 146, 154; *If I Could*, 146, 149; *In vastness of borrowed time (The taxing of a fruitful procession)*, 146, *147*, *148*, 149, 154; *I want you to know how hard I am*, 154, *155*, 156; *A Little Domestic Waste I*, 144, *145*; *A Little Domestic Waste VII*, 144, *145*; *Of This World Rather*, 154; *Siempre X*, 149